D1433052

WITHDRAWN

FATHERING THE NATION

FATHERING THE NATION

AMERICAN GENEALOGIES OF SLAVERY AND FREEDOM

Russ Castronovo

PS
217
.S55
C37
1995

#31607744
MNGA

1/31/02 BR

University of California Press

Berkeley · Los Angeles · London

University of California Press
Berkeley and Los Angeles, California

University of California Press, Ltd.
London, England

© 1995 by
The Regents of the University of California

Library of Congress Cataloging-in-Publication Data

Castronovo, Russ, 1965–
  Fathering the nation : American genealogies of slavery
and freedom / Russ Castronovo.
    p. cm.
  Includes bibliographical references (p.) and index.
  ISBN 0-520-08901-4 (alk. paper)
  1. American literature—19th century—History and
criticism. 2. Slavery and slaves in literature.
3. Slaves—United States—Emancipation—
Historiography. 4. National characteristics, American,
in literature. 5. Slavery—United States—
Historiography. 6. United States—Civilization.
7. Freedom in literature. 8. Memory in literature.
9. Narration (Rhetoric). I. Title.
PS217.S55C37 1995
810.9'3520625—dc20   94-42959
                                                           CIP

Printed in the United States of America

9 8 7 6 5 4 3 2 1

The paper used in this publication meets the minimum
requirements of American National Standard for
Information Sciences—Permanence of Paper for Printed
Library Materials, ANSI Z39.48-1984.

To my parents,
Michael and Frances,
and
to Leslie

Contents

Illustrations

Acknowledgments

Only by recovering repressed memories and forgotten citizens, this book argues, can the construct of America achieve realization of the challenging plenitude and differences in its national narrative. Thus genealogical investigation—a methodology devoted to examining sites of erasure and displacement—has tremendous importance here, and yet this book would only repeat the same myopic elisions and tragic disavowals that mark American narrative if I did not begin with an attempt to record another genealogy, remembering those people who gave so much to the ideas and spirit of this project.

Anthony Barthelemy, S. Paige Baty, Peter Bellis, Bud Bynack, Peter Euben, Susan Gillman, Tassie Gwilliam, Catherine Judd, Doris Kretschmer, Maria Teresa Prendergast, Tom Prendergast, Forrest Robinson, John Paul Russo, Roz Spafford, Frank Stringfellow, and Ingrid Walker Fields all contributed generously, offering invaluable recommendations throughout all aspects of this book from suggesting titles to helping me clarify and enhance my thinking and writing. Their rich and different presences as teachers, friends, and colleagues can be found on every page.

This book grew out of my doctoral dissertation, and my advisors' insight, humor, and guidance continue to enliven my scholarship. John Schaar is an indispensable mentor, and without his incisive political imagination, I would never have been able to begin a conversation about freedom. I am grateful to Hayden White whose unceasing intellectual enthusiasm and patient demystifications helped me see my way through the intricacies of critical theory and this profession. I am indebted to Michael Cowan: his love of interpretation is infectious, and his friendship unique. His understandings of America sustained and enriched both this book and myself at every turn.

Donald Pease and Karen Sánchez-Eppler accorded this project remarkable readings. They challenged my argument and ideas not merely as part of a scholarly exercise, but in ways invested with encouragement and thoughtfulness that helped make what I had given them so much better.

My research has been funded at important stages by grants from the University of California, Santa Cruz, and also by the Max Orovitz Summer Research Award at the University of Miami. An earlier version of chapter 4 appeared in *American Literature* 65 (September 1993), 523–27 with the title "Radical Configurations of History in the Era of American Slavery."

Any genealogy of this book naturally takes me back to my parents, Michael and Frances Castronovo who, for long as I can remember, have been giving me their confidence and understanding. Lacking their abiding influence, I would never have put pen to paper.

My deepest thanks are to Leslie Bow—my toughest critic and my strongest supporter. She has bestowed upon me a love and respect that extend far beyond this project to touch other memories and other stories.

"Adding Story to Story"

An Introduction to Parricide and Genealogy

We are a nation of inconsistencies;
completely made up of inconsistencies.
—Frederick Douglass, March 30, 1847

"Let every man remember that to violate the law, is to trample on the blood of his father," Abraham Lincoln admonished his audience at the Young Men's Lyceum in 1838. Lincoln's warning exerts a powerful appeal through the metaphoric association it makes between national allegiance and family respect. The fear of parricide operates as an injunction against social agitation and political disruption. Yet the context in which Lincoln reminded his listeners of this primordial taboo throws into question the sanctity and order of the patriarchal codes in American national culture. While what he called an "increasing disregard for law which pervades the country" prompted this jeremiad, his reproof materialized from the specifics of a "very short" story of a lynching in St. Louis. As if to emphasize America's volatile instability, Lincoln relates in a single sentence how a mob seized a mulatto, chained him to a tree, and burned him, "all within a single hour from the time he had been a freeman." Even though this African American noncitizen already "had forfeited his life, by the perpetration of an outrageous murder," the figurative killing of the father's law by vigilante justice caused Lincoln more concern, so much so that in the remainder of his speech he prescribes strategies for preserving a body politic conceived a generation before.[1]

That national body could not be abstracted from the specific body of the lynched mulatto. Seemingly only fodder for a rhetorical gesture, the mulatto nonetheless persists as a central though unruly presence in the overall economy of Lincoln's speech, as well as in the nation it addresses. While admitting that from one perspective, this act of mob violence had limited consequences, being "but a small

1

evil," Lincoln's reading of America could not find solace in the usual appeal to place union above all else and filter out from national debate the disruptive question of slavery. Unwilling to understand this lynching as an isolated local tragedy, he told the post-Revolutionary generation that the blood spilled when a freeman was "dragged to the suburbs of the city, chained to a tree, and actually burned to death" was embroiled with national history. Historical memory in the United States, like race, is thus disclosed as subject to miscegenation: the "blood of the father," symbolic and mythologized, mixes with an African presence, literal and violated, imperiling the task of remembering and perpetuating a nation.[2]

How could citizens ensure the success of this mission of preservation? "The answer is simple," states Lincoln. "Let every American, every lover of liberty, every well wisher to his posterity, swear by the blood of the Revolution." The sons' political duty required no special exertions; after all, they needed only to transmit a government that the fathers labored to establish. The genealogical character of this affirmation—the sons pledged themselves to a *"political religion"* committed to ancestral practices—was to guarantee that memory would be conveyed along the uncomplicated and unimpeachable lines of patriarchy. Despite this faith in the clarity of the Revolutionary "blood," the earlier emphasis upon racial intolerance reveals a confused legacy in which stories of ancestors and narratives of the nation compete with and interrogate one another. The political inheritance linking fathers and sons encounters episodic interruptions of another lineage evident in Lincoln's detailing of mob violence. His dismay at "the growing disposition to substitute the wild and furious passions, in lieu of the sober judgment of Courts" leads to a list of victims: "negroes, suspected of conspiring to raise an insurrection, were caught up and hanged in all parts of the State: then, white men, supposed to be leagued with the negroes; and finally, strangers, from neighboring States, going thither on business, were, in many instances, subjected to the same fate."[3] Though Lincoln casts doubts on an actual conspiracy, the larger preoccupations in his speech betray a suspicion that the history of white men is "leagued" with scenes of racial violence.

Disregard for the fathers' law, like racial violence, originates from two overlapping genealogies that express the miscegenated histories of the United States: one strand begins with patriotic fathers, and the other chaotically evolves from putatively rebellious slaves to threaten white freedom. Taken together these different stories stress the conflicts riding the currents of memory and blood coursing through the body politic. Lincoln's effort to tell his audience a straightforward lesson demonstrating the need of filial obedience is disrupted by a proliferation of stories that impart other morals, other imaginings of the nation. Revolutionary "blood" does not always follow predictable pathways and instead gets lost in questions of race and dismemberings of the fathers' law. Behind unprofaned fantasies of the "American mother" who teaches patriarchal reverence to her "lisping babe" remains this account of a lynching, hardly a pure enactment of filial remembrance.[4] What should be a simple story of remembrance now appears as a complex amalgamation in which parricide begins, not with murder of the fathers, but with a community's killing of a black man, an emblematic violation of the father's law. The metaphoric continuity of the nation in which the sons remember the blood of the fathers confronts the tangles of miscegenation, discovering the blood of the fathers in people whom the Dred Scott decision would later delineate as unprotected and unrelated to the founding promise.

Although Lincoln's goal was to preserve "the temple of liberty," moving from a mulatto to the founding fathers hardly grants his speech much stability. Rather, the course of Lincoln's remarks obliquely traces often hidden lines of descent and association. His analysis of antebellum memory emerges from a series of oppositions between past and present, remembering and forgetting, white and black, sons and fathers. So when he leaves his audience with the closing proposition "Upon these [memories] let the proud fabric of freedom rest," one wonders how secure or unified the foundation he has invoked could have been. Lincoln's purpose here was not ritual obeisance to the fathers; he, too, was guilty of "trampl[ing] on the blood of his father," of a figurative parricide, by suggesting the inadequacy of America's patriarchal ancestry: "like every thing else, they [memories of the Revolution] must fade upon the memory of the world, and grow more and more dim by the lapse of time. . . . *those* histories are gone. They *can* be read no more forever." He announces the death of the fathers, declaring their faded strength as figures that once seemed to knit together a nation as a family. Only faithfulness to the memory of the fathers—of which the lynching is a poor example—can guard ancestral patriots as viable forces in American civic life. Within this reconfiguration of an abstract America as a familial structure, within this redefinition of citizenship as a father-son dynamic, filial demeanor alternates from pious recollection to murderous forgetting, from prodigal amnesia to critical remembrance.[5]

This ambivalence toward national genealogy locates Lincoln as a representative of a pre–Civil War culture that experienced conflicting attitudes of pride and guilt in relation to its own past. At one moment, connections between the Revolutionary and antebellum eras tokened an unbroken legacy replete with authority, legitimacy, and coherence. The memory of the founding fathers could furnish a sense of continuity even at the height of national division. "We but tread in the paths of our fathers when we proclaim our independence," stated Jefferson Davis when he renounced his United States senatorial seat a month before he accepted the presidency of the Confederacy.[6] Yet the lines of genealogy produced disjunctive stories that failed to coincide under the promise of a single fatherly design. The votive son stumbled across a forgotten legacy of shame, and remembrance became a contradictory endeavor that assailed the antebellum cult of ancestor worship. Such disrupted paths of memory arose when Lewis and Milton Clarke recall their father, who fought for independence at Bunker Hill. The integrity of that legacy dissolve, however, when confronted with an institutional interpretation of their maternal ancestry. Sons of a slave mother, the Clarke brothers thus embodied a patriarchal history that legally could not be claimed; they descended from a history of freedom that enslaved them. Their 1846 slave narrative expresses these contradictions by returning imaginatively to the site of their father's freedom only to find reminders of bondage: "If I should creep up to the top of the Monument at Bunker's Hill, beneath which my father fought, I should not be safe even there. The slave-mongers have a right, by the laws of the United States, to seek me, even upon the top of the monument, whose base rests upon the bones of those who fought for freedom."[7] Even as they honor the father for his struggle for independence, these slave sons ironize the inadequacies and contradictions in his legacy. Their recollections of patriarchy are double, at once reverential and parricidal. Such bastard histories and aborted liberties resist unity and disrupt the organization of historical narrative.

Offspring of the Revolutionary generation, even though their descent was irregular, Milton and Lewis Clarke seem inspirited with the same principles of filial respect outlined in the Lyceum speech eight years earlier. Stating that there is sufficient devotion "in adding story to story, upon the monuments of fame, erected to the memory of others," Lincoln reminds his audience that while heroic action suited the founding era, modest and dutiful upkeep are the sons' chores. Whereas the founding fathers' "task . . . [was] to possess themselves, and through themselves, us, of this goodly land; and to uprear upon its hills and its valleys, a political edifice of liberty and equal rights," the sons should be content with that "edifice" as it stands, laboring only "to transmit" its promises to future generations.[8] These slave narrators seem to have heeded Lincoln's advice, maintaining a patriarchal tradition by reference to the antebellum generation's monumental tribute to the patriots of Bunker Hill. And yet, their memory is dangerously supplemental: as they reiterate the father's biography, they insinuate another legacy; as they invoke the symbolic dimensions of the monument, they suggest a memory of unexpected contours by adding another story. Against glorious deeds past, the Clarkes place their literal enslavement, a juxtaposition that embarrasses national memory, exposing the monolithic yet hollow protections it offers. In their formulation, supposedly potent patriotic relics—"the bones of those who fought for freedom"—take on a forlorn tone of futility and decay. "Adding story to story," as Lincoln suspected, did not increase the already great magnitude of the past, but produced an array of memories, diffuse and unstable, that did not easily coalesce with an overall unified narrative of America.

"Adding story to story" is the intention of this book: by doing so, I want to read and dismantle the architecture of national narrative and examine how fragmentation and unity as formal principles have been inextricably wrapped up in the most significant political issues, from representation to exclusion, from participation to disenfranchisement, from freedom to slavery. Reading such texts as Lincoln's Gettysburg Address, Melville's *Moby-Dick*, and Douglass's "The Heroic Slave" as instances of cultural criticism, I want to examine the ironies and inconsistencies that arose as patriarchal lineage administered a national narrative through the deployment of dates, biographies, memorials, and patriotic rituals.[9] Even though genealogical metaphors seek to fix citizens' memory along the authoritative lines of patriarchy, remembering the fathers in antebellum America unraveled into an ambivalent undertaking, recovering dissonant memories and bodies that did not comfortably mesh with ordered transcriptions of national history. National narrative, once assumed as the site of cohesion, can be seen to fissure into sites of contestation, exclusion, and repression. "Adding story to story" leads not to one larger story, but to dispersed histories that stand in uneasy relation to one another. As Homi Bhabha argues, "national memory is always the site of hybridity of histories and the displacement of narratives."[10]

Viewed as an amalgamation of stories, the narrative of "America" resists being told in terms of an intelligible story of uncontested descent; on the contrary, the nation's genealogy is inhabited by lost members, dispossessed bastards, forgotten orphans, and rebellious slaves.[11] At stake in reading America as a patchwork of stories is the possibility that the texts that we use to understand American culture may be reread in ways that thwart national narrative's compulsion toward coherence and homogeneity. By not acceding to the idea that American texts are threaded together by some underlying unity or political vision, interpretations may begin to tolerate varied experiences of citizenship, even those antagonistically founded upon contradiction and irresolution. If this scattering of memory dismembers the nation, it only creates more sites for the elaboration of different and competing political communities, none of which can claim final authority for its versions of history.

This dispersion of America results from a genealogical account of the nation. In this book, I use genealogy both as a descriptive term to suggest the father-son metaphor that saturated the politics, icons, and institutions of the antebellum period *and* as a method of investigation to uncover the disjunctions in the patriarchal imagining of the nation. Genealogy thus registers both the continuities and discontinuities that pervade inscriptions of a national past. Just as rumors of Jefferson's slave daughter undermine tales of free sons who honor Revolutionary fathers, just as Lincoln's Lyceum address structure internal contradictions into an obituary of *"now no more"* fathers, genealogy suggests a coherent history nonetheless always marked by irreconcilable memories that range from stories of devotion to parricide.[12] Genealogy is complicated by a tension that, on the one hand, seeks to delineate the nation with the order of patriarchy, and on the other, disorganizes any pretensions to transmit the nation via a singular, supposedly inclusive narrative that necessarily omits other lineages, such as the one between mothers and daughters. Only by preserving this tension can genealogy offer its diverse experiences and amputated memories without remembering those stories as just another American narrative of pluralism in which many (stories) make one (larger narrative). My own uses of genealogy in this book, which imply both an ordered account of United States history as well as its critical disarticulation, highlight the conflicts that accompany any memories that stem from the blood of the fathers.

In 1776, the founding fathers did more than establish a nation; they framed a narrative for the articulation of that nation. Although it may be difficult to imagine a more conflicted grouping than the figures of these last few pages—Lincoln, Jefferson Davis, and the Clarke brothers—their shared reliance upon family metaphors to allegorize the nation points to how patriarchal sanctions shaped politics, narrative, and race relations in much of mid-nineteenth-century America. Their statements issue from a cultural context where names, dates, phrases, and sites such as George Washington, 1776, "Give me liberty, or give me death," and Bunker Hill figured as the salient reference points of the foundational histories that structured national consciousness. America developed into a pietistic country where the lives, sayings, standards, and images of the founding fathers both validated and delimited political issues central to the maturing nation-state. Describing these conservative appeals to remember ancestral founders, genealogy provides this study with a historically specific metaphor, evoking the post-Revolutionary era's preoccupation with origins and authority. By the time of the deaths of John Adams and Thomas Jefferson, both on July 4, 1826, what Lincoln called "a *living history*" had slipped irrevocably into the past; sensing its own belatedness to national glory, the post-Revolutionary generation charged itself with a custodial duty of preservation. Almost "all important political, moral, and personal matters (and many matters that were not so important)," writes George Forgie, "were referred to . . . the heroic standards of the founding period and the lives of the founders themselves." Myths of a cherry tree, rebellious slaves who invoke Founding Fathers, novels of sons who repudiate the fathers, tales of orphans who recover a lost paternal legacy, public monuments to Revolutionary heroes, and scandalous stories of red-haired slaves at Jefferson's Monticello all contributed to a national narrative in which patriarchy ordered ownership and citizenship, political power and enslavement, aesthetic expression and experience.[13] Whatever the form of national narrative, whether patriotic legend, volume of history, or memorial column, fathers set prohibitions and provided rewards, circumscribed certain political possibilities and invalidated others, accorded structure and promised closure, all in order for their descendants to secure a destiny of liberty and empire.

In contrast to these impulses toward hierarchy and order, genealogy often fragments in its attempts to regulate citizenship, status, and power along the continuous lines of patriarchal hierarchy. "What tangled skeins are the genealogies of slavery!" exclaims Harriet Jacobs in *Incidents in the Life of a Slave Girl*. Just as Lincoln's Lyceum address could not escape the literal associations of a mulatto victimized by mob justice, genealogy also forcefully intersects with race. Disruptive and discordant, the practice of slavery frustrated attempts to articulate a coherent national ideology, prompting divisive speculations as to what sort of body politic the fathers first had imagined. Heroes of freedom, the founding fathers also loomed as progenitors of oppression. Patrilineal metaphors thus also insinuated a more radical sense of genealogy: in the words of Michel Foucault, "an unstable assemblage of faults, fissures, and heterogeneous layers that threaten the fragile inheritor from within or underneath."[14] Lincoln embodied this conflicted posture: even as he fulfilled the role of pious son, he foundered upon memories that discredited and eventually fractured the coherent image he held of his political fathers. Every act of homage contained insurgent suggestions of parricide.

Following Lincoln, who exalted parricide to a metaphoric dimension, I suggest that parricide—the most radical and ironic commitment to genealogy—interjected a disjunction into the smooth succession and tradition of ancestral fathers. Although Daniel Webster looked to the Bunker Hill Monument so that "no vigor of youth, no maturity of manhood, will lead the nation to forget the spots where its infancy was cradled and defended," historical amnesia did not pose the most dangerous challenge to the continuity of national narrative. What Lincoln and ex-slaves such as Lewis and Milton Clarke reveal is that remembering, not merely forgetting, initiates a practice of parricidal criticism. When, for example, Frederick Douglass honors the "solid manhood" of America's fathers in his famous 1852 Fourth of July oration, his recollections inevitably unearth what he calls "national inconsistencies." Or when William Wells Brown, reviewing in 1854 the glory of Santo Domingo and Toussaint L'Ouverture, offers comparisons to the American Revolution and Washington, he, too, discovers incompatible memories: "Toussaint liberated his countrymen; Washington enslaved a portion of his."[15] Refusing to be obedient to the memory of the founders, such parricidal criticism slayed the father's controlling metaphors, fracturing the unbroken linearity of national narrative.

Those nineteenth-century writers and critics who looked with murderous intent at the cohesion of ancestral lines engaged in figurative parricide by abandoning deference to either historical beginnings or continuity. The sacred aura of origins dissipated before the writer who recorded an alternate history in which, to borrow a phrase from Nietzsche, "beginnings were liberally sprinkled with blood."[16] This critical stance exhibits little filial piety, and as Foucault states, it does not hesitate to "laugh at the solemnities of the origin." In its search for what has been repressed, a genealogy of America returns to the site of national legacies and asks what has been erased in the writing of national narrative. Restored to the national-family tree, once excluded figures such as the slave and the parricide reveal the fatherly oppression that endures as an irredeemable yet constituent element of America and its democracy. Such a recovery of forgotten progeny crosses racial divisions, signaling how race, especially by its forced absence, has had tremendous impact upon any construction of the nation. Bred (retrospectively) to be pure, the national-family tree is miscegenated at its roots. Genealogy reveals that a patriarchal inheritance of freedom and memory were obliterated from the slave; and, at the same time, genealogy marks the African American presence as a subversive force that alters national legacies. As an integration of historical description and critical practice, racial genealogy illuminates how the dominant father-son metaphor of mid-nineteenth-century politics intersected with slavery, producing discursive acts that sustained America even as they unsettled and made inconsistent its national narrative.

Lacking the association between race, patriarchy, and layered understandings of parricide and genealogy, national narrative has been able to present an ossified story of unity, sameness, and or-der—a definition that necessarily precludes the possibility that na-tional narrative might be something other, such as an utterance of difference or heterogeneity. Demands for legitimacy then prevail over bodies and memories that speak against any narrative's ten-dency for finitude, closure, and incorporation. Consideration of one antebellum interpretation of the past helps reveal how an in-complete and fallacious practice of genealogy, like a truncated family tree that is assumed to be complete, eradicates the history of human subjects.

Notions of national descent supported the Supreme Court's 1856 ruling that the rights, duties, and protections of citizenship in no way extended to a black slave named Dred Scott. In his explication of the court's decision, Chief Justice Roger Taney often mentioned sacred documents of American history, but he refuses to ground his decision in landmark instances of history alone. Rather, Taney makes use of a national genealogy and seeks to guide the present by returning to the founding fathers, referring not simply to their well-known his-torical reputations, but to their more quotidian practices as well. Seemingly incidental branches of the family tree must be attended to: history, Taney declares, does not reside in single, distilled instances, but instead consists of a panoply of actions, words, and habits, all of which must be considered before allowing a judgment to emerge from the past. All the events surrounding the founding fathers, and not just isolated founding documents, deserve study. As a strategy of reading history, genealogical reverence causes Taney to approach the Declaration of Independence with a certain amount of hesitation. The transcendent quality of the Declaration easily allows the docu-ment to appear as a sublime moment of America, but for this reason it hovers in a rarefied context lacking depth and density, divorced from a more complete history vital to determinations of national character. Taney thus invokes the famous passage from the opening of the Declaration of Independence, "We hold these truths to be self-evident: that all men are created equal," only to suggest that unless these words are understood as originating from other words and actions, that unless these words are linked with the events and currents of history, one then runs the risk of flouting the nation's founding principles.

Application of the Declaration of Independence necessarily demands, in Taney's view, recognition that these "general words" of equality must be situated within the more particular context of "historical facts" and "fixed opinions" that surround the founders' attitudes toward "that race."[17] If the post-Revolutionary sons of America intend to draw conclusions from their legacy, then, as Taney counsels, the sons would have to consult the full character of that legacy. The sons would err if they based their actions upon a single epiphany of American history such as the Declaration; responsible judgment required that a generation debating the historical justification for slavery should conceive of the past as a sometimes contradictory, yet eventually continuous legacy in which political principles descended from prior events, exigencies, and practices. And this descent of practices from the founding epoch confirms for the Supreme Court the legitimacy and authority of the sons' institutions. Whereas history permits the citizen to consult isolated acts, genealogy implies to Taney the necessity of tracing the relations between various moments of the national past and how that past instructs the present generation.

Taney reminds the antebellum era that the Declaration is not an orphaned text unconnected to a larger inheritance. Instead, the Declaration originated from the founding fathers, who, it must be remembered, begat other decrees and deeds, many of which affirmed slavery as legitimate practice. Considered separately, "the general words above quoted [from the Declaration of Independence] would seem to embrace the whole human family," but considered equally with "the conduct of the distinguished men who framed the Declaration of Independence," the promises of 1776 did not speak to noncitizens, to black slaves, who entered the Constitution only as property. Contemplation of this fuller history accords the court the ability to isolate from "the whole human family" a distinct national-family tree.[18] In this restrictive sense, genealogy works doubly: it incorporates many daily acts into the historical record, but it ultimately makes this inclusive gesture in order to exclude those persons it deems nonhistorical. Recognition of family, which does much to uncover alliances based on the sameness of origin, is equally invested with marking those persons not embraced by its rights and rituals. Conflating family and nation, citizenship becomes as natural as birth—except that what counts as legitimate origin must fit a lineage narrowed by

patriarchal interpretation. Only through this retrospective exceptionalism can a national legacy be discovered, its narrative confirmed.

The chief justice's examination of the American legacy forms part
of a larger cultural context of ambivalent and conflicted voices surrounding the founding fathers. Discrepancies between the practice of
slavery and the promise of freedom unsettled the filial generation of
mid-nineteenth-century America. Canonical sons such as James Fenimore Cooper, Herman Melville, and Abraham Lincoln revisited the
foundations; patriotic sons such as George Lippard and Daniel Webster honored the fathers; unacknowledged sons such as Frederick
Douglass and William Wells Brown derided the paternal institution
of slavery; abolitionists and proslavery thinkers each invoked the
figure of Washington—all battled over the "correct" interpretation
of the patriarchal inheritance. Did the Compromise of 1850, allowing
for the extension of slavery into some territories acquired through
Manifest Destiny, represent a continuation or a tragic parody of the
design of the founding fathers? Would these fathers support popular
sovereignty if the citizens' voice called for the extension of slavery,
as Stephen Douglas argued, or did the founders' Northwest Ordi-
nance of 1787 indicate otherwise, as Lincoln stated? These questions
framing the most critical debates of the antebellum era contributed
to an encompassing ideological crisis that combined narrative and
politics: in what mode should America be narrated? Underlying yet
central to the American nation in the 1850s were the different strategies of either fabricating a narrative that had the order and resolution of romance, or narrating the country in a disjunctive mode that
eschewed the consistency and congruity of most historiography,
taking up instead stories shakily founded on dissonance, contradiction, and disruption.

Taney enters this fray and relies on genealogy to resolve apparent
inconsistencies within the national inheritance. Reading the Declaration as one of many elements of the founding legacy, Taney ascertains an underlying coherence between the language of equality
and an institution of racial inferiority and servitude. Even though
both freedom and slavery descended from the fathers, Taney uncovers in the national legacy a single, unifying principle confirming
the patriarchal authority of a national narrative. The "men who
framed this Declaration," writes Taney, "were great men . . . and
incapable of asserting principles inconsistent with those on which

they were acting. . . . They spoke and acted according to the then established doctrines and principles, and in the ordinary language of the day, and no one misunderstood them." According to Taney, the post-Revolutionary generation was temporally distant from the transparent days of Washington and Jefferson, and so it distorted the national legacy because it forgot the full history surrounding the Declaration. The problem lay not with the nation's origins, but with the present generation's inadequate and sketchy conception of those origins. Americans misconstrued their political inheritance when they compared the present to a single moment of the past instead of acting in accordance with the complete spectrum of history, a spectrum that united patriot with slaveholder. Citizens could transcend needless complications by remembering not simply a history, Taney implied, but an inheritance that connected them as sons to the unambiguous days of the fathers, when "ordinary language" prevailed.[19]

The post-Revolutionary sons, the first generation to succeed the founding fathers, both justified and criticized the present with reference to what Edward Said defines as *"filiation—*a linear, biologically grounded process, that which ties children to their parents."[20] Constructing men like Washington and Jefferson as the founders and defining dates like July 4, 1776 as the origin, Americans instituted authority for their own political system. Filiation plotted the national narrative of the post-Revolutionary generation along a course whose clear lines of succession and obligation promised no twists, internal contradictions, or dark digressions that could suggest a history that was anything but coherent. Just as with any story of fathers and sons, the father provided the son with authority and identity—as long as the genealogical line between the origin and successive generations remained intact and unquestioned. Of course, fathers cannot beget sons on their own, but erasing mothers from this genealogy both removed possible complications emanating from other legacies, maternally derived, and allowed the sons to prevent the diffusion (to daughters, to slave children acknowledged only by the mother) of an inheritance procured by the filial metaphors they applied to history. Tracing exclusive lines between fathers and sons invested the present with the stability of foundations set firmly in the past. The fathers bequeathed their posterity a coherence that extended to a past that forever would resist corruption, fixed in the security of completed history. Thus, Taney found that the furor created by a black slave declaring himself a free and independent citizen could be quelled if the sons correctly remembered the historical time of the fathers. The past, which reveals that "a perpetual and impassible barrier was intended to be erected between the white race and the one which they had reduced to slavery," would determine the proper course of action for the present. The political differences of the present would dissipate when sons like Taney posited a coherent past. Washington and the other founding fathers bore this reassuring relation to many endeavors of the filial generation, sanctifying nationalist projects such as Manifest Destiny and slavery by allowing citizens to claim that expansionism, for instance, figured prominently in the original design of America. Or, in other sectors, Alabama ideologue William L. Yancey could appeal to origins and confidently assert: "Your fathers and my fathers built this government on two ideas: the first is that the white race is the citizen, and the master race, and the white man is the equal of every other white man. The second idea is that the Negro is the inferior race."[21]

The Dred Scott decision amplifies one aspect of a layered understanding of genealogy that informs this project. As a descriptive term for the filial metaphors specific to the national narrative of the antebellum era, genealogy traces the language and rhetoric deployed in the construction of national history. Following the prominent examples of Herman Melville and Ralph Waldo Emerson, both descendants of Revolutionary forefathers, antebellum America configured itself as the adolescent, yet steadily maturing, male offspring of an original America engendered by Washington, Jefferson, and Madison.[22] The denial of suffrage to women and the legal definition of the black slave as the mother's child reveal patrifilial identification as the only valid metaphor of citizenship. Identifying origins along the line of the founding fathers at once invested history with patriarchal authority and guaranteed that the nation would continue as a bloodline from father to son. As Said points out, the term *authority* itself derives from patriarchal origins, its etymology suggesting *author* as a person who engenders, begets, or originates something. Moreover, in its connection to *auctoritas*, the term implies the maintaining of continuity.[23] Genealogy in this way verifies and perpetuates patriarchal power between father and son, between founders and citizens, between historical generations.

The fact that Taney's judgment addressed the historical legality of black slavery introduces a second significance of genealogy, one specifically marked by the complex of American race relations. Taney admits that the Declaration might "embrace the whole human family," but the question before the court, he states, is more narrow, concerning solely the status of blacks within what Taney calls the "new political family" of America. The placement of blacks within American genealogy concerned many other discourses of the antebellum era. Pseudoscientific ethnology, for example, denied African Americans a place in the human family, resorting to specious biology to "prove" the lack of full intellectual development or moral capacity in blacks. Meanwhile, biblical genealogy cursed slaves with the mark of Ham, and proslavery anthropology studied the history of man to "discover" the theory of polygenesis that gave blacks an ancestry separate from the white man's origin in Eden. Taney's concerns about national citizenship resonate with such discourses, though his conclusion makes a more particular appeal to historical foundations. The Constitution authored a "new political family" of free citizens who, sharing a history of independence and common political paternity, collected together in a nation. Blacks, in contrast, descended from a different political family; in Taney's opinion, "those persons who are the descendants of Africans who were imported into this country and sold as slaves" lack a history of freedom, and share no political blood with United States citizens. Failure to enfranchise blacks within a nation of free citizens hardly exposed the fathers as hypocritical or inconsistent; instead, this determination attested to the immediate status of the United States as a civilized nation. The founders "knew that it [the Declaration] would not, in any part of the civilized world, be supposed to embrace the negro race, which, by common consent, had been excluded from civilized governments and the family of nations, and doomed to slavery."[24] Genealogical recourse to the founding fathers at once explains the exclusion of blacks from this "new political family" and resolves potential contradictions within the national legacy. Exclusion, like the exceptionalism of this "new political family," secures coherence for the body politic. The history of the fathers, as the sons constructed it, validated those sons, making their decisions and institutions part of the heroic past rather than the product of interpretation and politics.

As a practice of remembering and constructing history, American genealogy inevitably has signaled exclusion: it identifies rightful members within ancestral paths, even as it omits those denied the originary authority of a patriarchal ancestor. Some have descended from fathers and therefore have a citizen's blood running in their political and social bodies; others lack a legitimate ancestor within the nation and can claim no prior authority to act as citizens. Within the specific context of a racially marked and disturbed nation, the metaphor of bloodlines acquired brutal literalness. As America confronted the ambiguity of miscegenation and the enslavement of children with white blood, the metaphor of civic freedom as an inheritance transmitted from father to son unraveled if those same fathers propagated slave progeny. If the familial nation, as Taney proposed, involves a comprehensive view of the founding father's words and actions, should moments of political and moral indiscretion be written as part of national history? Should the prevailing metaphors of political inclusion be rewritten so that the influence of mothers and daughters can be recognized as having a meaningful role in procuring the rights of citizenship? Should the genealogical tree of national citizenry also trace ignominious lines of bastards and forgotten offspring? Such disturbing questions did not remain isolated on plantations or in Taney's decision. The blood history of father-son relations only inflated miscegenation to national dimensions. Rumors of plantation patriarchs who fathered slaves spawned troubling questions about the descent of freedom. Once the existence of red-haired slave children at Monticello muddled the relationship between fathers and sons, at the national level slavery contaminated the legacy of freedom that passed from the founding fathers of 1776 to the antebellum sons of the 1850s. As with any story of fathers and sons, Oedipal tension, patriarchal prohibition, and filial rebellion punctuate the national story with moments of intense crisis.

In the face of such conflicts, one might longingly return to the authority of patriarchal origins for reassuring signs of coherence, order, and hierarchy. One could thus assume, as Taney did, that national foundations necessarily are as stable and legitimate as a genealogical tree. Allowing slaves the privileges of citizenship contradicted the appeals to genealogy made by the Supreme Court in this 1856 decision. According to this interpreter of America, a more complete history of the fathers, one that considers the exceptional decree of independence alongside daily acts of enslavement, proves slavery to be a policy wholly consistent with freedom because, after all, slavery and freedom had coexisted in the lives and homes of great men. The father-son metaphor of national history tracked no lines of connection or proofs of incorporation for black slaves descended from Africans who, in the eyes of antebellum America, had a separate and unequal genealogy. If slaves could inherit political rights fathered by Washington and Jefferson, then the unbroken line of filiation suddenly would compromise its own identity and unity to include political nonsubjects marked by difference and heterogeneity. For this reason, the enfranchisement of blacks, Taney argues, "would have been utterly inconsistent with the caution [the founders] displayed in providing for the admission of new members into this political family."[25]

To derive this conclusion, however, Taney could not apply genealogy in its most important and radical sense. Melville, Douglass, Brown, and Lincoln were American sons who implemented critical historiographies through parricidal remembrance. These political writers and actors turned to the past, but rather than resuscitate underlying principles of coherence, they articulate a disjunctive national history always fractured by inconsistency and contradiction. As with Taney's genealogical interpretation, they use family history as a metaphor to narrate American political history, yet the genealogical model they refer to lacks the purity and order of Taney's "political family." Alienated and disenfranchised descendants, bastards, mulattos, and forgotten sons all recur in their works as illegitimate people whose disqualified status challenges a national narrative based on seamless lines of genealogy. Fugitive slaves like Douglass and Brown and wanderers like Melville's Ishmael and Israel Potter represent parts of genealogical trees elided by Taney's decision and by other national narratives that gravitate toward unifying configurations of history. The story Brown tells of Jefferson's slave progeny in *Clotel* recovers an overlooked national daughter. But rather than resolve the outcast's unfortunate situation by returning her to her rightful position, Brown leaves this national daughter dangling, amputated from the security and identity of a genealogical line. What would be her rightful position? Hers is the conflicted identity of either a legal slave made free or a descendant of freedom reduced to bondage. Her paradoxical bloodlines defy uncompromised explanation; her story counters a legacy indebted to coherence and accord. Just as Ishmael's digressive musings deflect the imperious progression of the narrative of Ahab's quest, so, too, the story of Clotel impedes the seamless utterance of a national narrative based upon the sanctity of the founding fathers.

Melville, Lincoln, Douglass, and Brown recover stories and memories cast aside by authorized paths of history within the republic. They delineate connections that attested to an inheritance from American fathers, yet they do not insist upon incorporation within the customs, rituals, and official forms of national recognition. Melville's coupling of Ishmael's eclectic meditations with Ahab's teleological narrative is not an attempt to discern a cosmic unity between circular logic and linear progression, and Brown's novel does not relate the story of Clotel Jefferson with the melodramatic intent to restore her to her ancestral lands, either as heiress or slave.[26] This indeterminacy confers a countervalence upon the stories of Ishmael and Clotel; their memories are discounted, disqualified, and ignored. Such dispossessed and disenfranchised narratives, too, denote what Foucault, following Nietzsche, calls genealogy. In *Power/ Knowledge*, Foucault outlines a critical practice that examines subjugated and "differential knowledges," not in the hopes of unifying them with a single narrative as Taney did, but with the design of countering and disrupting singular articulations of history. Genealogy is an "insurrection of knowledges that are opposed . . . to the effects of the centralising powers which are linked to the institution and functioning of an organised scientific discourse within a society such as ours."[27]

Although Foucault has Marxism in mind when he mentions "scientific discourse,"[28] within antebellum America, historical discourse fulfilled these same functions, tending to install a set of homogeneous narratives as the story of the nation. A national mythology circulates: for Lincoln in 1838, the past identified his generation as "the legal inheritors of . . . fundamental blessings;"[29] for Taney, the standards of patriot fathers removed any qualms about the legality or morality of denying blacks those same "fundamental blessings"; and for Milton and Lewis Clarke, there was the faith that the father's freedom, if acknowledged in the pure spirit of its originary foundations, would offer them the protections guaranteed to all citizens. Each of these patriarchal plots appeals to a larger, more encompassing narrative that United States culture administered in the face of the political, racial, and moral crises of the 1850s. But by questioning how representative that narrative was, critics can discover ways to "emancipate historical knowledges from . . . subjection, to render them, that is, capable of opposition and of struggle against the coercion of a theoretical, unitary, formal and scientific discourse."[30] Taken in the context of American literature and culture, Foucault's comments suggest that by reading the national-family tree, not simply along the lines of hierarchy and primary relation, but with an eye to other affiliations such as those produced by miscegenation or domination, voices reappear whose once forgotten status enables them to discern the limits of the will to totality that makes narrative national.

But do these powers of discernment necessarily lead to radical opposition that can be sustained in meaningful ways? Many recent commentators have illustrated how Melville or even fugitive slaves sanctioned the dominant ideology. According to this line of argument, the American "genealogists" considered within this study acknowledged and, especially in their dissent, supported a narrative of America. Sacvan Bercovitch argues that Americans who criticize the nation nevertheless affirm a national ideology that always permits, allows, and consents to the voicing of dissent. He positions "classic" American writers within an inescapable circle of ideological containment in which criticism becomes "a mimesis of cultural norms." "The works of our classic writers show more clearly than others I know how American radicalism could be turned into a force against radical change," he states. Under this logic, writers who question an encompassing narrative fail to see how the nation once again encircles them by permitting their interrogations in the first place. What they think is an encompassing narrative is but part of the picture: their own perception and activism has been guaranteed by a more pervasive totality, which they cannot glimpse because their role as critic is always expected and already embedded in national culture. Bercovitch makes clear the flexibility of that culture by acknowledging his own enclosure within its system and confessing that any story he tells is a story that has already been imagined under the symbol of America: "I would like to declare the principles of my own ideological dependence. I hold these truths to be self-evident: that there is no escape from ideology." These wonderful sentences play upon the foundational language of the Declaration to underscore the point that any deviation from America necessarily remains indebted to an originary political rhetoric. Bercovitch thus self-consciously follows in a long line of antebellum dissenters—Thoreau, Frederick Douglass, working men, women's suffragists—who departed from America in their declarations of independence only to return to it by that very action.[31] The times, circumstances, and particular grievances may have been different in each case, but the underlying content of their protests still has consented to the "fundamental blessings" called forth by Lincoln.

But the truly radical aspect of such writers' work did not concern its content: it involved restructuring narrative form. They moved beyond radical rebukes of the content of American narrative—rebukes that Bercovitch understands as culturally affirming—to query the forms and modes in which that narrative was constructed and repeated. Instead of getting trapped in sterile complaints that only recapitulated national norms, they evaded quarrels that reaffirmed the content of America to concentrate on resisting the limits set on the stories they could tell about the nation. Melville, Brown, Douglass, and Lincoln formulated narratives that countered not just specific moments of history, but the more overarching structures of American history. Although such cultural critics were also not exempt from producing jeremiads against the state and its institutions, they nonetheless anticipated Bercovitch's point that employing American ideals to denounce America undercuts any apparent radicalism. In addition to worrying about *what* politics their culture practiced, they sought to antagonize the form of national narrative, asking *how* its preconditions (foundational beliefs, honored declarations, "fundamental blessings") dictated the stories one could tell. The issue is not so much whether one could tell different stories—indeed, Bercovitch shows the fallacy involved in this utopian optimism—but whether one could tell the same stories differently. Consent may disarm divergent content; however, ruptures in the form of national narrative are not so easily reconciled. So while dissent ineluctably reconfirms the logic of consent, many antebellum texts struggle against broadly configured narratives, whether they are rituals of assent, as in Bercovitch's account, or the country's monomaniacal insistence that history confirms its own righteousness. By probing American ideals and the political totality they implemented, genealogy inflicts a type of criticism that moves beyond countering official forms of American history to interrogate the parameters and modes out of which the nation is constructed.

By moving between literal and figurative understandings of genealogy, I hope to make clear the challenges it offers to the patriarchal lineage of the nation. Bercovitch writes: "Every ideology . . . breeds its own opposition, every culture its own counter-culture," and so criticism engenders consensus.[32] But given the accidental relations, unexpected ramifications, and uncontrolled resemblances that pervade genealogical trees, can America regulate its breeding? Certainly, the rigid rules and customs governing inheritance and enslavement attempted to do so, and yet as the orphans, bastards, and slaves who reappear in these pages show, these systems produced ambivalent figures whose illegitimate status necessitates asking: what form of genealogy can understand them, what shape must the national-family tree take in order to account for them? Perhaps that form has been provided by American literary history, which a century later enrolled Melville at the core of the canon, adding Douglass a few decades afterward, all the while holding Lincoln in place as the truest inheritor of the founders' promise? That is a dubious proposition, considering that once assimilated to the exchanges, conferences, and syllabi of higher education, these nineteenth-century voices accrue a prestige that makes their opposition national. Through what Jonathan Arac calls the "nationalizing of literary narrative," texts once deeply skeptical about America come to affirm the importance of dissent, reform, revolution and other norms.[33] Yet from genealogy we learn that "adding story to story"—or, in this case, text to canonical text—invites, not new canons, but new ways of talking about the canon. As an academic breeding ground of "classic" authors, the canon insures that its texts repeat certain lessons dear to the United States, but does it unequivocally control the ways they narrate America?

In *The American Jeremiad*, Bercovitch argues for the pervasiveness of canons and covenants, contending that "classic writers tended to uphold those [American] ideals even when they most bitterly assailed their society." His *Office of The Scarlet Letter* intensifies this critique by focusing on that dissenter, Hester Prynne, whose opposition to Puritan society "amounts to a code of liberal heroics," demonstrating that "radicalism has a place in society, after all." All of the writers studied here do repeat narratives of national culture.

However, repetition of national culture is not mere repetition, but repetition with a *difference*. While one may argue that Cooper's *The Spy* adheres to a dominant cultural image of Washington, and even that Douglass's "The Heroic Slave," by playing upon the name of Washington, contains its slave hero within an accepted historical framework, these narratives are not exact affirmations of national mythology. Repetition always includes something extra—an appendix, a preface, a disclaimer, an unlooked-for association—that supplements and alters overarching narratives. So while my orientation acknowledges the totalizing force of 1850s American culture and its ability to contain oppositional content, this study argues that ritualized and controlled reiterations of the nation nonetheless introduced subtle differences in each variation. And difference does make a difference. In other words, "adding story to story" no doubt provides reaffirming renditions of the sociopolitical order, and yet each story is not an exact replica of the foundational narrative. Though subsumed into what Bercovitch calls the "single most cohesive ideology of the modern world," these supplemental stories contain oppositional gestures that are not merely rendered inert. Agreeing with Foucault that "there are no relations of power without resistances," and with Jonathan Arac and Harriet Ritvo that "the resistances within a system of power may change that system," I hold that the formal incongruities found in this compilation of stories involve the stirrings of ambivalence and rebellion.[34]

As Homi Bhabha remarks in an essay entitled "DissemiNation," instances of repetition "add to" but do not "add up." While retellings of national culture augment national narrative, they do so in ways that cannot readily be factored into national narrative without altering it. Additions or supplements defy a logic that subsumes all experience or memory within homogeneous articulations; some trace remains too differential, too disjunctive, to fit into the covenant. Incorporation bears evidence of what needed to be assimilated. And in the racial terms so poignant in America, even as miscegenation assents to the same origin, it also registers a different history. Bhabha's insights into colonial discourse often center on acts of articulation that seem to mimic colonial authority, yet latent in any visible allegiance to national narrative lies a "discourse that is uttered *inter dicta*: a discourse at the crossroads of what is known and permissible and that which though known must be kept concealed; a discourse uttered between the lines and as such both against the rules and within them." What emerges from this relation is the "hybrid," which exerts a double pressure of recognition and difference. Even as the hybrid mirrors the colonial authority and "retains the actual semblance of the authoritative symbol," through *"the intervention of difference"* the hybrid resists the sameness to which it has subscribed. So Bhabha's statement that "the colonial presence is always ambivalent, split between its appearance as original and authoritative and its articulation as repetition and difference" illuminates American narrative, showing how articulations of ideological consensus nonetheless have remained resistant, harboring a double discourse conceived in subversion and heterogeneity.[35] Novels, autobiographies, and monuments that appear to reiterate the basic tenets of United States ideology no doubt have assented to "America," but they also have acted differently, refusing to return as part of the same narrative, and instead have entered the cultural field infused with darker, twin associations that cannot be reconciled to a pattern of the nation.

Coherent and consensual, national narrative is also split and ambivalent. Even the most dutiful son harbors murderous urges against the father. Such statements invite a reorientation of the perspectives used to survey American literary history. In addition to registering how oppositional texts of the canon inevitably flow into national ratifications, it is important to understand how even complacent and affirming texts such as patriotic biographies of Washington or monuments to Revolutionary fathers have stood uneasily upon a foundation of dissent. The aggregated stories that have produced ideological consent can also be taken as a form other than totality, as an array of fragmentary moments, offering not a continuous lineage, but sporadic returns and interjections from those pushed to the margins of Taney's "new political family." Bhabha's description of the hybridity of culture is helpful in underscoring this idea. Looking at "the scenario of the English book" in colonial India, he suggests that as this artifact of British rule met up with "the uncanny forces of race, sexuality, violence," it began to speak differently, to tell other stories even as it was still imprinted with the same, "universal" story it first had in England. Vulnerable to this sort of "estrangement," once authoritative and confident texts chart a "discontinuous history."[36] The artifacts of American rule, nationalist novels and founding fathers, likewise speak authoritatively, but they also speak in less sure tones, exhibiting all the same contradictions of citizenship, irresolvable issues of race, and unexpected criticisms of the nation found in the 1838 Lyceum address of a young man aspiring to become president of the United States.

This study thus understands antebellum America as a developing nation-state with its own narrative whose rituals of reiteration became compromised. Common patriarchal ancestors and shared legacies constituted a unity that corresponded to Thomas Hobbes's account of the covenant in *Leviathan*: an assumed artifice melding a people in the homogeneity of a single, national body. As Ahab puts the matter to his mariners: "Ye are not other men, but my arms and my legs; and so obey me." With the appearance of those subjects forgotten and overlooked by a myopic narrative, however, doubts arose whether the narrative as a covenant could apply (or should apply) to all the nation's citizens and noncitizens. What could genealogical history mean to those slaves denied patriarchal ancestors? What could the encoding of history within grand architectural bodies like the Washington or Bunker Hill monuments mean to those such as Israel Potter, whose scarred and forgotten bodies tell another story? What could it mean for Ishmael to remember how "all the individualities of the crew, this man's valor, that man's fear; guilt and guiltiness, all varieties were welded into oneness, and were all directed to that fatal goal which Ahab their one lord and keel did point to" while retelling the story of Moby Dick in an effort to separate himself from Ahab's doomed quest?[37] The chapters of this study trace the disjunctions and ruptures within the national narrative that made impossible coherent articulation of the covenant, that made incoherent such national representations of corporate oneness as George Washington, Thomas Jefferson, or the possessed crew of the Pequod.

Genealogy, in this critical aspect, helps undo the static, homogeneous presence posited by such representations. Unbroken lines of filiation splinter and branch off to recover obscured, illegitimate bodies and memories. The literal figure of the slave's body, like the mulatto invoked by Lincoln, for example, disrupts the more figurative corpus of George Washington within historical romance. And, at the same time, once genealogy draws attention to the shaky constructedness of a covenanted narrative presumed to be part natural and part divine, it can begin to implant counternarratives that substantially transform the history of a nation. Not only does inclusion of slaves and forgotten patriots alter the content of a national narrative committed to the renown of the founding fathers, but it also supplants the affirming, expository style of patriotic history with a more ironic mode given instead to doubleness and ambivalence. Genealogy as parricidal criticism rewrites the single history of the nation as a more diverse, contradictory, and conflicted set of experiences. These changes in the mode of narrating the genealogy of the American national body can effect a significant change in our understanding of what exactly amounts to freedom within America. A reassessment of this national narrative leads to a differentiated description of freedom as originating out of slavery, amnesia, and incompleteness.

The chapters in this book do not offer different perspectives on narrative and historical crises within the antebellum era so much as they chart a progression from the breakdown of freedom within the national narrative to the eventual recuperation of a different freedom through ironic constructions of history. From *eironeia*, meaning "dissemblance," and *eironikos*, meaning "deceitful," irony uses an evident meaning to camouflage a more subtle intent that rebels against that evident meaning. And when applied to history, irony subverts the constructed edifice of national narrative, disclosing the ways in which its homogeneity and coherence are the result of dissimulation. If one forgets the gaps and inconsistencies that are signs of this dissimulation, one can remember a straightforward, uncomplicated history; but, in contrast, if one remembers the signs of dissimulation, then a more ironic story can be told. In antebellum culture, as in all historical eras, history was a frame constructed for events fabricated with a series of causality, but what makes America perhaps distinctive is that the national narrative labored to forget the complications of constructedness. Critical genealogists, however, combatted the forgetting that history causes and remembered stories that lay alongside the more regular pathways of history. Melville, Brown, Douglass, and Lincoln made history ironic by exploiting the sanctified grandeur of unquestioned figures and moments from American history as a cover for memories, rumors, and insinuations that challenged the prevailing meaning of history. In much the same way, using literary texts, materials from popular culture, slave narratives, and political theory, I have plotted an ironic story that, although not chronological, exposes the construction of freedom and then seeks to reconstruct freedom within a more fractious and embattled narrative aware of its history of deceit and dissimulation.

Lest it be thought, however, that this book offers a thoroughly redemptive narrative without its own history of exclusion, I want to recognize that another genealogical line is largely absent from these pages. Matriarchal genealogy and maternal resistance also challenge the national lineage, and any consideration of slave women, republican motherhood, and agitation for women's suffrage further throws into question the adequacy of national narrative. Deep, generative discontinuities become exposed by examining both the extent to which patriarchal history sought to diminish women's role in the nation-family and the types of relations mothers and daughters created with institutions, history, and each other to combat their marginalization. By not more fully addressing this erasure, this study accepts the primacy of patrifilial relations in order to examine possible destabilizations of American patriarchy. Still, mulattos, bastards, and orphans are as much a product of mothering as fathering, and in the case of miscegenation, these sexual encounters add stories of forgetting and patriarchal power at their most turbulent and exploitative levels. Restoring the dispossessed to narrative is, for Frederick Douglass, a maternal project: scouring national history for traces of Madison Washington, Douglass compares his genealogical efforts in "The Heroic Slave" to those of "a wearied and disheartened mother, (after a tedious and unsuccessful search for a lost child)."[38] What needs to be noted, nonetheless, is that the American genealogists surveyed in this book, for the most part, were complicit with this elision of mothers and daughters. *Moby-Dick* thus examines how the perversion of democracy leads to racial exploitation, but it does so within an exclusively male, homosocial community; Lincoln's return to the birth of the republic understands such births only as male events; the slave mothers and wives whom Douglass mentions disappear when he begins to reconfigure freedom, a theoretical undertaking that for his heroic speakers is best performed in the arena of patriarchal history. Even as these writers suggest the inadequacies of a dominant political lineage, their reorientations of America did not discern how, in addition to an evasion of race and slavery, the suppression of women's legacies has been a constitutive absence in national narrative.

Chapter 1 examines James Fenimore Cooper's *The Spy* and others' juvenile biographies of Washington alongside sectional disputes and rhetorical conflicts in an effort to gauge the narrative authority of the founding fathers and the eventual dissolution of that authority. Prefiguring the highly ambivalent position of patriarchs in slave narratives, the politics of compromise within even such uncritical forms of patriotic literature disturb the coherence of Washington as the embodiment of the national covenant. Unable to contain the contradictions and incongruities of race slavery, the emblems of a unified, divinely bound America lose their currency. The chapters following this analysis of the breakdown of Washington as national signifier examine various genealogical projects that assail a historical narrative that had once held Washington pure, inviolate, and coherent. This fractured framework provides a context to consider an anti-teleological novel such as *Moby-Dick*, a strongly revisionary speech such as Lincoln's Gettysburg Address, and harshly critical American autobiographies such as William Wells Brown's numerous personal recollections.

"Queequeg was George Washington cannibalistically developed," announces Ishmael in *Moby-Dick*.[39] This statement counters the "facts" of various racist ethnological and anthropological discourses even as it further unsettles the authoritative narrative of the founding fathers. Chapter 2, "Covenants, Truth, and the 'Ruthless Democracy' of *Moby-Dick*," develops an argument that against a backdrop of pseudoscience and nationalist mythology, Melville reproduces aboard the *Pequod* the rituals of antebellum democracy. Race there arises as a scene of contestation, one moment galvanizing the crew in fraternal brotherhood, and the next inflecting differences that disrupt the crew and render the sailors susceptible to Ahab's exploitation. The complex of interactions between Ishmael and Queequeg, on the one hand, and between Ahab, the pagan harpooners, and the crew, on the other, recapitulates the demonology of American politics, in which symbolic rituals have masqueraded as political participation and in which demagoguery has replaced democratic principles. Conceived at the time of constitutional crises and the passage of the Fugitive Slave Law, financed in part by Lemuel Shaw, who enforced the Fugitive Slave Law, and written by an American son who, like the title character of *Pierre* is of "double revolutionary descent," *Moby-Dick* as political fiction critiques the rhetorical uses of founding fathers that threatened to make politics little more than fiction.[40] Melville's narrative thus performed the oppositional work that Foucault describes as integral to the practice of genealogy.

This type of countering maneuver inherent in the agonistic strife of genealogy can coalesce into revisionary narratives as well. The third and fourth chapters continue to look at Melville's works, not so much with an eye toward explaining the political character of his novels and tales, but with the contention that *Israel Potter* and "The Bell-Tower" served as theoretical reassessments of the narratives that emplot American history. The discursive skirmish between *Israel Potter* and what Nietzsche in "On the Uses and Disadvantages of History for Life" terms "monumental history" provides the focus for chapter 3. A wide range of cultural expressions, from sublime landscapes of Niagara Falls, to Emerson's transcendental reflections, to the literal embodiment of monumental remembrance in icons such as the Bunker Hill Monument established a mode of history that, taking a cue from the earlier discussion of nationalist mythology and *Moby-Dick*, can readily be described as Ahabian. Possessed by a powerful spirit and inexorably committed to national progress, monumentalism seriously threatened the possibilities of democratic action—just as Ahab adulterated the covenanted will of the crew. As expressions of monumental history, both the Bunker Hill Monument and Emerson's "transparent eyeball" in *Nature* enact national visions that obscure individual citizens. *Israel Potter* forms a line of resistance to monumental history by making ironic the transcendent, iconic forms of Revolutionary remembrance.

Such disjunctive remembering, as chapter 4 shows, became the primary mode for amending the American legacy. Fugitive slave William Wells Brown conceived of history as an ironic category susceptible to incongruity and inconsistency. With his several contradictory autobiographies and the speculative history in his novel *Clotel*, Brown exposed the discrepancies in the narrative of freedom. Elsewhere, Brown destabilized national foundations through scrutiny of architectural monuments and the sexual legacies of monumental fathers, uncovering a compromising racial context within the authorized paths of remembrance. Yet, as an examination of political speeches and popular antebellum legends about the Revolution proves, historical irony could also perform a preservative function as it restored coherence to historical narrative by bracketing off inconsistencies as rare aberrations having no power to invalidate the general "truths" of history. This type of preservative irony, as opposed to critical, genealogical irony, allowed Americans confronted with the sin of race servitude to dismiss slavery as an atypical, temporary episode of American history. Faith in the justice and truth of the national narrative could still prevail. Brown, Melville, and Lincoln retell the histories of political communities in ways that deal with this bad faith perpetrated by preservative irony. They work against affirming, popular legends of Revolutionary liberty by narrating genealogies that return to origins of freedom that simultaneously were origins of fraud, murder, and enslavement.

The final chapter, "Discursive Passing African American Literature," continues to identify race and slavery as the impetus for a genealogy of freedom. In slave narratives, however, genealogy describes more than a critical practice; it addresses a literal, continual concern of ex-slaves who seek to legitimate selves, memories, and freedom with appeals to a past that declares them illegitimate and unfathered. As Frederick Douglass states in *My Bondage and My Freedom,* "Genealogical trees do not flourish among slaves. A person of some consequence here in the north, sometimes designated *father,* is literally abolished in slave law and slave practice." Although Eugene Genovese argues that the notion of the absent slave father was in many ways more myth than actuality, most antebellum slave narratives are told by narrators who declare their lack of a father.[41] Historical actuality and narrative may differ, but as slave narrators so critically understand, narrative distorts real recollections and shapes new memories. Slave narratives stand as acts of self-authorship precisely because their authors had no patriarchal legacy that would inscribe their bodies and their memories with a citizen's rights, duties, or legitimacy. This constructed absence of a patriarchal legacy made for significant mutations in the legitimating discourses used by patriarchal institutions. Turning to their own bodies, often the illegitimate products of amalgamation, slave narrators experiment with amalgamation as a textual practice. Writing themselves within the legacy of the founding fathers, fugitive slaves adopt a historical discourse that has marked them and their descendants with silence, illegitimacy, and servitude. From these amalgamated circumstances, freedom emerges as a product of interbreeding whose parentage includes cruelty and compassion, enslavement and republican values, and contradiction and "self-evident" truths.

Not only do these African American inflections alter the content of consensual ideals such as freedom, but additionally, these elided and dispossessed accents reverberate throughout the structure of national narrative, casting doubts on whether that narrative can be told ever again in coherent fashion. Ralph Waldo Emerson believed that it could by construing the crisis over slavery as a temporary aberration, after which nation and narrative would resume onward to the promise of closure. "The Father of his country shall wait well-pleased a little longer for his monument," said Emerson in 1855, referring to the stump-like Washington Monument whose construction had slowed with the increase of sectional tension.[42] Like the monument, nation and narrative would find completion simply by returning to a course that supposedly had been laid out in the first moments of founding. Chapter 1, however, undercuts this optimism, exposing that it is predicated upon a belief that those origins are themselves coherent, containing none of the incendiary conflicts that disfigure Emerson's own era. In order for Emerson and other sons to wait upon the fathers, even when those fathers themselves were paralyzed by contradiction, antebellum historians, biographers, and novelists had to ignore their own narratival contortions in insisting upon father-son metaphors as a basis for theorizing and practicing politics. Though all metaphors demand such twists and turns, the patrifilial metaphors of America legislate a series of accommodations, distortions, and tangles that seriously circumscribe the possibilities of political experience and expression. Where a different trope—say a comparison of a poet's love to a red rose—does or does not correspond and cohere may be small issue, especially for an infatuated poet, but for a nation determining the character of its citizenry, the metaphor of descent becomes crucial when the story of father begetting son omits or obscures significant elements—such as slavery or blood—from the democratic experience.

1

Founding Fathers and Parricidal Textuality

Race and Authority in American Narrative

The soul of the Union is dead,
and now let its body be buried.
—*New Orleans Daily Crescent,*
December 1861

THE WASHINGTON CORPUS
AND THE SLAVE BODY

When, in 1795, one of George Washington's slaves ran away, the president directed that his name not appear on the reward poster. Pursuit of a fugitive slave might simply have been an affair of Washington's private, domestic management, yet the incident threatened to breed an embarrassing public situation by coupling the name of a patriot who had secured freedom for an infant nation with the body of the black slave. Though Washington prevailed in this case and preserved his national figure from unsettling contradictions, he was inevitably powerless to determine the ideological uses the nation would make of his mythic legacy. The private individual may have been resolute that patriots do not associate with fugitive slaves in public, but the corpus of metaphoric associations that made up the public image of the founding father stumbled against disturbing and indeterminate associations that saw Washington providing directives both for and against slavery. As members of the post-Revolutionary generation confronted this inconsistency, they continually rewrote the biography of the founding father in an attempt to articulate a national history that still promised coherence and closure.[1] And though corrections and changes of Washington's legacy seemingly assured the destiny of the nation in the face of increasing sectional division, these retellings, supplements, and prefaces to the narrative of the fathers undermined the coherent story of America by insidiously suggesting that its founding narratives were in some way inadequate and incomplete.

The president steered clear of the slave question, but after his death, abolitionist as well as proslavery factions never hesitated to couple his name with the bound body of the slave. "Alas! thought I," wrote an abolitionist who ran across a gang of manacled slaves en route to a pilgrimage to Mount Vernon. "The land of Washington!—her soil worn out—her children led away captive—surely a curse has fallen upon her." E. M. Hudson experienced none of this anguish over pairing slaves and founding fathers. Washington provided this Confederate polemicist with a fatherly blessing for race slavery in *The Second War of Independence in America*: "When we reflect that the greatest statesmen of America—as Washington, Jefferson, Madison, Monroe, Calhoun, and others—were slaveholders, and that they were distinguished by their moderation and mildness, as well as an ardent attatchment to freedom, we may well entertain a doubt that the influence of slavey upon the dominant race in America has been pernicious." For abolitionists and fugitive slaves, American history could not be articulated without voicing the contradictions of a freedom existing alongside the peculiar institution of race slavery. In the first African American novel, *Clotel; or, The President's Daughter* (1853), escaped slave and novelist William Wells Brown enforced sexual conjunction to act as national disjunction and dramatized the fractures in the American mythic narrative by placing the mulatto granddaughter of Thomas Jefferson upon the auction block. For Brown, remembering was hardly an exercise in patrifilial reverence; history was not a consolidated, indivisible domain. For slavery's apologists, however, figurative and even literal kinship between black slaves and founding fathers betrayed no lines of disintegration. Instead, the founding fathers became identified with biblical patriarchs, wisely overseeing their property, justified in sacrificing their children as Abraham did Isaac. George Washington's treatment of his "servants" instructed farmers in the proper management of their livestock, and slaves once owned by Thomas Jefferson were not a national embarrassment but a national resource capable of delivering valuable memories of the author of the Declaration of Independence. *The Memoirs of a Monticello Slave* easily sacrifices Isaac Jefferson's historical condition as slave to a higher mythic purpose: to remembering Washington's liberality ("He gave Isaac a guinea") or Jefferson's prodigious mind ("Isaac has often wondered how old master came to have such a mighty head").[2] Bound by the patriarchal institution, Isaac Jefferson remains textually enslaved to the history of the fathers, his own biography laboring to illuminate a receding legacy. A moral need to reaffirm the Abramic authors of the American covenant through such rituals of memory took precedence over any potential critique that might appear in the unreconciled voices and dissenting bodies—the cracks—of tradition.

Even though soliciting slave testimony might seem a risky historical enterprise, Isaac Jefferson's recollections affirmed new patterns of patriarchal authority that originated with the American experiment. In his study of American cultural consciousness from 1750 to 1800, Jay Fliegelman contends that the Revolution displaced traditional notions of patriarchal authority with more enlightened, more egalitarian relations between fathers and sons. Representations of Washington as a moral benefactor and citizen exemplar were consistent with liberal theories of education and child raising that began to be proposed in the eighteenth century. The young nation sought to devise a historical parentage that would not reinscribe Americans within the confines of a rigid patriarchal control. Antebellum biographies thus scripted a role of reformed, judicious authority for Washington by recording his adoption of Martha Custis's children—an action that found immediate extrapolation in the description of a national hero who, motivated by unselfishness, adopted and cared for an orphan nation. Washington's own childlessness proved oddly fortuitous to the history of the nation: freed of the restrictive lines of kinship, he emerged as the father of his country. "Far from betraying the Revolutionary ideology, the mythologization of Washington as founding father enthroned the antipatriarchal values that make up that ideology," writes Fliegelman. "The point is not that he is described as America's father, but rather what kind of father he is described as being."[3] The antipatriarchal Revolution toppled the stern, obdurate patriarch, replacing him with the benevolent father whose authority descended from his character and personal achievement. Washington met these requirements when he ushered America into its maturity, and then, as the classical comparison goes, like Cincinattus, he returned to his plow, leaving the citizens an inheritance of independence. He seemed to embody a pleasantly self-effacing authority who absented himself so the people could mature into their own rule. The problem arose, however, when Washington returned to his plow—and his plantation. The same kindly disposed father who watched over his citizens coincided with the apologists' image of the patriarchal planter overseeing his "children." The antipatriarchal ideology that Fliegelman describes also characterized the national father as slave owner. On the plantation, seeds of contradiction were sown that would disrupt the national narrative.

Such disruptive ambiguities did not plague the planter himself, as they did the legacy of the patriot that descended to the post-Revolutionary generation. His public silence on the slave question along with resilient yet dissimilar facts—that he led some human beings to freedom and independence, emancipated others, and owned as property still others—defied incorporation into a seamless story of America. Washington's private correspondence stresses a need for emancipation and is marked by such unequivocal declarations as "I can only say, that there is not a man living, who wishes more sincerely than I do to see a plan adopted for the abolition" of slavery. In the same letter, however, he apologizes for a lack of authority to implement his will autocratically: "But there is only one proper and effectual mode by which it can be accomplished, and that is by legislative authority." Washington's private resolution remains intact and unquestioned; at the national level, however, no closure extends to the corpus of representations that made up the icon of American patriarchal authority. Even when the owner of Mount Vernon made a decision in his will to emancipate his 317 slaves upon his wife's death, nothing was settled with respect to this corpus of public representations. In fact, an interpretative struggle began in which American culture labored to remember Washington's private life in a manner consistent with national policy. His Farewell Address's avoidance of the subject of slavery obeys an overall theme of his public career: the interest in national harmony oversees any protest that the figure of the black slave could articulate.[4] Rather than dissolve the story of America with a forced conclusion, Washington deemed it better to preserve the harmony and balance of the narrative itself, even if such a decision propagated ambiguity and inconsistency, keeping the nation's narrative suspended, prevented from realizing its errand.

For 1850s America, this irresolution had grown paralyzing. Citizens who would emplot the nation as Washington's biography in order to tell stories of promise and coherence found their tellings betrayed by stutters and traumatic gaps. Textual contortions, apologies, and rationalizations mar any coherence C. M. Kirkland achieved in her "private and familiar" juvenile biography, *Memoirs of Washington* (1857). Recounting how the seclusion of a snowstorm at Mount Vernon finds the general playing whist, she anticipates her young readers' delicate, impressionable sensibilities and quickly explains:

> But need we apologize for this amusement, which though disapproved in our day, was universally allowed in his time by the society in which he lived? Washington's habits require no apologies or concealments. He is not amenable in these matters to standards set up since his day. . . . He would have been slow to believe, probably, that the day would ever come when good people could be found who would condemn dancing, yet refuse to condemn slavery; who would consider card-playing a sin, yet utter no fulminations against what Washington himself, born and bred in the midst of it, calls "a wicked, cruel and unnatural trade."[5]

Kirkland's negotiation of the issue is apparent yet complex: on the one hand, she derides slavery, expressing disdain for those of her generation for whom moral outrage was a convenience; on the other hand, in deference to Washington, she trivializes slavery, mentioning it only by way of comparison to another "harmless" sin, an occasional fondness for cards. In similar fashion, Benson J. Lossing's *The Home of Washington* (1859) details dinner parties at Mount Vernon to imagine the docility of slavery under a proper national authority: "The dishes and plates were removed and changed, with a silence and speed that seemed like enchantment." Contained in silence and invisibility, slavery and its disturbing associations never risk impudence before company—whether it is dinner guests or a nation of readers. As with most other mid-century narratives of the founding father, *Memoirs* and *The Home of Washington* instill the belief that slavery was never problematic under Washington's patriarchal care and management. Dutiful and industrious habits equip Washington to carry masterfully the nation's share of the white man's burden of providing for what Kirkland sees as "the dilatory, inefficient and irregular people he had to deal with."[6]

Only after she has Washington dead and buried does Kirkland return to the question of slavery. "On the whole, the testimony of Washington against slavery is clear and explicit enough," she concludes, but the sense pervades the biography that slavery was not divisive while Washington lived. Her *Memoirs of Washington* turn to "Washington's opinions on slavery" only after the biography's plot has already effected closure, sealing the general in his tomb in the preceding chapter. This deferral and distancing of slavery in Washington's life did not occur only in popular biography. Even Washington Irving's *Life of George Washington* (1859), a more historically serious treatment, postpones the complication of slavery until the multivolume work has laid Washington to rest. In the final chapter of the work, once "the body was deposited in the vault," Irving confronts the presidential planter and attempts to sort out the "insuperable difficulties" that prevented immediate emancipation of his slaves.[7] The national narrative—ordered around the coherence of Washington's life—displaces slavery until after the story is ended in the resolution of Washington's burial. This return of the oppressed after the founder's death expresses more than Kirkland's or Irving's trauma; insurgent reconsiderations of the founders' story during the antebellum era mark the strained seams of faulty closure in a biography made national. Attempts to negotiate slavery involved a retreat to the past, a retreat to the storied coherence of Washington and his era that predated the affixing of any unsettling appendix. Yet text and culture suffered the same problematic: each sought to distance an uncertain present by retelling a narrative whose plot promises order and closure, but as juvenile biographies demonstrate, death failed to seal the nation's fate in unity and innocence. A postscript emerges, attached to the original plot, supplemental to the father's biography. This appended legacy describes much more than textual inconsistency within these 1850s biographies; for the antebellum sons, the present seemed a disjunctive appendix to the glorious era of the fathers.

Increasing numbers of citizens in the antebellum era returned to the memory of when Washington lived as a way to evade the threatened incoherence of comparing whist and slavery, of reconciling contemporary morality and founding exigency. The "problem of slavery impinged upon all others, producing a national ideology riddled with ambiguities and tensions, and year by year distorting the course of democracy," writes Eric Sundquist.[8] Beginning with the constitutional crisis of the 1850s, America sought to stave off disruption by rededicating itself to its original foundations. Bills were introduced for the completion of the Washington Monument and the restoration of Mount Vernon; first drafts of Washington's Farewell Address, stressing the need for national unity, were discovered and purchased by Congress, which ordered that copies be circulated among the populace. Anxiety and indecision about the coherence of the nation fueled this zealous return to narratives of the founding fathers. Henry Clay, who introduced the Senate motion to purchase the Farewell Address, hoped that "amid the discordance and ungrateful sounds of disunion and discord which assail our ears in every part of this country," Washington's parting counsel to overcome sectional differences would placate citizens. As early as 1792, Thomas Jefferson had looked to his fellow Virginian to sustain the putative unity of national narrative and suggested that the infant sections of the nation would endure by being suspended bodily from the hands of their father. Urging Washington to a second presidency, Jefferson wrote, "North and South will hang together as long as they have you to hang on."[9] The metaphoric dimension of Jefferson's plea stems from an understanding that nations are not solely defined by topographic contours. The nation arises from tropographic contours as well.

Much recent critical work has addressed the narratival aspects of the nation. The "National Symbolic," "an apparatus of cultural fictions," "the nation as narration," and the "imagined community" all highlight intersections of literary criticism with cultural studies of nationalism.[10] For instance, although important differences exist between Benedict Anderson's analysis of the novelistic historical consciousness of the modern nation and Etienne Balibar's description of the "whole system of translations" that produces for a nation a "fictive ethnicity," these conceptions posit the nation in relation to techniques and strategies associated with fictional construction. Whether the nation emerges from a "new cartographic discourse," as it does in part for Anderson, or whether critics privilege an account that is geographic, biographic, or tropographic, the key commonality is that the nation is graphic, a written space whose dimensions are set, confines illustrated, borders advanced, and citizens collected by linguistic imaginings.[11]

American political thought, as Jefferson's utterance makes clear, has long been characterized by metaphoric configurations of community. Aboard the *Arbella* in 1630, John Winthrop theorized that the covenant binding a community needs be represented symbolically by a body. Winthrop sanctified the community by casting it as the New World inheritor of a covenant God had first made with Abraham. Members of the community, Winthrop suggested, do not so much cohere by devising a covenant among themselves, but rather are knit together in a civil body serving as a worldly incarnation of Christ's body. As "the body of Christ whereof we are members," the Puritan settlement established unity; through metaphor, this prototypical American community imaged itself as coherent. Through this imagined relation, the colonists could "mutually participate" in a shared symbolism that outlined the contours of the community and gave it order. Individual citizens might deem others "as disproportionate and as much disordering as so many contrary qualities or elements," but the metaphor of the body activated a symbolic image capable of organizing differences and contradictions into a single, homogeneous whole. *E pluribus unum*, indeed. Metaphor allowed the community to enter the symbolic realm of politics and accomplish a type of coherence that was unavailable in a context tainted with division and disarray. It was more than a case of representation by metaphor: fictive bodies do not simply mirror a desired national order; as John Beverley writes, literature also produces and constitutes political realities. Metaphor has the figurative power to regenerate sundered entities, for as Winthrop promised, a community founded upon love "gathers together the scattered bones of perfect old man Adam, and knits them together into one body again in Christ."[12]

Although the Puritan experiment would eventually fail, its failure gave way to a much larger federation—America—still indebted to achieving consensus through another noncorporeal body, the narrativized body of the founding father. At this point, it is helpful to turn to another theorizer of the covenant, Thomas Hobbes, who contended that large, stable forms of political community must be mediated through the fictional representations of a body. Chapter 16 of *Leviathan* proposes that in the unity of the representative actor, people are made one as a civil body. The representative always contains a fictional component, configured as an "Artificiall Person" who bears the symbolic manifestation of the community along with or in place of his or her natural body. This desubstantiation of historically and physically bounded bodies corresponds to what Michael Paul Rogin, working through Hobbesian distinctions between the sovereign's natural body and the mythical body of the king, has called "political demonology." With Washington's death in 1799, the bounded body vanished, only to find resurrection in the "Artificiall Person" of the father of his country who represents and regenerates the American civil body. Winthrop's Christ returned as an American father; in one of the first biographies of Washington, Parson Weems imagines the "prophetical remark" of a farmer who, chancing upon Washington in prayer, muses, "I am greatly deceived—and still more shall I be deceived if God do not, through him, work out a great salvation for America."[13]

Race has infiltrated the political demonology of American politics. Discussing presidential figures including Lincoln, Nixon, and Reagan, Rogin demonstrates how the notion of the king's two bodies has permeated political imaging, creating situations such as occurred during the 1980s, when the president's real body had a tendency to project itself not only in the fictive framework of the Hobbesian representative, but within the cinematic space of the Hollywood movie. With the death of Washington, however, any tension between the hero's two bodies vanished with the interment of his corporeal form. A single body, a narrativized form preserved with the formaldehyde of myth, remained. Biographies effaced any lingering disjunctions by serving up the general's private life, detailing his domestic routine, making it national. But with this total inclusion, unassimilable elements—like the fugitive black slave Washington preferred not to acknowledge—posed serious discrepancies for a narrative affirming itself as single and unified. Providing messages of freedom as well as examples of proper domestic management of one's slaves, Washington defied the coherence so crucial to narrative closure by standing in two radically opposed positions at the same cultural moment. The father's confused identity could reveal only a narrative fraught with unresolvable contradiction; rather than solidifying an American identity, Washington functioned as a telling symptom of a national inconsistency, of an incoherent American body.[14]

As a figure of national narrative, Washington might act as a metaphor for the promise and unity of the American civil body, but he could in no way support the ideological weight of the bound body of the black slave. He double-crossed the national narrative, signifying the inability to forge cohesion. As the sons returned to the figures of the fathers for solace and confirmation of their own political righteousness, they discovered that the fathers themselves were hardly coherent enough in their beliefs and practices to legitimate a stable mid-nineteenth-century America. Bred with a reverence for their political origins, members of the antebellum generation were shocked to learn of an illegitimate genealogy in which enslavement appeared as the undeniable twin of freedom. They uncovered a fundamental contradiction: ideas of freedom originating in the conditions of slavery. Edmund Morgan emphasizes this point in his study of colonial Virginia, which argues that so many planters spearheaded the cause for independence, not in spite of, but because slavish dependence to an oppressive patriarch was a daily sight. "Virginians may have had a special appreciation of the freedom dear to republicans, because they saw every day what life without it could be like," states Morgan. Harriet Beecher Stowe thus imagine a white child in 1776 rejecting the suggestion that his father obey the king with the scoffing exclamation, "Father a slave!" This portrait of "The Altar of Liberty, or 1776" is disrupted by the following view, "The Altar of ———, or 1850," in which a fugitive slave is remanded to his master in Georgia. The absence, the missing political legacy in Stowe's diptych, suggests how for the post-Revolutionary sons the contradictory kinship of freedom and slavery signaled a divisive rent in the narratives that articulated and preserved a nation. By the 1850s, territories acquired from the recent war with Mexico sparked heated debate when it came time to decide if those lands would enter the Union as either free or slave states. Which course did the narratives of the past advocate? What did the now ambivalent representative body of Washington advise?[15]

In the midst of this debate, abolitionist and antislavery factions took up positions along the tropographic contours of national narrative. While one Unionist called upon those flinging threats of dissolution to recall that "dismemberment" would trample "the spirit of Washington," Senator John C. Calhoun prophesied that the South would follow the legacy of the same, yet another Washington, who rebelled against an oppressor nation without hesitating "to draw his sword, and head the great movement by which that union was forever severed." Contrary to those who believed that the first president had left an enduring inheritance of union, Calhoun read Washington's secession from England as "the great and crowning glory of his life," a radical legacy to be remembered by his "latest posterity." Outside the halls of Congress, E. Cecil's *The Life of George Washington, Written for Children* (1859) called upon readers to remember how the national father "fought not for Virginia only, not that he himself might be free, but for all the States, for all his countrymen, and for us," while south of the Mason-Dixon line, poets would soon sing the praises of Robert E. Lee via comparisons to the national father. The loyal referent for national union switched sides and became a banner for political rebellion:

> Rebels! 'tis our family name—
> Our father, Washington,
> Was the arch-rebel in the fight
> And gave the name to us—a right
> Of father unto son.

Even a year after Appomattox, Melville looked upon Lee's appearance before the Reconstruction Committee and mused: "Who looks at Lee must think of Washington."[16]

Such contradictory appeals to Washington were not aberrations; instead, as George Forgie argues, recurrent scenes of guilt, ambivalence, and resentment typified the 1850s. In *Patricide in the House Divided*, Forgie scans antebellum magazines, congressional speeches, and electoral debates to diagnose the split consciousness of a filial generation that embraced the legacy of the founding fathers even as it staged an Oedipal rebellion against those same fathers. Under this rubric, Forgie offers insightful readings of such moments as Lincoln's discomfort with the fathers in his debates with Stephen Douglas. As Fliegelman points out, however, Forgie's "overreliance on the apparatus of psychohistory" skews his interpretation so that vital historical and political issues are subsumed by Freudian explanations.[17] In addition to encountering the drawbacks of Freudian interpretation, *Patricide in the House Divided*, like Fliegelman's study, underestimates the kinship between the founding fathers and American slaves. Although Forgie acknowledges that the founders failed to bequeath a coherent narrative for or against slavery, his discussion glosses the centrality of race slavery in antebellum culture. Concentrating on the recognizable heirs of the founding fathers, Forgie ignores those unacknowledged sons—America's slaves—who had received no inheritance of freedom. Whether slaves used patriotic discourse or were represented within it by others, they disrupted the legacies integral to coherent tellings of national tradition.

Frederick Douglass makes clear the necessity of foregrounding the racial underpinnings of antebellum discourse. In an 1852 Fourth of July address, Douglass excuses himself from singing the praises of the national narrative: "I leave, therefore, the great deeds of your fathers to other gentlemen whose claim to be regularly descended will be less likely disputed than mine!"[18] Saying he has no authority to engage with the legacy of the founders, Douglass nevertheless implies that the incongruity of the slave's ironically spoken silence is a fundamental element in any rendition of national patriarchy. Invoking the fathers even as he refuses to discuss them, Douglass reconfigures his lack of authority and exclusion as critical commentary. His inability to pay tribute to the fathers acts as ironic authorization to juxtapose the figure of the muted slave with the verbose tradition of patriotism. Speaking by not speaking, Douglass argues for the centrality of race in any meditation on American nationalism. His formulation echoes in Toni Morrison's recent conclusion that "the metaphorical and metaphysical uses of race occupy definitive places in American literature, in the 'national' character, and ought to be a major concern."[19] Biographies of the national father did not ignore the peculiar institution—in fact, in these volumes the master rebukes, gives instruction to, and punishes his plantation slaves—yet in virtually every instance, slavery as political referent keeps its place, standing in the background, the slave's presence a silent emblem of Washington's wealth, authority, or kindness. Douglass and Morrison, in contrast, argue that this presence may not be so secondary or docile, but rather is discursively unruly and historically recalcitrant, latent with insurrectionary potential.

With the increase in sectional tension, concerns over the body of the slave now coincided literally with the death of Washington. John Norton's *Life of Washington* (1860) recounts the general's fatal sickness in a manner consistent with other biographies in the prewar years. Under a section entitled "More thoughtful for a servant than himself," readers learn how Washington awoke cold and sick one winter night, but, like any self-sacrificing patriarch, refused to call the "colored woman" to make a fire. Too considerate (or too guilty) to trouble a slave woman, Washington instead suffers bodily.[20] The next day finds him being bled by none other than the plantation overseer and lapsing into death—not to mention into a good deal of historical irony. In the didactic tone of Washington biographies, as well as their tendency to rewrite biography as national allegory, readers learn that the heritage of Washington could be preserved and the Union made to cohere if the nation ignored the fuss over slaves.

America's inability to settle definitively such questions and reach consensus imperiled the destiny of the national narrative, forestalling any promise of closure. The sundering of Washington's narrative between plots of enslavement and plots of freedom told of a nation beleaguered by its own incoherent memory. The Puritan typology that inscribed the community within the Exodus framework of a chosen people destined to be delivered out of the wilderness into the promised land could scarcely be coherently or confidently articulated when the tellers themselves could not agree on the character of their own fathers, let alone on the political character of Kansas and Nebraska as free or slave. Wendell Phillips expressed this divisive ambiguity when he said of the founding fathers: "I love these men; I hate their work. I respect their memory; I reject their deeds. I trust their hearts; I distrust their heads."[21]

Even though Washington stood divided, even though authorizing cultural referents lacked stability, narratives of the American nation nevertheless appeared to achieve closure. By their very status as narrative, stories of America impel themselves to closure, wrapping up any loose discrepancies along the way to a promised ending. As Frank Kermode suggests in *The Sense of an Ending*, human actors who find themselves stranded in the midst of uncertain authority and "disquieting gaps" rush forward with "fictive concords" to suture hints of inconsonant experience.[22] Such fictive concords—which readily compare to Hobbes's and Winthrop's uses of a symbolic, covenanted body—dispel the insecurity of an aimless present by affixing it to origins and ends invested with legality and legitimacy. In 1850s America, what Hayden White sees as a psychological "desire" to use narrative as a means of structuring "an image of continuity, coherency, and meaning in place of fantasies of emptiness," led back to the fathers who, in the sons' eyes, had become woefully inadequate and sorely compromised.[23] Fictive concords, like mythologized patriots, seem to reconfirm the nation by narrating stories and biographies of promised, seamless closure. But any narrative capable of representing American freedom alongside of American slavery that attained closure was too perfect to be true. Anxious insistence for narrative closure ended in national disarticulation. The fictive nature of the concord threatened to expose itself as fictive; the artificiality of the covenant became heightened by uncontrollable social actualities and difficult memories, calling into question the reliability of its authority. Although American national narratives may end, they find no resolution, falling short of the freedom, social harmony, or political legitimacy associated with closure.

To understand how the relentless demand for closure affects narrative, I would like to work through certain theoretical insights on the interrelationship of narrative and authority found in Melville's *The Confidence-Man* (1859). "True, it may be urged that there is nothing a writer of fiction should more carefully see to . . . than that, in the depiction of any character, its consistency should be preserved," writes Melville's duplicitous narrator. Even as he makes this statement, the narrator eschews consistency, deeming it the mark of "untrueness." The narrator thus declares that a fictional apparatus "incongruous in its parts" or "at variance with itself as the caterpillar is with the butterfly" offers a more accurate representation.[24] But as *The Confidence-Man* amply illustrates, Americans, ever diligent in their search for seamless stories, experience "distaste" for narratives whose inconsistency precludes the promise of closure. They instead place confidence in characters as coherent as Hobbes's "Artificiall Person," who can effect unity and resolution. Such confidence, however, is a tenuous fictive arrangement that always threatens to unravel into deceptive artifice and fraudulent representation. "Truth uncompromisingly told will always have its ragged edges," Melville later elaborated in *Billy Budd*.[25] Whether it is the problematic representation of Captain Vere's authority, which leads *Billy Budd* to attempt four endings, or the total lack of authentic authority in *The Confidence-Man*, which causes the narrative to trail off into scenes of ambiguous despair, Melville's often inconsonant fictions contend that closure stands in opposition to "truth." Narrative closure exists as the product of cultural confidence, the result of a fiction that privileges consistency, unity, and harmony above all else.

Aboard the ironically named *Fidèle*, where protean inconsistency in character as well as narrator fleeces passengers and confuses readers, closure is forever denied by *The Confidence-Man*'s final sentence: "Something further may follow of this Masquerade." Likewise, in *Billy Budd*, where authority uneasily oscillates between unfeeling tyranny and judicious command, any sense of narrative closure needs to remain suspended. Only authority can cut the "ragged edges" and place the events aboard the *Fidèle* or the *Bellipotent* to rest. Interestingly, *Billy Budd* does contain a moment of closure when "News from the Mediterranean," described as "an authorized weekly publication," finds a tidy explanation, ending with the assertion that the "criminal paid the penalty of his crime."[26] Once a moral has been fixed, once the evil receive their comeuppance, the news story can gratify the demand for closure. Authority intercedes in the stalemate between "truth" and narrative closure; authority rescues narrative from the paralyzing effects of open-ended and ambiguous "truth," providing and producing closure. The account given in "News from the Mediterranean" achieves closure because its concern is authority, not truth. In contrast, the "Counterfeit Detector" that appears at the end of *The Confidence-Man* has no authority, since it may itself be counterfeit. And the narrative ends—but does not find closure—as a nefarious character leads a confused old man into the dark. Melville reveals how within narrative, authority and closure exist in tautological relation to one another: authority ensures closure; yet without closure and with the persistence of ambiguity, there can be no authority. "Truth," as Melville understood, enters nowhere into the equation. In nineteenth-century America, no equivalence between truth and authority existed; the two remained separate and unequal. As Carolyn Porter writes, "Melville found that the truth lacked authority, and that authority—the authorized discourses of his era—lacked truth."[27]

Narratives of America end not so much in a geographic destiny as in a moral landscape that grounds Americans' sense of moral purpose and political legitimacy. Milk and honey are more than tokens of prosperity; they also symbolize essential virtues. Narrative is thus in itself a moral action; the closure inherent to narrative can only come laced with a meaning that validates its social context. As Hayden White asks, "Could we ever narrativize without moralizing?"[28] In Melville's comments about "truth" we find the answer:

yes, we could certainly tell a story, indeed, even appeal to cultural authority to articulate coherent resolution, but finding closure that guarantees an unambiguous vision of equality, justice, or freedom is quite another matter. American narrative in the mid-nineteenth-century, written in the context of race slavery, did find endings, but endings without closure, as though it were cut adrift, out of sight of the terra firma of unambiguous moral principle.

THE RECUPERATION
OF PATRIARCHAL AUTHORITY

Narrative may lead to a moral landscape; a story may rededicate the American people to that primordial saga of Exodus whose ending promises a land of unlimited abundance and a harmonious civil society, shining as a city upon a hill. Narrative commands the authority to order events into a story and carry it along through its wanderings to an affirming conclusion. But from where does this authority to create and enact closure come? If we answer "the author," we hazard repeating a version of the intentional fallacy. It is impossible to consider an author, especially an American author in the era of slavery, apart from a social context. Even Thoreau, self-stranded at Walden, lived close enough to Concord to hear the Fourth of July celebrations. Fiction attains closure by means of cultural authority; how well the narratives of a culture cohere influences how securely fiction can rely on a smooth teleological progression from beginning to end. Fulfillment of a promised destiny—whether it is a narrative's pledge to deliver a story to its ending or a nation's design to settle a New Canaan—is dependent upon the coherence of cultural narratives (such as the covenant to read a fictive, biographic Washington as national representative) that contain and express the body politic. Neither narrative nor nation—as articulation—can be completed when nonrepresentative bodies whose silence and interruptions speak differently, "betwixt and between times and places," as Homi Bhabha puts it, and sidetrack the headlong rush for closure. Race denied redemption of the pledge to reach a satisfying end for mid-nineteenth-century America; the black slave stalled and redirected the narrative that the body politic would tell. If, as Toni Morrison argues, "the process of organizing American coherence" occurred "through distancing Africanism," then, the return of that textually and politically repressed presence renders national narratives incongruent.[29]

National narratives are tenacious of coherence and order, however. In the face of unlooked-for ironies and inconsistencies, covenanted bodies remain committed to a fictional apparatus that ignores, silences, or renders docile disruptive agents. This disposition encouraged George Washington Parke Custis's *Recollections and Private Memoirs of Washington* (1859) to affirm the absence of any contradictions within the narrative corpus of the founding father: "As a master of slaves, General Washington was consistent, as in every other relation of his meritorious life."[30] Four years later, in the midst of civil war, Washington could hardly have been expected to provide unity with the same ease that the fictive representativeness of the Hobbesian sovereign melds an ordered community. Even so, 1863, which witnessed Chancellorsville and Gettysburg, saw the publication of Uncle Juvinell's *The Farmer Boy, and How He Became Commander-in-Chief* in Boston. Rather than thinking that either of these battles, which amassed tens of thousands of deaths, bolstered Northern confidence enough to reaffirm an American narrative, we should interpret this cultural artifact in another way: doubts over the preservation of the grand design gave rise to this volume of juvenile literature. Uncle Juvinell conjured up the figurative body of Washington in attempt to efface gaps within the body politic. That is, following Fredric Jameson, who reads narrative as a socially symbolic act resolving tensions and conflicts within society, we need to read this document of popular culture as a narrative recklessly providing surety to a social network that is without firm backing or sure heading.[31]

A spokesman of God, the Reverend William M. Thayer, prefaced Uncle Juvinell's work by saying *The Farmer Boy* is "so well adapted to the exigencies of the times."[32] The narrative's status as a biography written for adolescents and children preserves the coherence of *The Farmer Boy*, allowing its plot to overcome the rebellious intimations of Thayer's preface and arrive at the promise of closure. Its author's design for it comes to fruition, though not because Uncle Juvinell, as "the blind bard of Kentucky," could lay claim to the divine inspiration of sightlessness as did Homer and Milton. Conventions of genre come to the rescue of this potentially disrupted narrative, anchoring its teleological course. The farmer boy does grow up to become commander-in-chief. An old, blind man sees the assurances of national history encoded within the structure of mythic biography. Romantic history permits Uncle Juvinell to wear blinders and glimpse only the security of the already completed past, but not the irresolute nature of the present. Supported by this generic foundation, Washington overcomes the doubts of Reverend Thayer, as well as the nation's disintegration, to occupy a position of authority. He accords the text both a centered focus and a clearly ordained sequence of events to follow. His biography is the narrative of America; he enacts the mythic course of humble origins expanding to sovereign dimensions. In this Washington, individual biography and national history coincide, each attaining the moral destiny that national narrative promises.

Washington's life authoritatively guides *The Farmer Boy*, just as he guided the young nation to a reputed freedom. But since the figure of Washington embodied such a resilient example of patriarchal authority, it was no longer necessary that he tell the truth. His fatherly benevolence may have led to a confident biographical narrative, but as Melville argues in *Billy Budd*, "truth" is another matter. Washington's reputation as truth teller may oblige Uncle Juvinell to say that "we must keep within the bounds of true history, and content ourselves with the knowledge of that which really did happen," yet his patriarchal authority as a storyteller to children allows him to escape his own words. Uncle Juvinell thus reshapes the story of the cherry tree, itself already an invention of Parson Weems. Surveying his plantation, George's father sees the fallen cherry tree, and in turn, he sets upon the bodies of his slaves. But as Uncle Juvinell informs his listeners, his bondsmen deny the trespass, rolling the whites of their eyes in buffoonlike protestations of innocence. Yet Father Washington's undisputed authority as master and expert on slave demeanor allows him to dismiss the slaves' truth. Knowing the character of his slaves, he selects the most likely villain and makes ready to apply the switch to the slave boy's backside. Indeed, as Uncle Juvinell tells the tale, George's sire is correct in his actions, even if his judgment is wrong, for the elder Washington is well aware of the slave's "natural" propensity for rascality: "Now, you must know there was not a more audacious, mischief-making, neck-or-nothing black brat than this same Jerry to be found on the banks of the Rappanhannock, which is a very long river indeed." Salvation appears in the figure of the young George, who intercedes just before Jerry's punishment: "O papa, papa! . . . don't whip poor Jerry: if somebody must be whipped, let it be me; for it was I, and not Jerry, that cut the cherry-tree."[33]

Whereas the "tragic mulattoes" of *Clotel* parade both the blood of founding fathers and black slaves as part of an effort to denounce the inconsistency of democratic institutions, Uncle Juvinell's purpose in pairing young George with an ill-mannered slave is more benign. Washington becomes the savior of Jerry by substituting his body for the slave's; through his body, the slave can become part of a community knit together in the symbolic body of this Americanized Christ. Father Washington kindly counsels his slave congregation: "Look on him, my black children, look on him, and be as near like him as you can, if you would have the love of your master and the good-will of all around you." In no way, however, does he urge an egalitarian community; authority and hierarchy remain clearly delineated. Washington symbolizes a covenant that places, again to use the words Winthrop, "some high and eminent in power and dignity; others mean and in subjection." As a political relic charged with religious overtones, Washington signifies the logic that makes some masters and others slaves—if Winthrop's understandings of hierarchy and Christian charity are severely perverted along racial lines. Under the master's interpretation, George not only martyrs himself to regenerate the black slave, he also redeems a patriarchal authority that has fallen into the ways of poor judgment. Father Washington has falsely accused one of his "black children," and although the law sanctions a master's wrongful punishment of his slave, the son proves the righteousness of that authority by allowing it to be exercised upon his own body.[34] In the very moment that George disagrees with his father's judgment, he submits himself to that same judge. Although young George tells the truth, his object is not truth alone; rather, he sacrifices himself to reaffirm his father as authority by submitting to his father's punishment. More impossible than telling a lie would be for the son to subvert the authority of the father.

The Farmer Boy tells its tale self-consciously, in that it is the story of a kind, elderly man narrating the life of Washington to his nephews and nieces one Christmas. This narrative frame reiterates the lessons of authority that George's example teaches. Uncle Juvinell commands attention because he is the storyteller, and in his tale the children are bound in a community of listeners. Washington's narrative provides a communal vision with clearly marked social positions, just as his body serves as the locus of morals for the slave children along the Rappanhannock. The audience respectfully listens to the teller as though he were speaking the truth. As every evening begins a new chapter, the reader watches the rambunctious children settle down, lulled into proper behavior by the narrative. The girls listen as ladies, pressing their uncle for details of balls and dresses, and the boys listen as men, hankering after fights with Indians. And as every evening begins, a servant named Black Daddy caters to the wants of this little gathering, bringing treats and refreshments on a tray. Although never explicitly labeled a slave, Black Daddy caters to the narrative of hierarchy as well; like Jerry, who finds his place in the example of young master, the avuncular slave unobtrusively hovers at the edges of the narrative frame. Though named as father and affectionately marked with a paternal sobriquet, Black Daddy exercises no authority; he is an instrument of those who participate in the national myth of Washington. In a manner similar to the non-narrative appearance of slavery in many Washington biographies (that is, slavery appears only after Washington has died), Black Daddy enters only before and after each night's storytelling, never barging in during the middle of Uncle Juvinell's narrative. Race remains excessive to the narrative frame of the biography lest, like the mischievous Jerry, the ambivalent legacy of slavery becomes disruptive in the context of Uncle Juvinell's antebellum present.

Young George and father Washington enact a didactic tableau to convince the rebellious slave of the moral propriety of white authority; in contrast, Uncle Juvinell's generation, alarmed by its own belatedness, falters in its attempts to convey a similar lesson. The past can effectively manage contradictions like Jerry; however, the present narrative frame encircling that storied past cannot control its racial context as forthrightly as father Washington manages his slaves. At the temporal site of subsequent tellings, race can appear only in the margins, subdued by displacement. Exiled to the complacent margins of the peculiar narrative frame, slavery exhibits none of the impertinence that could question the storyteller's authority;

instead, as a cultural reference, slavery cowers before the necessary coherence of the national narrative.

This story of Washington and the story of his narration mutually reiterate accounts of community that in 1863 stood as relics of a broken past. Slavery in the text is as well-managed as Black Daddy's presence among the listeners to Uncle Juvinell. Yet the memories and figures that had been placed at the margins of both *The Farmer Boy* and the antebellum present return from narrative exile in critical fashion. Slavery—no matter how docile Jerry or Black Daddy might appear—alters filial demeanor, making even the most obedient sons and prefaces into rebels.

THE NAME OF THE FATHER
IN COOPER'S *THE SPY*

Washington revealed a coherent American identity at a time when cultural authority resolutely brought the national narrative toward closure, when Jacksonian democracy represented the myth of the common man's enfranchisement, increasing governmental centralization, and unprecedented territorial expansion. In James Fenimore Cooper's *The Spy: A Tale of Neutral Ground* (1821), only Washington can resolve ambiguous identities because his is unequivocally the identity of the true American father. And as national father, he judiciously exercises the authority to lead Cooper's narrative to closure. An overnight success that in its equally celebrated stage adaptation ran until 1852, *The Spy* supplied the nation with nativist themes, establishing Revolutionary romance as a legitimate American genre. "'The Spy' is lurking in every closet," says the male narrator at the outset of Lydia Maria Child's *Hobomok* (1824). From this popular mingling of narrative and history, the romance figures as a "nation-building novel" whose plots, themes, and resolutions strive both "to fill in a history that would increase the legitimacy of the emerging nation and by the opportunity to direct that history towards a future ideal."[35]

The Spy unfolds a story of deception and ruse by centering on the travails of the aristocratic Wharton household smack in the middle of contested territory. Burning barns and saber battles surround the family's ill-chosen retreat from the horrors of war. Travelers and guests visit the Wharton estate, yet no one knows if they are for the king or for the colonies. The Wharton's neighbor, a Yankee peddler named Harvey Birch, is the most enigmatic character, communicating with both sides, slipping ghostlike past sentries and pickets, and espousing no definitive political alignment. Although Birch really is a "useful agent of the leaders of the revolution," that usefulness depends upon his appearance as a mercenary sympathizer to the king. To be the patriot, Birch has to act the part of the traitor. The Continentals curse Birch as a fiendish spy and pursue him with a noose throughout the novel. Masquerade abounds. When the son, Henry Wharton, visits his family, he does so disguised by a red wig and an eye patch. A British colonel poses as a bachelor so that he can engage in bigamy and wed the eldest of the Wharton daughters. The peddler cross-dresses as a common washerwoman, a black slave disguises himself as a British officer destined for the gallows, and a condemned spy escapes by assuming the identity of a black slave— all are incidents that make the narrative space as unstable as the boundary between British and Continental territory over which the two armies battle. In Cooper's world of revolutionary espionage, where appearances deceive, Washington has the authority to tell the truth. By relying upon Washington, *The Spy* corrects the history of many people who

> wore masks, which even to this day have not been thrown aside; and many an individual has gone down to the tomb, stigmatised as foe to the rights of his countrymen, while, in secret, he has been the useful agent of the leaders of the revolution; and, on the other hand, could the repositories of divers flaming patriots have been opened to the light of day, royal protections would have been discovered concealed under piles of British gold.[36]

Only Washington possesses the authority to reposition everyone in a secure identity. "Washington can see beyond the hollow views of pretended patriots," the actor playing Harvey Birch told theater audiences. In the novel, the general sees through the disguise of the British captain, Henry Wharton, and later he cancels the orders demanding the arrest of this dutiful son, whose only crime was visiting his family. Like young George in *The Farmer Boy*, the mature Washington confirms patriarchal authority by perceiving that Henry's motivation in passing undetected into territory controlled by colonists is not military subterfuge, but the simply the desire of a son to return home. Cloaked in the identity of Harper, Washington sanctions Henry's deliverance; he tells Wharton's sister with characteristic candor that refuses any imputation of pride or duplicity, "Miss Wharton, that I bear no mean part, in the unhappy struggle between England and America, it might now be useless to deny. You owe your brother's escape, this night, to my knowledge of his innocence, and the remembrance of my word" (407). The supreme judge, Washington divides the innocent from the damned with his own "word," with his own name.[37]

Wharton's masquerade of his own identity has created precarious divisions where national union and narrative closure once seemed imminent. If he is executed as a spy, marriage between Southerner and Northerner will never occur, and hopes for union—whether conjugal and national—will never come to fruition. Wharton's best friend, Major Dunwoodie of the American forces, has eyes for Wharton's sister, but if Major Dunwoodie's troops hang Wharton, certainly no alliance can occur. Washington's signature removes the enmity between friends and grants Dunwoodie permission to return to his plantation, where Wharton's sister can act as his nurse. Holy union, previously stymied by political differences between families, comes courtesy of Washington's fatherly influence. Wharton's salvation and his reconciliation with Dunwoodie symbolically magnifies in significance to represent a coherent national narrative. The New Yorker, Wharton, and the Virginian, Dunwoodie, put aside their differences and become kin, a legacy they pass on to their sons who, at the end of the novel, appear as comrades in arms during the War of 1812. Sectional dissimilarities vanish as North and South join in holy matrimony, making clear how both antebellum household and national culture located authority in the figure of the father. Washington's power to secure a propitious resolution for family and nation in one stroke proves the bonds of national union to be as strong as those cementing domesticity.

The name of Washington releases Wharton from the stigma of being a British spy. Cooper prefers not to relate second-hand that this redcoat passes unmolested, but includes the text of Washington's letter, authorized with his own signature, as a source of narrative authority. Key conflicts and decisions find resolution and justification in letters and orders that end with the indisputable seal of American authority: "Washington." Cooper relies upon the cultural authority of Washington's legacy to supply episodes of his narrative with verisimilitude and satisfying moral resolution. Under Washington's auspices, Cooper imprints historical romance with "truth"—though *The Confidence-Man* must make us uneasy about any conjunctions between "truth" and authority, even Washington's. So sacred is Washington's signature that to corrupt it represents the most grievous sin, payable with one's life. Dunwoodie apprehends Wharton traveling with forged credentials that nevertheless bear Washington's authentic signature. Although "this name is no counterfeit," Wharton's own identity as an honorable soldier falls under suspicion for coupling the true signature of Washington with the "fictitious name" he has assumed to pass the American picket (84). For this offense, Wharton must accompany Dunwoodie to the highlands, where a military court sentences him to death. Tampering with this American authority threatens to render murky the distinction between authentic and counterfeit. Unable to tolerate the ambiguous state of affairs generated by the treasonous pilfering of Washington's signature, unable to have confidence in a situation where a patriot's virtues may be only appearance, the court eradicates these spurious doubts by commanding the most determinate closure—"recommending him to be executed by hanging, before nine o'clock on the following morning" (353).

So sacred is Washington's affidavit that Birch swallows it as though he were partaking of the host. Captured by Dunwoodie's troops as an agent of British general Sir Henry Clinton, Birch refuses to divulge the truth that would allow him to escape the gallows. Saying this, he reaches into the folds of his shirt and produces a document that the reader knows to be Washington's verification of the peddler's loyalty to the American cause. Rather than show this sacred signature to the Continentals, Birch swallows the paper, and is then thoroughly prepared for death. Having eaten the patriotic host, the spy calmly accepts his fate, assured of eternal deliverance for his service to Washington. As a Christian martyr who dies rather than renounce Christ, Birch chooses death rather than forswear his faith in the icon of the nation. Later, as he helps Wharton to escape, Birch recalls the times of temptation when he has been plagued by doubt and despair: "There was no pity, no consolation near, to soothe my anguish. Every thing seemed to have deserted me. I even thought that HE had forgotten that I lived" (390). Although Birch's echo of Christ on the cross suggests that God is "HE," the text poses another alternative—that "HE" is the supreme commander of the American forces. Birch has emphasized the third person singular only one other time in the novel: confronted with execution, he takes solace in the faith that *"he* will do my memory justice at least" (230). The stage directions for this scene in the play, which script Birch with hands clasped "in energetic devotion" and eyes cast toward heaven, further encouraged Americans to affiliate Birch's *"he"* with an ever-watchful patriarch.[38] With Godlike authority, Washington will rescue Birch from perpetual ignominy and secure him the salvation of honor after death. Like those who refuse to utter the divine name, Yahweh, this humble peddler will gladly die a martyr to patriotism rather than speak the name of the final American authority.

Because of his stubborn faith, Harvey Birch never reveals his true identity while alive. The text threatens to end the narrative of his life, an American spy, without a clear sense of resolution. Whereas Washington repeatedly signs his name in *The Spy*, his signature acting as the standard of patriotic loyalty, Birch can communicate information to the Continentals only anonymously. His messages and warnings have no author, and hence Birch himself has no authority to verify his true character. Denied even the authority to sign his own name, the spy obviously lacks authority to name others; he understands he can never exercise the patriarchal authority of a father. Telling the presumed traitor that the day of judgment will arrive when Harper "will not blush to acknowledge you in his true character," Washington then gives Birch a certificate proving his identity as an American patriot, saying that while the document may be of no use to the peddler himself, "it may be serviceable to your children" (453, 454). Birch is destined to die alone in the world; no kin will clear his name and bring a final justice to the tale: "'Children!' exclaimed the peddler, 'can I give to a family the infamy of my name!'" (454). Forever denied patriarchal authority, Birch sadly yet resolutely accepts the ultimate unhappiness that is to be his reward. Leaving no descendants who will discard the legacy of alienation and integrate happily, marrying into a community, Birch nevertheless prepares the way for a conjugal romance between families of Southern patriots and Northern loyalists that re-affirms the national project.

Even though Birch's life ends short of any resolution except death, *The Spy* as narrative achieves a perfect sense of closure. The final page unmasks all pretenders and removes the stigma from the graves of supposed British agents. It comes as no surprise that it is Washington who accords the narrative the authority to legislate closure. For the sons of the Revolution, who in this case are the male descendants of Wharton and Dunwoodie, now united in resisting the British at Niagara Falls during the War of 1812, Washington speaks from beyond the grave to perform the last rites for the forgotten patriot, securing him a national destiny. On the dead body of Harvey Birch, his last years no doubt spent as an outcast, an Ishmael howling alone in the wilderness, the American soldiers find a note reading,

> Circumstances of political importance, which involve the lives and fortunes of many, have hitherto kept secret what this paper now reveals. Harvey Birch has for years been a faithful and unrequited servant of his country. Though man does not, may God reward him for his conduct!
>
> —Geo. Washington (463)

Now complete with a signature as awesome and sublime as the cataract that frames this ultimate revelation of American identity, Cooper's narrative can end. Although a single sentence does follow this authorizing signature, Cooper has no authority to offer any new information that would propel the story forward beyond Washington. He writes in lapidary fashion, "It was the SPY OF THE NEUTRAL GROUND, who died as he had lived, devoted to his country, and a martyr to her liberties" (463). Significantly, this final sentence is declarative; it has the air of completion and finality that marks history as an authoritative telling. Only Washington has the authority to act upon history; in contrast, the narrative cannot act without Washington. All that follows Washington's signature is a summation of the action that Washington has already resolved. *The Spy* refuses to proceed where Cooper's Washington has not tread. Rather than detailing new events, the text returns to its own finished history. Departing from the textual past inscribed by Washington would be for a historical romance to cast off genre and precedent and venture into the neutral ground of narrative without authority. Once blessed with Washington's word, *The Spy* stops developing, now content to tell itself its own history.

RACE AND THE PARRICIDAL PREFACE

Washington's actions of reconciliation and redemption in Cooper's text allow *The Spy* to operate as a "nation-building novel" in which Southerner weds Northerner and sires children who, unlike their parents, have a national rather than a regional affiliation. But by 1850, the figure of Washington no longer could tell this national "truth" of union and future homogeneity. Firebrands like Calhoun rejected reading Washington as an icon of federal harmony and offered another interpretation of the founding father that said the narrative was not national but sectional. Washington's status as slaveholder provided Calhoun and others with the legitimacy to dissent from the overarching apparatus of national narrative. A few weeks after Clay in 1850 introduced measures for Congress to rededicate the American public by distributing Washington's Farewell Address, Calhoun offered these words in the Senate:

> Nor can the Union be saved by invoking the name of that illustri-
> ous Southerner whose mortal remains repose on the western bank
> of the Potomac. He was one of us—a slaveholder and a plant-
> er. . . . Nor can we find any thing in his history to deter us from se-
> ceding from the Union, should it fail to fulfil the objects for which it
> was instituted, by being permanently and hopelessly converted into
> the means of oppressing instead of protecting us. On the contrary,
> we find much in his example to encourage us, should we be forced
> to the extremity of deciding between submission and disunion.[39]

Within this context, *The Spy*'s continuing popularity with nineteenth-century audiences no doubt testifies to a desire for repeated rituals of national affirmation, but alterations in later editions questioned the authority of original narratives, insinuating fractures in the bodies, myths, and plots that articulated the American body politic. Consider how the 1849 edition of *The Spy* opens on a far different note than the original 1821 text. In an introduction written for the later edition, Cooper addresses the reader, but he does so without a convincing sense of authority. Gaps and ruptures imply a lack of control: the narrative about to be received is not a seamless discourse of fictive American history. Absences unceremoniously interrupt the text. Cooper can begin only with the subjunctive, insinuating a corps of doubts: "The author has often been asked if there were any foundation in real life, for the delineation of the principal character in this book" (v). He continues to relate the circumstances of the novel's publication and appeals to one "Mr. ———." as witness to the factual nature of *The Spy* (vii). But like Harvey Birch, the identity of "Mr. ———." remains in question. According to Cooper's remarks in 1849, the narrative is true, derived from an unnamed authority—but how authoritative is a source that cannot avow itself? Repeatedly mentioned, the lacuna "Mr. ———." undermines the text's authority. By the end of the novel, however, the signature of Washington fills this space, sealing up any textual rupture, thereby reestablishing faith in narrative authority. In fact, in the 1849 address to the reader, Cooper explains Washington's role in securing closure for his narrative. Financial considerations dictated that "the last chapter," closing with Washington's signature, "was actually written, printed, and paged, several weeks before the chapters which precede it were even thought of" (ix). Though lacking a complete vision of the story's course, Cooper finds in Washington the authority to resolve what was incomplete and deliver the narrative—just as Washington had delivered the nation—to the promised land of closure.

This patriarchal authority supports a hierarchal vision in which any suggestion that could disrupt the course of narrative is contained by a textual apparatus of silence and insignificance. Waiting obsequiously in the wings of *The Spy* until his comic presence is called for stands the Wharton's black slave, Caesar. He occupies the same abject position as Black Daddy in *The Farmer Boy*; both receive representation not so much as human figures but as buoys marking the limits of an authority that is at once textual and cultural. Given the strong presence of Washington as well as an overall commitment to the national mission in both stories, neither Caesar nor Black Daddy utters any critique of the narrative that encapsulates them. Plantation master and founding father will not suffer any impudence. Throughout, Caesar remains firmly in his place, voicing all desires and fears in a thick dialect. Even the potentially subversive situation when the slave, Caesar, and the master, Henry, exchange costumes and identities, even a situation that may radically suggest affinities between black and white rather than emphasize differences, ultimately fails to delegitimize constructed distinctions. Cooper makes the reader privy to the masquerade, in which artifice obscures the "natural" facts of each man's identity. If any resemblance between the heroic white soldier and the subservient black man arises, it is merely the effect of Cooper's unnatural stratagem. It is notable that in other scenes where race is not a factor, Cooper expresses no scruple about duping the reader with disguises, making the reader occupy a position of ignorance, permitting him or her to see past the ruse no sooner than any of the astonished characters. In this instance of racial cross-dressing, however, by letting the reader know a masquerade will occur, the text removes the possibility of any confusion that could cause an obfuscation of the "real" distinctions between master and slave. Whereas Mark Twain employs racial cross-dressing in *Pudd'nhead Wilson* to interrogate the imposition of arbitrary categorizations, Cooper's intent lies elsewhere. The man who wrote "Slavery may actually benefit a man, there being little doubt that the African is, in nearly all respects, better off in servitude" would not question the prevailing racial hierarchy.[40] And even if Cooper wanted Caesar to articulate an indictment of race slavery, Washington's silence on the question of slavery would refuse him authorization to do so.

Despite its title, *The Spy* engages in hardly any covert ideological action. Still, because of his conception of the American public as often unthinking and usually misdirected, Cooper doubted that his readers had understood the messages encoded in his fiction. Deeming it necessary to spell out his thoughts on the American republic, Cooper interrupted his career as a novelist. In 1838 he published *The American Democrat* as an unequivocal commentary on civic life in the United States. The democratic gentleman, whom Cooper took as his own self-image, stands as the hero of this treatise. Central to his definition of democracy is an explanation of the functioning of authority. The principal lesson Americans needed to learn, Cooper believed, was that authority does not and should not lie with the people. Apprehensive of "an unauthorized publick" that nevertheless considered itself justly endowed with the power of popular opinion, Cooper wrote against what he perceived as a democracy's natural tendency toward radicalism. When he looked at the Revolution in *The Spy*, he charted the fortunes of an aristocratic family who mingle only with characters of equal station. Cooper revised the Revolution as a novel of manners, rescuing history and his reading public from the "madness" of abolition sentiments. Washington's actions in the novel do not just preserve a family, his paternal authority protects ladies and gentlemen whose foresight to remove to a secluded country manor backfires when the battle shifts to the neutral ground outside their front door. The commander-in-chief's converse with a mere peddler is justified not only by military necessity, but by the inherent nobility of Harvey Birch, who often sighs with pretensions to a Byronic loneliness of soul. Military discipline and class status, heavily emphasized in the novel, reinforce the American chain of being, with the paterfamilias at the top and the black slave at the bottom. According to *The American Democrat*, "men of really high social station" perceive that a democracy based upon law, not on shifting public opinion, preserves the status quo. Gentlemen do not crudely read the American promises of freedom and equality as prescriptive statements; instead, they understand the finer point that the "celebrated proposition contained in the declaration of independence is not to be understood literally. All men are not 'created equal' . . . since one has a good constitution, another a bad; one is handsome, another ugly; one white, another black." Cooper's representation of authority in this tract culminates in the same hierarchical vision as that expressed in both *The Spy* and a racialized reading of Winthrop's *Model of Christian Charity*. Relying on scriptural "truths" about relations between master and servant, Cooper structured his interpretation of American society around patriarchal authority and thus could assert: "It is quite possible to be an excellent christian and a slave holder."[41]

Negotiations between Cooper and the cultural text of Washington figure as a synecdoche in which issues of authority, closure, and race found in *The Spy* represent fictional strategies for sorting out these issues within the narrative of America. Black Daddy is securely positioned by his serving tray, and Caesar is continually harried by racist ascriptions of cowardice and servility; however, America would soon undermine the narrative and patriarchal governance that kept such unruly ideological bodies in place. Exertions of patrifilial memory, though designed to assuage conflict, were infused with irony: repetitions of founding narratives were not exact, but involved a critical supplementing of the nation with prefaces.[42] Citizens as diversely minded as Abraham Lincoln and Jefferson Davis theorized that closure, either as union or division, would appear, not by following the nation to its ending, but by remembering its beginnings. Only a return to national foundations could provide final moral authority because so putatively perfect were those origins that they already contained the wisdom of their own conclusion, just as Cooper knew his novel would end with Washington's signature even before he had finished it. Likewise, in Uncle Juvinell's bedtime story, the farmer boy does not slowly mature and change into the commander in chief; his boyhood is narrativized as an unquestionable premonition of greatness. Resolution for sectional conflict lay at the beginnings, yet all that descended from those beginnings—Jefferson's slave children, Washington's equivocal legacy, the expansion of slavery, and political compromise—exerted a supplemental force that could not be reconciled in any coherent ending for the national narrative.

While the nation labored to be "borne back ceaselessly into the past," to invoke F. Scott Fitzgerald, it aggressively contradicted its temporal odyssey with a territorial imperative that promised continental closure in a future of conquest and expansion. As America annexed the promised land in the name of Manifest Destiny, contradictions of freedom and bondage latent in Washington's biography became even more apparent, and debates as to whether that promised land would be admitted to the Union as free or slave states grew harder to contain. Adding to the nation may have sounded victorious cries in the halls of Montezuma, but it also incited interrogations like that of fugitive slave Samuel Ringgold Ward, who charged: "The war with Mexico was conceived and brought forth, on purpose to lengthen the cords and strengthen the stakes of slavery."[43] A narrative such as *The Spy*, or even the nation's narrative, that had freely circulated in 1821, found itself restricted by uncontainable contradictions by the 1850s. The original text, whether Cooper's historical romance or the American union, forfeited ideological coherence as prefaces responding to race slavery—author's introductions and congressional compromises—undercut the ability of narrative to stand alone. Both Cooper's 1849 introduction and the Compromise of 1850 prefaced original narratives as a response to a growing awareness that these narratives of historical romance and historical nation needed further explanation and support. Foundational texts no longer stood inviolate in the security of their own declarations. Informed by contradictory motives, these prefaces implied a frailty and lack of authority within original patriarchal narratives in what proved an ironic attempt to bolster the texts of the fathers.

What afflicted the coherence of narrative was not so much actual contention in the political arena, but the narrative itself, splintered into preface and text. Jacques Derrida's commentary on the subversiveness of the preface can help us to explore further this tension within narrative. Derrida suggests that a filial relation like that of father and son exists between text and preface because the preface is always sired by the text after its completion. Even as the preface pays homage to the text, it is seized by an Oedipal urge and questions the text's self-sufficiency, insinuating doubts about the father's authority in which it originated. In other words, because of its very existence, the preface as son questions the ability of the text as father to stand alone. Sustaining the father, the preface implies an act of parricide. Returning for a moment to *The Farmer Boy*, we see that even a good-natured and innocent text can harbor the parricidal preface. Thayer's introduction, which commends the text as "so well adapted to the exigencies of the times," simultaneously works at cross purposes to Uncle Juvinell's stories. Published while "our nation is groaning and travailing in pain to bring forth a future," *The Farmer Boy* strives to recollect a prosperous union; however, this memorial rite uncomfortably juxtaposes past and present, creating a comparison that was mired in the anguish of the country's looming dismemberment.[44] The generative processes of the founding father have degenerated into national abortion. Tales of Washington engendered a community of malleable, youthful citizens, but Thayer's preface rebels against this scene of political contentment by ripping the narrative from its framework of a comfortable Kentucky home and thrusting it into a context of an American community at war with itself, unheedful of Washington's pleas for union.

In a similar manner, *The Spy*'s narrative authority maintained its hierarchical vision without incident—until the 1849 edition introduced a preface. In that year, surrounded by debates and events that would lead to passage of the Fugitive Slave Law and the Compromise of 1850 as well as to John Brown's raid on Harper's Ferry, *The Spy* initiated an insurrection against itself. A narrative that was coherent in 1821 found itself struggling to contain the self-wrought division of a parricidal revolt of preface against text. Paying homage to an America he had seen expand and strengthen since *The Spy*'s original 1821 publication, Cooper reaffirmed the narrative of the republic, rededicating himself with zeal to the national mission. Indeed, he claimed, the recent triumph over Mexico should have granted every American a full store of patriotic confidence, with recollections of "guns that filled the valley of the Aztecs with their thunder" (xii). The victor's spoils, however, sparked national debate as it came time to determine if slavery should extend to these new territories. The effort to resolve the issue returned America to a futile search of the founding fathers for some authoritative directive regarding slavery. Unable to find any instruction, America wrote the Compromise of 1850 and the Fugitive Slave Law as prefaces that supplemented (and thus doubted) narratives of the nation's origin. Immediately after reveling in the national glory of the Mexican-American War, Cooper's introduction moves toward its conclusion, and yet closure remains far off in the romantic distance of the Revolutionary past. Cooper writes: "There is now no enemy to fear, but the one that resides within" (xiii). No foreigners threatened America; only the spies of its own ideological contradictions could act as insurgents within the authoritative narrative of Washington.

Even more incendiary than Reverend Thayer's unintentional subversion of Uncle Juvinell in *The Farmer Boy*, Cooper's 1849 supplement fosters doubts about its predecessor even as it pays respects to its textual father. This filial rebellion of preface against text permits an understanding of narrative beyond psychological interpretation. It provides insight into the peculiar political situation of the post-Revolutionary sons, struggling to expound interpretations of slavery that would be consistent with the legacy of the founding fathers. In this way, then, problematics of father and son, text and preface, cease to be understood as purely textual matters confined to historical novels and biographies. The preface's insurgency occurs within a larger field of discursive contestation involving the narration of patriarchal authority integral to American politics and culture. At stake is nothing less than the structure, coherence, and consistency of America's articulation of its past. Remembering that the preface is always born after the origination of the text, American history can be read, not along chronological lines, but along lines of textuality, where issues of race, containment, and power come to the forefront. Thus, the original text of America that was declared to have begun in 1776 did not precede the 1850s embattled by guilt over race slavery. Rather, the 1850s, composed after that original text, are properly the preface. Disregard for the chronology of national history no doubt overturns notions of order and causality, but what now appears is a glimpse at the workings of power, strife, and negotiation that inform any narrative. As preface to the originary articulations of 1776, the 1850s unsettled the national narrative. Irreconcilable debates over slavery, even works like the Compromise of 1850 and the Dred Scott decision that seemed committed to preserving the memory of the founding fathers, nonetheless bear a critical relation to the original text of freedom that inspired the American narrative in the first place. Slavery, itself stemming from patriarchal authority, rebels against the fathers who found freedom in its shadow. American narrative, disgusted by its return to the fleshpots of oppression and injustice, revolts against itself, splintering into preface and text.

The preface need not work critically, however. Its supplemental commentary is liable, according to Derrida, "to be reappropriated into the sublimity of the father," and it is this patriarchal containment that appeases marginal and excessive figures such as Black Daddy and Caesar. After all, the patriotic and moralistic tones of the prefaces to *The Farmer Boy* and *The Spy* evince the sublimity of national narrative, making it at first difficult to say if doubts about the antebellum present (which is also the textual occasion for these belated appendices) instill a subversive lack of confidence or if uneasy allusions to instabilities in the narrative frame ultimately are assuaged by the traditional closure of national narrative. Derrida's description of the father's facility in "mastering his seed" seems to remove these doubts, recording how the preface often drops its critical impetus and carries out the text's designs. But a purely textual account nonetheless takes on added historical valence when translated to the antebellum context: narratives of Washington are thoroughly yet conflictingly committed to this "mastering," whether it is correcting the rascal Jerry or filling the lacunae in Cooper's foundational fiction. The figure of Washington works narratively to domesticate the excessiveness of race, to bring unruly slaves back within the patriarchal household as well as to disarm unseemly prefatory asides to the crisis over slavery. The historical extension of Derrida's formulation becomes a dangerous sexual and political postscript when it is remembered that his "mastering" is transitive, acted out upon "his seed."[45]

Although no intimations of Jeffersonian miscegenation attached themselves to Washington, and assuredly Jerry is not young George's kin, in terms of national narrative, his legacy of nonaction and ambiguity engendered a filial generation that sorely needed his fabled guidance. In the context of a nation founded upon democracy and slavery, Washington's legacy of mastery is ambivalent; his authority, as textual figure, cannot evade its own history of a compromised racial inheritance. Hoping to dispel these contradictions and make coherent the legacies that uncertainly validated their own political existence, the sons produced legal decisions, congressional acts, biographies, and historical romances that worked at cross-purposes, retelling stories of the father's authority while reproducing the circumstances that undercut that authority.

Although America continually returned to honor the originary text of its history, such a move undermined that history's authority. Prefacing foundational fictions with fictive resolutions for social ills that descended from the original fathers, the sons of the American Renaissance instigated a textual rebellion of monumental dimension. Even a statesman sworn to uphold the design of the fathers might conceive of national origins in ways that radically disfigured their imagined political purity. A few months before troops fired upon Fort Sumter, Lincoln penned a fragment that interpreted the Constitution as the preface to the Declaration of Independence. The fathers' belated commentary in 1789 to their own founding in 1776 makes dubious any claim for national consistency; parricide as national-textual supplement began with the fathers themselves. Seemingly a gesture of concern and homage, a document designed "to *adorn*, and *preserve*" the Declaration, in Lincoln's formulation, the Constitution ironically endangers "the principle of 'Liberty to all,'" threatening "to *conceal*, or *destroy*" what the fathers themselves had promised.[46] Arguing that the Constitution provides a supplement to the Declaration of Independence, the president-elect formulated a critical understanding of the nation as divisive and conflicted at its origin. Reexamination of democratic origins, as Lincoln would so dramatically discover in the next four years, sets in motion a genealogical search for origins that disrupts not only beginnings but also endings, fissuring possibilities of closure. Reading the history of their fathers, American sons like Cooper and Calhoun, William Wells Brown and Abraham Lincoln, Uncle Juvinell and Herman Melville, had no choice but to amend and revise, to preface and supplement, in short, to interpret critically the legacy they had inherited. The narrative bequeathed by the fathers seemed riddled with irreconcilable contradictions between promise and praxis; it was a narrative that in its retelling demanded a preface, an amendment, to make proper adjustment for the social actualities of the present. And although some necessary and proper amendments were not publicly ratified until after Reconstruction, the cultural crisis of the 1850s stood as a preface voicing serious reservations about the narrative from which America descended. The 1850s descended from the glorious days of 1776, but the debates, fiction, and biography generated during the antebellum years articulate an insurrectionary preface to the ideals promulgated by the founding fathers. As writers and politicians remembered the original inception of the Union, they both inadvertently and intentionally authored a subversive filial rebellion questioning the very tradition from which they had nevertheless derived their authority. No matter how laudatory or affirmative its inspiration, no matter what body bore the national fiction, American historical remembering foundered in its attempt to apply fatherly authority to silence the rebellion that unacknowledged textual and racial sons instigated.

No work of the post-revolutionary period better prefaces the history of 1776 than Melville's *Moby-Dick*, which does violent homage to the founding father with the comparison that "Queequeg was George Washington cannibalistically developed." This last sentence, however, is merely a preface to the argument of the next chapter.

2

Covenants, Truth, and the "Ruthless Democracy" of *Moby-Dick*

*But the Declaration of Independence
makes a difference.*
—Herman Melville, *Letters*

THE NARRATIVE COVENANT

Moby-Dick (1851) constantly retraces its steps, backtracking in the progression of its narrative to provide amendments and prefaces to the story it is telling. Ishmael often confesses his negligence and atones for his sins of omission by reversing course to sketch details and provide supplemental information. "The Sphynx" thus commences by referring backward: "It should not have been omitted that previous to completely stripping the body of leviathan, he was beheaded."[1] The chapter "Ambergris" contains an apology from Ishmael that he may have unjustly assumed the landsman reading his tale to have a familiarity of certain practices common to the whaling industry: "I have forgotten to say that there were found in this ambergris, certain hard, round, bony plates" (317). Or consider how "The Dart" opens by flinging itself backward: "A word concerning an incident in the last chapter" (230). As a sailor, Ishmael seems given to this same predilection; when on deck at the tiller, he fixes on the ghastly madness of the tryworks and then turns himself about. His negligence threatens to capsize the *Pequod* by running her into the wind. Looking backward jeopardizes the stability and safety of the ship's crew, just as Ishmael's narrative retracings and circlings back run counter to the imperious linearity of Ahab's hunt. In this sense, the narrative's use of allusive names like *Rachel* or Ahab causes the reader to turn back to prior textual sources, searching after a textual foundation to find support and meaning. Such references impede the reader's progress into the story with vague suggestions and half hints like those Elijah speaks to detain Queequeg and Ishmael momentarily before they board the cannibal craft. *Moby-Dick's* tacking back and forth indicates how narrative must be built on prior sources, but even as it returns to textual foundations, the novel exposes a concern about the stability and desirability of narrative in the first place.[2]

Using a strategy prone to forgetfulness and a prose interrupted by hiccups of memory, Ishmael problematizes the act of narration. Fully aware that he is telling an American odyssey in pursuit of an ending, Ishmael engages in a covert insurrection against his own narration, stalling the narrative whenever possible. His digressions and deferrals more than stall disclosure of Ahab's mission: such devices obstruct the seemingly irrefragable course of narrative that threatens to invest him as teller with the same fatherly authority that guides and governs Cooper's national narrative of the Revolution. When Melville wished "that all excellent books were foundlings, without father or mother," he expressed Ishmael's desire to orphan his text, to sever his book from the originary sources of privilege and status, to send off his story as a wayward articulation.[3] If Melville was in one sense the originator or father of *Moby-Dick*, Ishmael was to be his parricide. Under the guise of a scrupulous attention to detail and the apologies for his somewhat absent-minded narration, Ishmael plays the idle philosopher, amateur biologist, temperance reformer, dabbler in jurisprudence, historian of the sperm-whale fishery, all to conceal his critical examination of the patriarchal authority that secures narrative progression and closure. Harboring this project, Ishmael manipulates *Moby-Dick* to interrogate the nature of narrative (not to mention the narrative of nature), resisting a destiny that can lead only to, if not ideological closure, then at least a plotted ending. He tries to find exception to what the essence of narrative authoritatively demands; he wonders if stories, like nations, need move toward the promised land of a final page. In other words, Ishmael constructs a politics of narrative through which he can take issue with the covenant the author makes with the autocratic structure of narrative in order to impart his tale; he questions both the terms as well as the feasibility of attaining the promises to be fulfilled with the completion of narrative. This line of interrogation implicates citizens as well, leading Ishmael to examine critically an implacable covenant that requires consent to American national narrative as a precondition of encountering and attaining meaningful political experiences such as freedom and community.

At times, Ishmael seeks to circumvent the teleological narrative of metaphysics. From the first paragraph, Ishmael desires to deny his own essence in suicide. Likewise, his status as an orphan frustrates the implicit teleological quests of genealogy, history, and biography. For Ishmael, Ahab heroically embodies this rejection of the classical narrative of metaphysics by chastising the gods and fates for assuming that they can determine his destiny. Elsewhere, Ishmael's retrogressions insinuate doubts about the sanctity of historical narrative. "Fast-Fish and Loose-Fish," like many chapters in *Moby-Dick*, starts with a return to a preceding episode: "The allusion to the waifs and waif-poles in the last chapter but one, necessitates some account of the laws and regulations of the whale fishery, of which the waif may be deemed the grand symbol and badge" (307). What seems an innocent correction of a whaling story develops as a critical examination of American narrative. Ishmael amends the expanding history of the American experience by pointing to the expansionist tendencies of its own inception: "What was America in 1492 but a Loose-Fish, in which Columbus struck the Spanish standard by way of waifing it for his royal master and mistress? . . . What at last will Mexico be to the United States? All Loose-fish" (309–10). The unavoidable colonialist impulses of Manifest Destiny become part of this chapter, whose inclusion encourages a reexamination of the text that has preceded it. Not only do we turn back to "The Grand Armada" to consider "waifs and waif-poles"; we also review other textual ancestors, the founding principles of an American history, which in telling us of a liberty secured from a colonial oppressor point to 1850s America's hypocritical regard for its origins. Rather than simply smoothing out the narrative by amending it with background information, the history supplied here suggests the inconsistencies between inherited ideals and current governance. As Ishmael informs us that the regulations of fast fish and loose fish determine what is "fair game," he reminds us that the game is not fair, but a "masterly code" whose lawful wisdom translates into imperial domination (307). He interrupts a plot seemingly bent upon monomaniacal conclusion to impede another plot devoted to grandiose designs; he politicizes the interruption of a whaling voyage, using it to imply a subversion of the teleological vision of Manifest Destiny.[4]

Whereas an ardent believer in the Union like the author of *Teachings of Patriots and Statesmen; or, the "Fathers of the Republic" on Slavery*

(1860) hoped that his countrymen would "steadily pursue the path marked out by the fathers, and perpetuate the principles" of the Union, a conciliatory sentiment seconded in Henry Clay's proposal that Washington's Farewell Address be ritually reread, Melville cherished no expectations that filial returns to founding fathers would rededicate the nation to either consensus or justice.[5] National retrospection, as the willy-nilly backward glances of *Moby-Dick* suggest, may not delineate any clear "path," but instead lead to an unrelated series of halfhearted investigations that end up nowhere. In fact, the search for a stable history can backfire and uncover further, more profound division. Characterizing Ahab, Ishmael warns against excavations of the past if one is looking not to find a parricidal supplement, but further testaments of purity and guidance: "from your grim sire only will the old State-secret come" (155). Genealogy may lead to unsuspected discoveries that contradict or simply complicate the legitimating and linear story genealogy proposes to trace. Ishmael's lack of patriarchal faith readily sets him apart from the pietistic counselor of the *Teachings of Patriots and Statesmen*, who prefaces his volume with a frontispiece of Washington as though the sight of the founder could provide the clarity of vision to secure the national and narrative conclusions that Melville suspected (Figure 1). This engraving of the national father, bearing a facsimile of the general's signature that exercised such authority in *The Spy*, establishes a firm foundation for what is no doubt a rocky issue. The image and name of Washington steers a course between "extremists, both North and South," guiding the sons through the fractious present by appeal to the stability of texts from the country's past. *Moby-Dick*, in contrast, can only assemble an array of abortive prefaces over which shakily preside "a late consumptive usher" (9) and a "mere painstaking burrower and grubworm" (11). Ancestry thus has little sway in *Moby-Dick*, not the least because of Ishmael's efforts to undermine the coordinates of order and authority, whether maritime, narratival, or cultural.

From its beginning, *Moby-Dick* tackles the sources, origins, and genealogy of narrative precisely because it does not have a beginning, but multiple beginnings whose sheer plurality renders narrative authority a circumspect force in the novel. An etymology prefaces Ishmael's appearance. Ranging across thirteen languages, this entry tries to derive the linguistic essence of the whale, mirroring

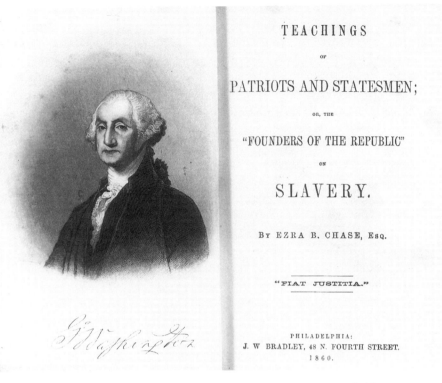

Fig 1.   The claims to authority implied by the frontispiece and title page of Ezra Chase's work starkly contrast with the suspect array of prefaces that open *Moby-Dick*.

Ahab's fanatic drive to pierce the life of Moby Dick and clutch at physical and spiritual mysteries. The gamut of possibilities, from the Latin *cetus* to the English *whale* to the unfamiliar and fanciful "Feejee" *pekee-nuee-nuee*, makes leviathan indeterminate, a protean entity changing across different cultural imaginations. In this ironic attempt to muster a comprehensive linguistic knowledge, Melville marshals the support of lexicographers, yet each contradicts the other, citing different origins of the English word *whale*. The etymology fails to resolve the ambiguity that arises from the title itself. *Moby-Dick; or, The Whale* poses a question just as much as it announces the novel. The hedging either/or quality of this self-declaration undercuts *Moby-Dick* by immediately placing it under revision with its identification as one of a certain species of animal. *Moby-Dick* falls short of being intelligible by itself; it needs to be amended with *The Whale*, a term that then comes under scrutiny and fragments into the Babel of the etymology. Unlike a national primer anchored by the singular presence of Washington, Melville's novel gets under way pulled at by crosscurrents set up by the effort to put it into motion.

Linguistically unable to moor itself in any sovereign meaning, *Moby-Dick* next searches after cultural authority in the "Extracts." In this second preface, a sub-sub librarian amasses an impressive array of references stretching from the Genesis account of divine authorship, "And God created great whales," to *The New England Primer*'s reiteration of God's authority, "Whales in the sea / God's voice obey," to Hobbes's study of civil authority in *Leviathan* (12, 15). Despite the exhaustive length of this compilation, not to mention the great length of leviathan himself, these extracts exact little authority. Melville prefaces this preface with a short note designed to provoke ridicule and skepticism of "higgedly-piggedly whale statements" that the "grubworm of a poor devil of a Sub-Sub," the antithesis of the mighty whale, has painstakingly arranged (11). After this, the narrative proper begins: "Call me Ishmael." Maybe that is the narrator's name or maybe not; after the sham endeavors of the etymology and extracts, he would fain make a claim for authenticity. At the very moment that Ishmael issues an authorial announcement of his own identity, we take his statement as a warning that we need beware a possible deception from a narrator telling a tale under an assumed name. Lacking any textual foundation, having only the vacillating nature of the novel's either/or title, Ishmael can inscribe his own being only as a moment of doubt and suspicion that quickly degenerates into a desire for suicide. Any appeals to authority that he might make are undermined with the confession that *Moby-Dick* merely forestalls self-annihilation, that a sea voyage and the telling of it are "my substitute for pistol and ball" (23). Ishmael internalizes the filial rebellion of preface to text and contemplates murderous rebellion against the sovereign authority of his being.

Sailing the *Pequod* into the wind or proceeding backward via prefaces and textual emendations imperils both the mariners and the narrative, undercutting the planned course of any expedition. These prefaces, in both their supplemental succession one after another and their dubious communication of information, compile doubts about the text's origins and stage a rebellion against the narrative that follows. The rebellion is even more insidious because it does not appear to be a rebellion. The prefaces pretend to shore up the narrative by making an appeal to linguistic and cultural contexts, only to engage in a textual insurrection. Questions arise that produce a lack of confidence in the integrity of the narrative project: where has the author gotten his authority to narrate his story? From his own personal experiences? From history? From a culture that accepts such a mythic telling? As we have seen, Cooper faced such doubts in the introduction to his own novel of the Revolution: "The author has often been asked if there were any foundation in real life" for his narrative. Ishmael hopes that these notes supplied by "a late consumptive usher to a grammar school" and "a sub-sub librarian" will answer such questions, but he covertly desires that this attempt to establish authority will undermine it. The array of prefaces and false starts allows Ishmael to interrogate his own patriarchal authority to tell his tale by expressing deep-seated reservations about the project of narrative itself: can the author narrativize solely by relying upon a willful cultural authority unconcerned with democratic models of narrative, what Melville called "truth"? In other words, does narrative need only a will as irrefutable as Ahab's, which has no scruples about manipulating the cultural power of prejudice, stereotype, and superstition, in order to bend covenanted listeners to its articulation and enactment?

In "Hawthorne and His Mosses," Melville undertook to answer these questions, describing the strategies an author must use to avoid surrendering truth to a culture whose concern is not truth, but power and authority.[6] In order to tell a tale, an author has to make a covenant with authority: he or she agrees to cede truth in exchange for the cultural authority to narrate. Words, allusions, tropes, icons, and symbols can all serve as part of the artist's literary arsenal if he or she lets go of pure, unadulterated truth and filters it through the vehicles of discourse that culture has so graciously offered. According to Melville, without the legitimation or protection of truth by these filters of cultural authority, "truth is forced to fly like a sacred white doe in the woodlands; and only by cunning glimpses will she reveal herself." Once borne by these tropes circulating within cultural discourse, however, truth no longer needs be bashful precisely because it is no longer untainted and delicate truth, having been perverted and encouraged to lie. If truth is forced to fly outside of the domain of culture, it is eventually tracked down and secured within the authoritative discourses of that culture. In this way, the argument in "Hawthorne and His Mosses" anticipates Foucault's analysis of discursive truth. Like Melville, Foucault understands that truth cannot exist in the wilds, unfettered by culture, but that truth must always be positioned *"dans le vrai,"* (within the true). Foucault gives the example of Mendel, who spoke the truth only to be dismissed because he failed to speak within the truth ordained by contemporary biological discourse.[7] In contrast to Mendel, ethnologists of Melville's era could authoritatively describe the symptoms of drapetomania, a mental aberration that caused black slaves to run away, because such a disease fell *dans le vrai* of a discourse permeated with notions of racial hierarchy and ethnocentrism. American statesmen similarly spoke the truth when they described the annexation of slave territories as a project to "extend the area of freedom" because such claims were made within the authorizing tenets of an American narrative plotted with Manifest Destiny. No matter how much truth desires "to fly like a sacred white doe in the woodlands," *Moby-Dick* reminds us that truth, despite its transcendental aura, is always connected to society, is always saturated by an array of political, nationalist, biological, or literary discourses. As Foucault writes, "Truth is a thing of this world: it is produced only by virtue of multiple forms of constraint. And it induces regular effects of power. Each society has its regime of truth." Once caged in this manner, truth can reveal itself only in spaces not supervised by culture. "You must have plenty of sea-room to tell the Truth in," writes Melville. As the land disappears in *Moby-Dick,* Ishmael sings an epiphany to the handsome sailor, Bulkington, who shuns companionship ashore: "Know ye, now, Bulkington? Glimpses do ye seem to see of that mortally intolerable truth; that all deep, earnest thinking is but the intrepid effort the soul to keep the open independence of her sea; while the wildest winds of heaven and earth conspire to cast her on the treacherous slavish shore?" (99).

But it is not always possible to sign up for a whaling cruise and leave behind the lee shore; besides, even when one has moved beyond sight of the land, a demagogue named Ahab can arise, charismatically insisting that musings abroad the wide ocean be coordinated around the hunt for a white whale. Melville thus posits that truth resides in the darkness of voices tinged with madness or evil that resist "slavish" codification. Everyday citizens do not possess such voices; indeed, as Melville writes in "Hawthorne and His Mosses," "it were all but madness for any good man, in his own proper character, to utter, or even hint," of the darker realities that underlie the metaphysical and political aspects of life on the "slavish shore." The citizen "speaks the sane madness of vital truth" in the marginal, uninhabited spaces that exist within culture. Within the Puritanic gloom of Hawthorne, the frantic despair of Lear, the sanctioned idiocy of Pip, or the undecipherable message of Queequeg's tattoos, one can see, like Bulkington, into the depths of "that mortally intolerable truth."[8] Only within the paradoxical incongruity of "sane madness," only within a consciousness ironically positioned against itself, can the citizen utter truth. Obscured by a culture's authority, truth will appear only in the "cunning glimpses" of ironic and parodic representations of authorized discourse.

Ishmael skeptically approaches selling the soul of truth to narrative in exchange for authority; before he enters the narrative of *Moby-Dick*, before he agrees to the covenant that will authorize him to tell the tale, he affixes a series of prefatory amendments indicating his hesitancy about the project of narrative in the first place. Ishmael has a prejudice against narrative, which, in its peculiarly American incarnations, produces an inexorable drive to capture a conclusion, no matter what the consequences. Other captains, similarly authorized by the notion of the quest, who "systematically hunted out" notorious whales, lead Ishmael to suspect that massacre and extermination are symptoms of larger narrative and cultural imperatives (170). This teleological drive, this monomania for closure, does not only encompass the *Pequod*'s mad captain, but describes the founding imperatives of American civilization. Ishmael thus specifies the single-minded and relentless pursuit of "New Zealand Tom" and "Don Miguel": "as in setting out through the Narragansett Woods, Captain Butler of old had it in his mind to capture that notorious murderous savage Annawon, the headmost warrior of the Indian King Philip" (170). Whether whale hunting or Indian hunting, each practice is legitimated by a teleology that admits no quarter. This convergence between the present history of whaling and the annals of colonial settlement initiates a double movement that is at once laudatory and ironic: at one moment, whaling is ennobled by its placement within a narrative of American progress that triumphs over the "savage";

at another, the earliest episodes of nation building appear driven by a sophisticated mixture of commercial speculation and genocide. As the present looks to its ancestors for confirmation, as Ishmael tries to discover historical precedents for his current enterprise, the past itself falls under suspicion. Historical returns can only be critical, only parricidal. And, now, aboard a ship named for an extinct tribe of the "Narragansett Woods," Ishmael finds himself replicating yet another American quest. Compiling whale statements and whale etymology, in addition to beginning his narrative with an anonymity that jeopardizes narrative authority, Ishmael delays disclosure of a story that in its maddest moments learns nothing from history and repeats the nation's uncompromising mission of racial trespass.

Rife with antifoundational paradox and misdirections, Ishmael's prefaces initiate a novel in which narrative authority is not total, but ambivalent, in which comments and characters can, if only for brief moments, escape the vortex of speaking *dans le vrai*.[9] In terms of the novel's events, Ishmael's evasion of the "regime of truth" and search for a non-negotiated truth can be undertaken only amid moments of great ambivalence. He forms a friendship with a pagan cannibal whom he at first distrusts and then later forgets; he criticizes Ahab's political authority even as he finds himself lured by the magnetic quality of his captain's rhetoric. Although these falters make Ishmael an unlikely hero, in terms of an American narrative, such ambivalence exerts a critical force and instills resistance to the tacit assumption that nations and narratives should pursue destinies and endings that place truth within practices and institutions justified by cultural authority. The question becomes: why should a people follow Moses out of the wilderness if to do so it exterminates native tribes of that desert, imports slaves into the desert, and, finally, seizes all of that desert as though it were theirs by divine promise? The impetus of narrative, unchecked by prefaces, moves authors, readers, and citizens along so quickly in an "unfaltering hunt" for a promised closure, a white whale, or a Manifest Destiny, that they have little time to question critically the consequences of their own progress (166).[10]

This preference for prefaces did not make Melville an authorial isolato in his day. His narrative techniques and the issues he thematized have led literary scholars to federate him and other artists along the keel of an era commonly known as the American Renaissance. Shared concerns such as the complication of the legacy of

Puritan morality, the often problematic dramatization of race relations, and the wariness about the individual's incorporation into the community produced a certain insecurity and anxiety about the narratives being authored in mid-nineteenth-century America. That is, the stories told seemed to lack authority because of their often critical and ambiguous renderings of America. Authors sought to compensate for their stories' dubious authority by constructing extratextual appeals to authenticate and verify the narratives. Before Hawthorne can tell the dark romance of the New World that opens with a prison door in *The Scarlet Letter* (1850), he finds it necessary to author "The Custom House" preface, which both delivers an account of the writer, to provide "proofs of the authenticity of a narrative therein contained," and sketches the historical Surveyor Pue, who "authorized and authenticated" the documents to whose outline his narrative adheres. Yet as many readers have commented, Hawthorne's efforts backfire, registering a host of unsettling anxieties that include his worries about descending from a line of Puritan oppressors as well as his preoccupations about the menacing federal eagle perched above the Custom House door. This preface bears a relation not simply to the text as father, but to Hawthorne's own patriarchal ancestors and the national authority governing his career in Salem. Concurrently tracing family history and federal power, "The Custom House" literalizes Derrida's observations about the preface as a "seminal *différance*" prone to reabsorption within the authority of fatherly figures, from "stern and black-browed Puritans" who would belittle Hawthorne's idle artistic efforts, to "Uncle Sam," who capriciously provides him employment, to Inspector Pue, whose papers are his textual foundation. Edgar Allan Poe's *The Narrative of Arthur Gordon Pym* (1838) responds to similar concerns about authenticity by appending a preface in which Pym, himself a fiction, declares that a real person, Poe, published parts of the narrative as fiction so that they would have "the better chance of being received as truth." Such ironic twists and turns perversely add to the authority of the text in a manner that is more supplemental than coherent. With some people doubting a slave's ability to read and write, with some believing their narratives to be the shameless propaganda of abolitionists, and with still others doubting the actuality of the events related and the severity of the conditions described, ex-slaves preceded their narratives with introductions from renowned white people. William Lloyd Garrison of the *Liberator* provided the authority Frederick Douglass could not claim because of his blackness, and the renowned woman of letters Lydia Maria Child asserted that Harriet Jacobs's *Incidents in the Life of a Slave Girl* (1861) was no fiction. Garrison confirmed that, despite its poetic skill, *Narrative of the Life of Frederick Douglass, An American Slave* (1845) was the authentic production of a black slave, and Child apologized for the "execrences" within the story of a slave girl pregnant at fifteen. In addition to authorizing slaves' stories compromised by their authors' identity, these editors lent support to narratives compromised by their own critical politics; the prefaces provided surety for narratives that critically represented the fathers' land of liberty.[11] But that support and surety came at the expense of the slave narrator's discursive independence. Douglass readily recognized that Garrison's prefatory efforts worked inversely, threatening the ex-slave's ability to stand alone as author and procreate a text, a problematic I explore in chapter 5. These contradictory positions of affirmation and textual undercutting, of filial worship and parricidal desire, recur several times over in *Moby-Dick*, even before the narrator introduces himself with the words "Call me Ishmael." But insofar as Melville understood that the unabated contradictions of slave-holding within democracy produced these gaps in narrative authority, he would have found only Douglass and Jacobs sharing his insights about the racial connections between narrative and political form.

Nevertheless, Melville remained something of an isolato among both the reading public and the New England literati. "What a madness & anguish it is, that an author can never—under no conceivable circumstances—be at all frank with readers," complained Melville the year before he began work on *Moby-Dick*.[12] Indeed, the public picked up on that "madness & anguish," and reviewers, in the wake of *Mardi* and *Moby-Dick*, intimated that the author was plagued by a nervous disorder and should seek rest in an asylum. In all of America, Melville found he could be frank about his beliefs in truth and democracy with only one person, Hawthorne. And yet traces of embarrassment and hesitation mark even his exuberant letters to Hawthorne. Melville's distaste for missionary programs and temperance crusades kept him aloof from the likes of John Greenleaf Whittier and Harriet Beecher Stowe. He differed with his Pittsfield neighbor, Oliver Wendell Holmes, whom he unfavorably rendered as an exacting scientist in "I and My Chimney"—which, as Carolyn

Karcher suggests, may have been in response to Holmes's interest in racist ethnology that held blacks to be a distinct, less evolved human species. "Poignantly attesting to Melville's sense of isolation is the almost total silence he maintained on the subject of slavery in his letters to family members, friends, publishers, and fellow writers, even while he was formulating his impassioned fictional indictments of it," argues Karcher.[13]

Nor did Melville find support for what he called "unconditional democracy in all things" among his ancestors or his present family. Melville's double Revolutionary descent, boasting of a maternal grandfather who successfully defended Fort Stanwix against the British and a paternal grandfather who dressed up as an Indian and dumped tea in Boston harbor, graced him with Titan-like forefathers. True, these ancestors testified to Revolutionary greatness, yet these fathers also achieved a distinguished, if not aristocratic, status for the Melvilles and Gansevoorts that no doubt contradicted faith in an "unconditional democracy." His father died when he was twelve, yet he hardly found a surrogate in his father-in-law, Lemuel Shaw, chief justice of the Massachusetts Supreme Court. Unlike Cooper's representation of the union between the Whartons and the Dunwoodies, the alliance between the houses of Melville and Shaw no doubt created discomfort for Melville when Judge Shaw surrendered escaped slave Thomas Sims to his master in Savannah by upholding the Fugitive Slave Law. That Shaw not only helped support Melville's father's widow and her children but patronized Melville's own artistic endeavors certainly acted as a restraining order upon his son-in-law's political beliefs. Melville no doubt accrued advantages from these natal and adopted family legacies that echoed national history, yet at what point did remembering these debts suffuse "the open independence" of his sea with prescriptions of an already written filial identity? As Melville complained in an ambivalent expression of parricidal longing and patriarchal impossibility, "No one is his own sire."[14]

Donald Pease suggests that *Moby-Dick* is not a work of isolation but a "collective" project dedicated to Hawthorne in recognition of their shared understanding of the often specious character of American political rhetoric. Although he inscribed *Moby-Dick* to Hawthorne, Melville must have viewed Hawthorne's support of Franklin Pierce's proslavery presidency with aversion. In a letter of June 1, 1851, Melville assumed that his belief in a "ruthless democracy on all sides" would cause Hawthorne to shy away from him. One critic has called this letter Melville's declaration of independence from Hawthorne. In the same letter that Melville warned Hawthorne of his adherence to "unconditional democracy in all things," he proclaimed his alienation from antebellum cultural expression: "What I feel most moved to write, that is banned,—it will not pay. Yet, altogether, write the *other* way I cannot."[15]

What way, then, did Melville write? Positioned within a family committed to juridical, national, and ancestral discourses, indeed positioned *dans le vrai*, one would suppose that he had very little "sea room" to tell and narrate a "ruthless democracy." Only an equally ruthless narrative strategy that could tolerate irony, paradox, and discontinuities like "sane madness" could offer glimpses that momentarily evade prescriptive "slavish" discourses and approach the freedom of Bulkington's vision. Only "ruthless democracy" could counter the "regime of truth."

THE TRUTH OF POLYPHONY
AND THE FRAUD OF ETHNOLOGY

Somewhere between the poles of free will and necessity, somewhere within authorized discourse, Melville developed a strategy he called "the great Art of Telling the Truth,—even though it be covertly, and by snatches"; he wrote fiction using a narrative strategy whose authority was rendered suspect in its own telling. Somewhere between his sardonic suggestion to "Try to get a living by the Truth,—and go to the Soup Societies" and his conviction that American political discourse spoke with authority but not with the truth of democratic principles, Melville incorporated the truth not as subject matter, but as the very mode of telling. Truth does not surface in the story of a fated captain demonically pursuing a dumb brute in the face of prophetic warnings; instead, truth lies in the narrative used to tell the story of that captain and that whale. Ralph Ellison thus observes of Melville: "Whatever else his works were 'about' they also managed to be about democracy." The content of Melville's narrative form is a truth that can be expressed only in the hardly utterable contradictions of racial heterogeneity besieged by American democracy.[16]

Slavery played no part in Melville's "ruthless democracy." As both idea and practice, it sullied the democratic body politic and democratic narration. Like slave ships that "run away from each other as soon as possible," slavery had no companion concept among the fraternity and freedom of his oceanic democracy (195). Frederick Douglass censured American politicians who acted "like hungry sharks in the bloody wake of a Brazilian slaveship," and four years later, Melville called upon the same image to suggest the solitary, anticommunal pathways of bondage, commenting that only sharks, voracious and self-devouring, "the invariable outriders of all slave ships crossing the Atlantic," provided a community for slavery (235). Melville's unsettling commitment to "ruthless democracy" impels his narrator to radical actions and even more radical strategies of narrative. Lacking any model or precedent, Melville constructed a novelty entitled *Moby-Dick* that created a polyphony, not simply in terms of the culturally diverse voices of the crew, but in terms of the diverse forms of narrative Ishmael uses to tell his and his shipmates' story.[17]

As the novel ranges from transcendental meditations upon existence to democratic choruses, Ishmael flits in and out of the story. Soon after Ishmael selects a cannibal named Queequeg for his bosom friend, the narrative ceases to be the story of a young sailor, as is *Redburn*. Rather, it becomes the story of different ways to tell the story of a crew sailing after glimpses of democracy, glimpses that are dangerously susceptible to Ahab's demagoguery. Unlike Ahab, Ishmael does not invent ways to make the crew, in its heterogeneous composition, coalesce around his story of the *Pequod*. He relinquishes suicidal autobiography to the dramatic democracy of "Midnight, Forecastle." While the delegates of the choruslike crew speak and exchange thoughts, Ishmael remains silent, much in the same way that later he loses track of himself among the ecstatic utterances of an unctuous community of shipmates squeezing spermacetti— "Squeeze! squeeze! squeeze! all the morning long; I squeezed that sperm till I myself almost melted into it"(323). Ishmael dissolves into the crew, becoming one of their number, engaged in the common quest. After he boards the *Pequod,* he blends into the rigging of the communal narrative, relinquishing his own authorial and sovereign "I" to refocus the narrative's concerns on the many and diverse elements of whaling, as well as the heterogeneous composition of the crew.

Melville's narrative style and polyphonic discourse employ modes of telling particularly suited to situations marked by such heterogeneity and difference. Only through what Richard Brodhead calls "a conflict of fictions" could a "ruthless democracy" be represented. Brodhead argues that Hawthorne and Melville remained in continual tension with "constitutive conventions of their genre"— the novel—and this tension caused them to eschew any single narrative mode. *Moby-Dick* resists generic imperatives "to subsume varied material into a unifying and homogeneous narrative mode," privileging instead diverse representational strategies. If democracy is to be "unconditional," as Melville suggested in his letter to Hawthorne, then the narrative that transmits unconditional democracy must shirk off any conditions or conventions that allegiance to one fictional style demands. Only heterogeneous composition could represent the heterogeneous bodies forming the *Pequod*'s crew.[18]

Melville employed this composite narrative form as a political venture: not simply to tell a different story of America, but to *tell differently* a story of America. As Ishmael fades in and out of the narrative, he initiates, in the words of Carolyn Porter, a "discursive democracy." Drawing upon Bakhtin's ideas of polyphony, Porter argues that Ishmael speaks in a "double-voiced discourse" that appropriates authorized discourse at the same time that he parodies that discourse, undermining the validity of the tongue he has chosen to speak. In the same way that the parricidal urge in national narratives of Washington at once acclaims the text and thwarts its coherence, Ishmael acts as a textual insurgent, acknowledging a recognized discourse only to plunder it of its authority. Melville accords Ishmael an ironic authority capable of subverting dominant cultural authority. For example, in both "The Advocate" and "The Affidavit," Ishmael employs legalistic discourse to undermine its own credibility with faulty and exaggerated examples about the sperm whale fishery. Whether the prevailing discourse is legalistic, scientific, or philosophical, Ishmael siphons off the discourse's authority by subjecting it to a mixture of irony and parody. Each discourse corresponds to a vision/version of reality, so that, according to Brodhead, "no representation of reality can pretend to a final validity." Without "final validity," there is no consummate authority, and the crew resides in a democratic narrative, precariously prone to incorporation within Ahab's political rhetoric. For the time being, however, the unmanageable sum of these irreconcilable and discordant visions promotes an egalitarian consciousness that relinquishes control of the narrative so that others may speak; Ishmael embodies a narrative consciousness that speaks as one sailor among the thirty-man crew, as one more isolato forming the "Anacharsis Clootz deputation from all isles of the sea, and all the ends of the earth" (108). Ishmael's voice is "a virtual sponge, capable of soaking up an infinite number of voices and squeezing out their discourse into a pool as large as the ocean he sails," writes Porter.[19]

Yet radical democracy causes Ishmael embarrassment. It is a political, sexual, and cultural vision that cannot be sustained without breeding dangerous conflict and acute self-awareness for its practitioners. Thus, while squeezing sperm, Ishmael finds himself apologizing to his shipmates for his reckless and transcendental passion, which leads him to mistake their hands for "gentle globules" (323). But rather than apologize to the reader or confess a sense of embarrassment for his fraternal feelings, Ishmael interrupts "A Squeeze of the Hand" in midcourse to speak of the stark preparations of the tryworks, whose mechanical violence mutilates the harmonious universalism just related. He descends into the blubber room among the barefoot cutters, whose stumps that were once toes replace affectionate fingers squeezing sperm. The impulse that leads Ishmael to squeeze "the very milk and sperm of kindness" becomes the source of bodily amputation (323). If the spademan "cuts off one of his own toes, or one of his assistants', would you be very much astonished? Toes are scarce among veteran blubber-room men" (324). The rhetorical question encourages us to answer that, no, these common amputations being so ordinary do not astonish us, though, Ishmael, we are surprised at your mad and exuberant language of squeezing sperm. The quickness with which the narrator's jubilations of fraternity dissipate as the crew prepares the ship to become the factory at sea causes Ishmael and his reader to look back upon the episode of squeezing sperm as the embarrassing ramblings of a utopian dreamer.

Melville the letter writer presents his democratic ideals with similar apprehension to the more politically conservative Hawthorne. He sees with an Ishmael-like timidity his own tendency toward the arrogance of Ahab: "It is but nature to be shy of a mortal who boldly declares" unflinching faith in radical democracy, he wrote to Hawthorne. But Melville could not bridle that Ahab within from autocratically taking up Ishmael's ideas about democracy and transforming them into parricide of national dimensions. Melville thus "boldly declares" to Hawthorne that "a thief in jail is as honorable a personage as George Washington." And within *Moby-Dick*, George Washington becomes as honorable as a pagan savage who peddles shrunken heads. In the famous passage where Ishmael experiences salvation from his misanthropy as well as from the cultural prejudices of Christianity, he describes the magnificence of his bedmate Queequeg by way of the unabashed comparison we have already noted:

> With much interest I sat watching him. Savage though he was, and hideously marred about the face—at least to my taste—his countenance yet had a something in it which was by no means disagreeable. You cannot hide the soul. . . . Whether it was, too, that his head being shaved, his forehead was drawn out in freer and brighter relief, and looked more expansive than it otherwise would, this I will not venture to decide; but certain it was his head was phrenologically an excellent one. It may seem ridiculous, but it reminded me of General Washington's head, as seen in the popular busts of him. It had the same long regularly graded retreating slope from above the brows, which were likewise projecting, like two long promontories thickly wooded on top. Queequeg was George Washington cannibalistically developed. (58)

To counteract the potentially jarring nature of his metaphor, Ishmael here puts forth a comparison tentatively developed. Just as the stares of the New Bedford citizens accost Ishmael and his bosom friend as they make their way through town streets, Ishmael the narrator knows his description will provoke, at the very least, the astonishment of the reader. Proceeding with clauses to explicate and clarify his position, all of which delay the final rushed assertion, he confesses his conceit is "ridiculous." His authority is ironic not simply because it subverts authorized discourses, but because it participates in its own destabilization. Ishmael takes on the same embarrassed tone Melville used when he communicated to Hawthorne his sentiments about Washington, admitting that the analogy was "ludicrous." Yet Melville goes on to affirm the "Truth" of his brash egalitarian comparison, knowing all the while it lacks any authority in the patrifilial culture of antebellum America: "This is ludicrous. But Truth is the silliest thing under the sun." As narrative, as an attempt to speak political "Truth," "ruthless democracy" will not be logical, even, or regular—otherwise it could easily succumb to the regime of truth.[20]

In the same way that Harvey Birch's association with Washington testifies to the spy's true nobility, here, Ishmael's metaphor seemingly works to the enhancement of Queequeg and not to the discredit of Washington—and if it does, Ishmael is quick to apologize. He adopts the prose of exuberance, licensed to use hyperbole. The metaphor works to uplift Queequeg, and Ishmael hopes that his statement can accomplish its missionary purpose without tainting Washington. Ishmael thus knows that what he says "may seem ridiculous," but certain it is that his analogy contains a radical, nay, sacrilegious, political dimension. If audiences found undignified Cooper's coupling of Washington and a common peddler-spy, Ishmael's parallel hardly would appease anyone when it threatened the symbolic father of freedom by rhetorically chaining him to a dusky pagan. The urbane planter thus collides with the uncivilized islander, who, as Eleanor Simpson suggests, is described as a Negro.[21] The fool's unauthorized description often speaks the truth: Ishmael's likening of Queequeg to Washington, "ridiculous" though it may be, conjures up the dark side of American narrative, a side marked simultaneously by truth, uneasily straddling democracy and slavery, and by a lack of authority to tell that truth. Though Ishmael first displaces Queequeg to the imaginary Kokovoko and not Africa, the conjunction of the father of his country with an idolatrous pagan nevertheless indirectly points to the incongruity upsetting both Washington as an authoritative symbol and American narrative as legitimate promise. That Ishmael reports Queequeg's native island lies to "the West and South" leads the reader from New Bedford, not to Polynesia, but to the territories received from the Mexican-American War as the bounty of Manifest Destiny, whose identity as free or slave was in contention. Geographic crises replicate and reproduce themselves on the symbolic landscape, miring Washington's identity, as well as the identities of his descendants, in the incongruous personalities of a civilized free man and the islander whom Bildad curses as the "son of darkness" (87).

Ishmael, however, can imply this truth only by way of displacement.[22] In the abyss separating Melville's own truth lacking authority from the national authority lacking truth, displacement arises as an effective strategy. Not just in terms of a subversive content that sports with fantastic islands as political allegory, but in his very mode of telling does he come at truth "covertly, and by snatches." That is, in order for Ishmael to reincarnate Washington in the body of a heathen, he must undermine his own authority and apologize for the truth he presents as though it were an oddity of his own brain. Indeed, for Ishmael to speak the truth, he must extricate himself as best he can from an America in crisis; he must, like Bulkington, reject the "slavish shore" that impedes the perception of truth. Ishmael is last seen, shipwrecked, but still afloat in the middle of the Pacific, yet as an author, Melville still inhabited the "slavish shore," and he lived, at the time of *Moby-Dick*'s composition, both in the family that upheld the Fugitive Slave Law by returning Thomas Sims to a public whipping and in an America debating the Compromise of 1850. Though like his narrator, Melville may have stood apart as he perceived a social fabric of narrative and nation where democratic practices corrupted democratic ideals, he was still *dans le vrai* of authorized discourse. The power of America's discourses proved particularly effective in allowing Congress, faced with same disjunctive controversy, to legislate an artificial yet authoritative closure to effect a compromise declaring freedom and enslavement compatible and mutually enhancing. Congress narrated an expanding vision of America that permitted California to enter the Union as a free state but fell back upon the idea of popular sovereignty to permit slavery in the other territories acquired from Mexico and passed the Fugitive Slave Law. The Compromise of 1850 certainly preserved America through the legislation of consensus and accord, yet as it did so, it unavoidably called into question the totality and storied perfection of the national narrative. Nation and narrative could continue expansion if the gaps in founding logic were overlooked. In other words, in 1850, promise became compromise.

The principles that once initiated perhaps the most remarkable attempt at intentional community were revised and reworded in popular consciousness: during this era of supplemented and amended narrative, the *Richmond Enquirer* explained this alternative reading: "In this country alone does perfect equality of civil and social privilege exist among the white population, and it exists solely because we have black slaves. Freedom is not possible without slavery." Slavery, if one compromised democratic discourse, did not appear to be incongruous with freedom, but, in fact, made for a more profound experience of civic freedom. "The situation of the slaveowner," wrote a supporter of the Confederacy, "qualifies him, in an eminent degree, for discharging the duties of a free citizen. His leisure enables him to cultivate his intellectual powers, and his condition of independence places him beyond the reach of demagogues and corruption." If America could compromise in this way, Melville and Ishmael could compromise Washington with comparisons to thieves and cannibals. Their ability to make these comparisons reflects a culture whose authority to enforce a narrative—especially one that told an inconsistent story as though it were consistent—was as titular as its symbols. Ironic subversion thus presented itself to Melville and his narrator not only out of the gap between truth and national authority, but out of the seams of that authority itself. Melville and Ishmael spoke discourses that repeated American national authority, but, to recall Bhabha's account of colonial discourse, the discourses they reproduced were "uttered *inter dicta*." It is in one such eruption or moment of "sane madness" that Ishmael compromises the patriarchal founder of America, likening Washington to his cultural opposite. His patriotism is one among many ritual repetitions of Washington, but it is also one of the most "ridiculous"—that is, if parricide is a laughing matter. In the contradictory echoes of homage as criticism, promise as compromise, and Washington as Queequeg, patriotic repetition takes on a subversive, if not murderous, intent toward the patriarchal myths, legacies, and institutions that undergirded the nation.[23]

Whereas the *Richmond Enquirer* adjusted the principles of the narrative to fit the times, other discourses, scientifically developed, functioned as critical commentaries that amended social actualities to fit the new narrative. In his *Treatise on Sociology* (1854), Henry Hughes concluded: "In the United States South, there are no slaves. Those States are warrantee-commonwealths." Bridging divisions between the industrial ethics of the North and the agrarian ideology of the South, Hughes stressed economic affinities, calling the slaveholder a "prudent capitalist." Ethnologists like J. C. Nott and George R. Gliddon shored up the makeshift narrative with a spurious mixture of biology, history, and anthropology. South Carolina senator John C. Calhoun found ammunition in their ethnological substantiation of racial stereotypes, using their arguments to encourage expansion of the peculiar institution. Nott's and Gliddon's exhaustive study *Types of Mankind* "proved" the superiority of the Anglo-Saxon race over others whose physical and mental inferiorities supposedly threatened the continued advancement of civilization. America was not to understand literally Paul's words that God "hath made of one blood all nations of men," for indeed the white and dark races, as ethnology's interpretation of biblical history and anatomy attested, were physically distinct and should remain so. "The Negro and other unintellectual types have been shown . . . to possess heads much smaller, by actual measurement in cubic inches, than the white races," reported Nott and Gliddon. Democracy, said the antebellum ethnologist, can be implemented successfully only among whites, for only they are historically and biologically conditioned for self-determination; in contrast, "*dark*-skinned races, history attests are only fit for military governments." This discourse implied that founding principles needed to be reexamined in the light (and darkness) of these new findings in the human sciences. Apparent contradictions between freedom and enslavement were only the "facts" of nature and biology, not the result of human failing or hypocrisy.[24]

Ishmael's perception of Queequeg's high and noble brow refutes the ethnologist's narrative that acted as a varnish on the disintegrating national narrative. Both the "son of darkness" and the founding father exhibit the cranial capacity to conceive of democratic principles. Even Ishmael, prone to "deliberately stepping into the street, and methodically knocking people's hats off," can experience the regeneration of democracy (23). Despite having a cranium choked with grim Puritanic loomings, Ishmael, too, can conceive of ideals like brotherhood and universal fraternity. Queequeg provides the impetus for his redemption, demonstrating the equality of their crania—and thus their equal capacity for freedom, democracy, and good—when he clasps Ishmael about the waist and "pressed his forehead against mine" (59). And Queequeg concretely reaffirms his commitment to the fundamental ethics of the joint-stock company of humanity by repeatedly saving castaways, among them an African named Daggoo trapped in the sinking head of a whale, a white landlubber who has just called him "the devil," and a refugee from the merchant marine stricken with a bout of misanthropy (65). Once Queequeg's actions indicate the fallacious nature of racist biological classification, Ishmael employs his double-voiced discourse to appropriate and subvert ethnology's authority. That is, through Queequeg, a dark-skinned heathen whose visible being renders him suspect in the Puritan vision, Ishmael finds the impetus to examine the cultural authority of his era. Queequeg, who lacks any authority while on the mainland of the United States—even when he tries to use a cultural artifact like a wheelbarrow, he shows his distance from a basic cultural literacy—ironically provides Ishmael with the authority to parody and undermine the discourses of that dominant culture.

Just as ethnology distinguished three types of mankind by identifying the black race, the sons of Ham; the brownish yellow race, the sons of Shem; and the white race, the sons of Japeth, Ishmael proposes the classificatory system of cetology. His system allows him to discriminate along with Linnaeus: "I hereby separate the whales from the fish" (117). With meticulous and scientific care, Ishmael divides his study into books, folios, chapters, and subheadings. Textual classification becomes biological classification and allows this amateur naturalist to discriminate authoritatively between sperm whales, baleen whales, and porpoises. Yet Ishmael soon undercuts his newly pilfered authority by extending it too far, using it to make untenable hypotheses. He parodies the authority that permits one to make discriminating judgments between types of whales or types of mankind.[25] Of humpback whales, Ishmael the taxonomist writes: "He is the most gamesome and light-hearted of all the whales, making more gay foam and white water generally than any other of them" (121). The improbable nature of sketching an entire whale group's personality repeats ethnology's fraudulent categorization of a "light-hearted" race, or William Smith's conclusion in *Lectures on the Philosophy and Practice of Slavery* (1856), which ascertains from an assumption of black "intellectual inferiority" that slaves "are the most cheerful and, indeed, merry class of people we have amongst us."[26]

The socially enmeshed "truth" that props up observation—whether it is a description that "foam" is "gay" or slaves inferior—leads to untenable conclusions that force Ishmael to view suspiciously the foundations of his governing classification. Thus, Ishmael, like any good researcher, tells us his sources, in this case, Linnaeus's "System of Nature, A.D. 1776" (117). What seems a scrupulous piece of scholarship is in actuality an error. Linnaeus's *Systema Naturae* first appeared in 1735, and the important tenth addition was issued in 1753. Under the guise of scholarly authority, Ishmael substitutes the date of the Declaration of Independence for the date when the Swedish botanist separated whales from fish. Rather than producing skepticism about Linnaeus, Ishmael intends to question the meaning of 1776, to classify it as a year that, despite its pretensions to equality, never instituted practices to actualize the dictates of freedom. Disagreeing with Linnaeus by asserting that "the whale is a fish," Ishmael abjures separation, proposing in its place a system of inclusion where types of fish are not segregated: "By the above definition of what a whale is, I do by no means exclude from the leviathanic brotherhood any sea creature." (118) Ishmael consents momentarily to speaking *dans le vrai* of biological discourse so that he can then misuse its authority to deflate an uncritical political discourse. By the ironic authorization of a cetology, we learn blacks are not separated from whites, but integrated, as whales and fish are, as Queequeg and Ishmael are, in a universal fraternity.

"Unconditional democracy in all things," Melville realized, was a radical project requiring that Ishmael encode his ideas about democracy in the discourse of taxonomy. Indeed, he was doing no more than the humanist researchers writing *dans le vrai* of ethnological discourse who "discovered" historical and biological predeterminations for black slavery. An all-important difference, however, lies in the fact that Ishmael remains an isolato, floating above the depths plumbed by his parodic discourse, while ethnologists existed as part of a federation where various discourses (biological, legal, historical) intersected and supported one another. Not only did ethnologists like Nott and Gliddon find compatriots in the ranks of a social critic like Hughes, or in the pages of a political commentator like James Fenimore Cooper, or in the impassioned rhetoric and magnetizing presence of an orator like Calhoun. They were also part of a historical brotherhood that stretched back to the founding fathers. In *Notes on the State of Virginia*, Jefferson established a textual foundation upon observations of geography, plants, and animals to comment, however tentatively, upon his black slaves' animal-like sensuality and intellectual slowness. In contrast, Ishmael stands alone and embarrassed in the desert of his own rhetoric, able to associate with other discourses only in a "ludicrous," if not subversive, manner.

Radical truth telling demands consideration of a cautionary postscript, however. Ishmael's beliefs about democracy could cause more than embarrassment and alienation; such a democracy is fraught with the danger of its own "ruthless" and frantic nature. Ruthlessly democratic form leads to discursive experiments like "Midnight,

Forecastle." Here, Ishmael, the narrative authority, disappears, and the text presents unmediated the crew as chorus, a central element of drama in Athenian democracy, now the polis of the *Pequod*. They alternate between joining together under the textual designation of "ALL" and reasserting their individual characters with their opinions about whaling, the sea, and women. The chorus thus unites an assortment of thirty men into a crew that nevertheless preserves the diversity of sailors from Malta, Nantucket, China, and Tahiti. But this democracy, including whites and blacks, splinters over racial conflict. The chapter ends in a scuffle echoed by an atmospheric squall: nothing more can be told; the communally spun and diverse narrative stalls; the reminiscing about Tahitian girls, the speculations about Ahab, the singing of mariners' songs, indeed, the development of the dramatic chorus, dissipates as the Spanish sailor comes at the African Daggoo with a knife. "Unconditional democracy" may be too radical; it may join together racially different citizens who can interact only in a volatile and violent manner.

THE POWER OF BLACKNESS

More dangerous to democracy than the racial strife among the crew is the threat Ahab poses. Because his command seems egalitarian, Ahab's leadership becomes that much more insidious to the collective consciousness of the crew. He makes none of the distinctions based upon the social hierarchies of race or class that circulate on shore; he admits Pip to the intimacy of his cabin as readily as he sheds a furtive tear telling Starbuck of his wife ashore. His rule is democratic, degrading no man because of his condition. The only exception to his thinking is himself. As Starbuck cynically comments, "Aye, he would be democrat to all above; look, how he lords it over all below!" (143) Ahab adopts the role of charismatic leader whose proud defiance summons up a heroic Prometheus of the American spirit: "Talk not to me of blasphemy, man; I'd strike the sun if it insulted me. For could the sun do that, then I could do the other. . . . What I've dared, I've willed; and what I've willed, I'll do!" (139, 142). Against the frontier, savages, or British pharaohs, a man of Ahab's stature leads the people out of the wilderness through the exertion of his indomitable will. In him, we see the American hero; his sheer presence, burning with "an infinity of firmest fortitude, a determinate, unsurrenderable willful-

ness," fascinates Ishmael and the crew (110). Ahab "is the *shaman*,"
writes Richard Chase, "that is, the religious leader [who] . . . attains
some of the knowledge and power of the gods. The *shaman* is usually
deeply neurotic and sometimes epileptic—the savior with the neu-
rosis. Again, Ahab is the culture hero (though a false one) who kills
the monsters, making man's life possible."[27] Ahab appears as the true
demagogue in contrast to Gabriel of the *Jeroboam*, a false prophet
whose mysticism suppresses a group of frightened and superstitious
sailors. Gabriel is the demagogue as rabble-rouser; Ahab, on the other
hand, at first suggests an older meaning of demagogue—a leader of
the people.

Skillful oratory, awe-imposing presence, mental prowess, and a
vision all constitute Ahab's political genius. Yet all these qualities
that compel the thirty men to follow his will, recreating them as the
crew of the *Pequod*, would remain inert if Ahab did not possess a
symbolic vehicle to articulate and manifest his power. Through his
brilliant understanding of ritual, Ahab reveals his will and word with
potency. In "The Quarter-Deck," Ahab conflates the rationality of the
social contract with the demonic dynamism of religious communion
to mold the crew to his purpose. Even the narrator adheres to this
pact, dropping the narrative of his friendship with Queequeg to clasp
hands with the other seamen already stuck fast to Ahab's vengeance.
Ishmael's retrospective narrative may intimate moments of discursive resistance, but he must admit "my shouts had gone up with the
rest; my oath had wielded with theirs. . . . A wild, mystical, sympa-
thetical feeling was in me; Ahab's quenchless feud seemed mine"
(149–50).[28] This single-minded quest whittles away other narrative
possibilities, leaving only an American story of progress that ignores
digressions, such as a pagan's Ramadan or the political lessons of
whale classification. Any episodes that depart from the unyielding
linearity of the hunt, any ironies that twist expectations or interject
variations of the captain's mission, are left ashore at the Spouter Inn.
Unlike an authority such as Ishmael's, which derails itself in its own
subversion, Ahab's authority is imperious, wholly consumed by
pursuit of an undifferentiated mass of whiteness.

Under Ahab's command, narratives become narrative, and the
challenges of cultural difference are included in this subsumption.
Within his ritual orchestrations Ahab continually invokes the race of
his pagan harpooners—yet because it is ritual, this invocation re-

duces their being to only a symbolic dimension. In the ceremonial rites of the political shaman, Queequeg, Daggoo, and Tashtego forfeit their varied humanity to the democratic gathering Ahab convenes. In other words, the symbolic import of their skin replaces the truly human essence in Queequeg that Ishmael discovered out of prejudice and fear and that provided the ground for interracial friendship. Thus, although Ahab calls Queequeg, Daggoo, and Tashtego "my three pagan kinsmen" because like him they have seen and pulled after the white whale, his interest lies in neither brotherhood nor difference (141). He understands the harpooners neither as men nor isolatoes, but as symbolic entities he can exploit to ratify his quest. In Ahab's political demonology, the three become satanic cupbearers who lend pomp and mystical shamanism to the ceremony played out in "The Quarter-Deck." "Ahab is Conjur Man. He invokes his own evil world. He himself uses black magic to achieve his vengeful ends," writes Charles Olson.[29]

Transforming these nonwhites into "sweet cardinals" and redefining their harpoon irons as "murderous chalices," Ahab presides over a barbaric communion. Gone are the heterogeneous stories of fear and desire that populated the forecastle at midnight. In Ahab's words the sailors ordain themselves into an "indissoluble league." "The frantic crew" responds uniformly to the ritual, drinking together as one body from the inverted harpoon tips of Queequeg, Daggoo, and Tashtego (141). Later, in "The Forge," these same three find their bodies manipulated to baptize Ahab's hunt; confronted by the crew's questioning of the pact they have formed, Ahab reaffirms the oath of "The Quarter-Deck" by symbolically sanctifying his imperial mission with blood drawn from heathen flesh. Tempering his harpoon with this blood, Ahab acts as the mad priest: "Ego non baptizo te in nomine patris, sed in nomine diaboli!" (373).[30]

Melville took Ahab's blasphemous ritual as the informing principle of his own writing. Warning Hawthorne that "this is a rather crazy letter in some respects," he wrote on June 29, 1851, "this is the book's motto (the secret one), Ego non baptiso te in nomine—but make out the rest yourself." He desired to make a heroic Ahab-like assertion of willful independence, but the Ishmael within was too reluctant to continue. Melville refused to utter the word *patris*, for his book undermined the patriarchal authority of American scientific, legislative, and political discourse; it was an omission that prepared the conditions for "ruthless democracy" even as it left the narrative project susceptible to the insertion of diabolic evil. Apprehensive that Hawthorne would not embrace his views, Melville ended the letter at this point. Yet in doing so, he forced Hawthorne to "make out the rest yourself" and scorn the father; Melville subtly enrolled his friend in that democracy by insisting upon his participatory interpretation, leaving him to complete the parricidal sacrilege. Later, in November of the same year, Melville's awareness of the demagogue's ability to galvanize the people to a darkly conceived mission caused him to confide again in Hawthorne. "I have written a wicked book," he confessed, without apologizing or asking forgiveness, "and feel as spotless as a lamb." Still, Melville could not forget the lesson of Ahab: a false demagoguery can warp the democratic promise into a tale of reckless dimensions that the people nevertheless follow because of their adherence to the original covenant as given by national narrative. Whether citizen or shipmate, each retains enthusiasm for a compact that promises to realize the final, moral end of a destined narrative.[31]

This ambivalence—acknowledging a malevolent intent alongside of virtuous, lamblike self-conviction—reproduces itself as a complex political stance that allows Ishmael to affirm the narrative compact even as he recognizes the bankrupt nature of national narrative, even as he dissents from the final revelation of its ending. Ishmael consents to Ahab's vengeful quest, admitting that "my shouts had gone up with the rest," yet this affirmation does not compromise his ability to articulate intellectual dissent from Ahab. As with any citizen of national culture, Ishmael realizes, like Melville, that one must first consent in order to dissent, that one must first enter a discourse to thwart the truth claims of that discourse. Thus, in the chapter following his admission of participation in Ahab's "quenchless feud," Ishmael manipulates the narrative to separate himself from the captain's plot: "What the white whale was to Ahab, has been hinted; what, at times, he was to me, as yet remains unsaid" (157). Likewise, Melville as a citizen who took pride in his double Revolutionary descent at the same time vented deep-seated reservations about an American narrative indebted to plots of imperialism, Indian removal, and slavery. The author of *Moby-Dick* may have felt "as spotless as a lamb," but as a citizen of the United States expanding slavery under the doctrine of Manifest Destiny, Melville ineluctably saw the underside of the American narrative—a moral blackness without integrity that sinfully compromised the legacy of the fathers.

As unregenerate pagans who can make no similar claim to spotlessness, Queequeg, Daggoo, and Tashtego embody a diabolical darkness—a cultural assumption Ahab exploits with his understanding of the "great power of blackness." Melville had powerfully figured the dimensions and effects of a metaphysical blackness in the year preceding *Moby-Dick*'s publication in the "Hawthorne and His Mosses" review. Although Ahab himself ignores the forebodings of the reversed compass needles or the coffin used as a life buoy, he knows the dark side of the Puritan mind and its weakness for allegory. Through his knowledge of man's fixation upon "blackness, ten times black," he manipulates the democratic consciousness of the crew. To a mind like Ishmael's, steeped in the Puritan legacy of "Innate Depravity and Original Sin," blackness generates a certain compulsion and attraction. Reviewing *Mosses from an Old Manse*, Melville spoke of his own inexplicable and Ishmael-like desire to investigate blackness: "Now it is that blackness in Hawthorne, of which I have spoken, that so fixes and fascinates me." In addition to Melville, crew members like Ishmael, Bulkington, and Ahab peer into blackness in their searches for truth. The depths of the sea allure them, as do dark figures exterior to discourse *dans le vrai* who, because of their marginalized status, hint at a nonprescribed truth. Ishmael chooses as his friend the non-Westerner Queequeg, whose tattooed skin transmits "a mystical treatise on the art of attaining truth," and Ahab showers paternal kindness upon the castaway Pip, who "saw God's foot upon the treadle of the loom, and spoke it; and therefore his shipmates called him mad" (368, 322). Perhaps ever undecipherable, truth may reside in these alien and black forms, and thus they hold a certain fascination for the crew and for Ishmael's narrative. But as Ahab represents the harpooners and Pip to the crew, as Ahab translates their intuitive capacities of revelation into political rhetoric for his quarrel, the harpooners and Pip cease to promise truth. Their blackness does not lead to depth, but to a superficial appeal designed to rally the crew around the demagogue's inexorable hunt.[32]

Unable to claim the divine calling that authorized the Puritan errand into the wilderness and the American continuation of these labors, Ahab requires a religious symbology to shroud his nefarious errand in authority. He becomes a political sorcerer who combines ritual and alienation to convert the literal blackness of these natives' skins into the symbolic "blackness of darkness beyond."[33] During the religiously charged rituals of "The Quarter-Deck," "The Forge," and "The Candles," Ahab reifies the skins of the Indian, African, and Polynesian into an image of a potent, spiritually symbolic blackness that he then uses to exploit psychologically the wills of the crew. The harpooners act as attendants who perform a perverse sanctification of their captain, becoming iconic embodiments of blackness to which the crew is susceptible. In the same way that a forest gathering at midnight demonically attracts the faith of Young Goodman Brown in Hawthorne's story, Ahab's masterful ritual coerces Ishmael and the other sailors to adhere to his chosen destiny. Ahab addresses the crew through the symbolic bodies of the pagan harpooners, who make manifest his incontrovertible will and the possessive quality of his power. They are powerful black forms—after all, they fling the iron into the life of leviathan—who surrender their physical, human being up to Ahab, becoming metaphysical indicators of his prowess that the crew cannot deny. Each man of the crew drinks "the fiery waters" (141) poured into the harpoon sockets; each man affirms this covenant, made not from the promise of God, but forged out of the dark side of free will. Like a member of the Puritan community, the seamen individually consent to the contract proposed by Ahab; but like Young Goodman Brown, who chooses to attend the coven at midnight, they are manipulated by their own human susceptibility to the symbolism of the harpooners' marginalized, dusky forms. The dark sailors catalyze Ahab's bonds with the crew; they become the conduits through which the men affirm the covenant.

During the electrical storm, when the crew raises "a half mutinous cry," Ahab corrals their passion within the proven strength of ritualistic politics (385). He snatches up the harpoon tempered by heathen blood and waves it above the heads of the crew, reminding them of the covenant they have wildly ratified: "All your oaths to hunt the White Whale are as binding as mine" (385). He swears "to transfix with it [the harpoon] the first sailor that but cast loose a rope's end" in defiance (385). Ahab not only threatens physical violence to "transfix" or impale the first transgressor of the covenant, but he also promises to "transfix," to captivate, the wills of those who oppose them—just as Hawthorne's blackness "fixes and fascinates" Melville.

And Ahab fulfills this latter promise: in this crucial situation, he returns to ritual; he manipulates the flaming harpoon sanctified by blackness to incarnate a political symbol that reminds the crew of a host of previous rituals to which they have already consented. Awed by the symbolism of the Black Mass, the men can do no more than murmur their dissent; the ritualized arena of politics leaves no space to formulate a will counter to Ahab's. The captain has shrewdly removed debate and dissent onto the irrefutable ground of ritual. Ahab performs what Donald Pease calls "cultural persuasion," a rhetorical strategy that effects "the displacement of potentially disorienting political arguments onto a context where the unquestioned ground—the ideological subtext justifying political dissent—can empty them of their historical specificity and replace them with ideological principles."[34]

Under Ahab's dominion, the racial identities of the harpooners are displaced in this manner, their culturally specific humanity subsumed by a symbolism that ratifies the whole. Queequeg climbs from the rank of harpooner to become the representative of which Hobbes spoke: that is, his black body represents the body politic, bearing and articulating the covenant to the crew. Like the other harpooners, he surrenders his body to the domain of political demonology where ritual alienates him from his body, abstracting it until it acquires a symbolic dimension. Queequeg shares more with Washington than the head size noted by Ishmael; he, too, is a narrative surface where a collectivity reads the covenant. Yet a major difference between founding father and noble savage cannot escape notice; unlike the Washington figured by the antebellum era, Queequeg is alive. In becoming political in this symbolic sense, Queequeg is abstracted from his humanity, reduced to a representative body that slavishly carries the significances Ahab intends. Queequeg's body, inscribed with a truth in the form of tattooed "hieroglyphic marks" he himself cannot read, vanishes, and what remains is brought *dans le vrai*. As represented to the crew by Ahab, Queequeg is contained within a political rhetoric whose regulations and significances Ahab alone controls.

Queequeg occupies the position of the American slave denied autonomy of his body, defined as a lesser human by the prevailing authorized discourses of antebellum culture. Even within the discourse of abolition, the black body surrendered up its physicality to become an alienated surface articulating agendas foreign to the slave's interest. Female abolitionists often rhetorically exploited the figure of the black slave, forcing it to transmute its own statements of freedom into women's concerns for suffrage or a testimony of the transcendental inner purity of religion. Although *Uncle Tom's Cabin* takes its name from a black slave, that slave lacks any physical dimension; for Stowe, Uncle Tom is a metaphysical embodiment of Christian dogma; his character is based upon the denial of his flesh that suffers. For James Baldwin, the theological and sentimental aspects of Stowe's novel that make the dark-skinned slaves superficial and inhumane representations of blackness tell "a lie more palatable than the truth." Devoid of the humanness whose recognition serves as the basis for democracy, Queequeg and his fellow pagans seem empty shells incapable of voicing a subjectivity, of making manifest a being who suffers as all citizens do. Each harpooner is reduced to a rhetorical configuration after the manner in which Foucault speaks of the body politic: "the body is also directly involved in a political field; power relations have an immediate hold upon it; they invest it, mark it, train it, torture it, force it to carry out tasks, to perform ceremonies, to emit signs."[35]

In addition to the harpooners, Ahab makes the body of the cabin boy, Pip, a body politic in Foucault's sense, a rhetorical surface upon which the captain dramatizes his command to the crew that watches. Carolyn Karcher suggests that Pip holds out to Ahab the possibility of a redemptive friendship similar to the understanding between Queequeg and Ishmael. If Ahab would remember the "man-rope" linking him to the castaway Pip, he, like Ishmael influenced by the "monkey-rope," might abjure his vow of vengeance and turn to the pursuit of a relationship as strong and as meaningful as "cords woven of my heart-strings" (394). Despite Karcher's suggestion, the potential within the relationship of Ahab and Pip contains little of the promise embedded in Ishmael's friendship with a pagan. Whereas Queequeg is a magnificent figure whom Ishmael likens to George Washington, Pip remains an idiot playing a tambourine, shunned by the crew, the lowest of the low. Hardly an egalitarian association arising from mutual respect, Ahab's intimacy with Pip represents to the crew the sympathetic capacity of Ahab's paternalistic care. The noble captain will provide refuge for even the most forlorn of the democratic mass. Although the gods may be indifferent to the fate of poor Pip, Ahab proves himself the humane ruler who can provide succor to all. Listening to Pip's ramblings even as the Manx sailor assaults the cabin boy, Ahab seeks to convince the crew of his connection to the truth expressed in Pip's insanity. The lunatic utters a masked truth that Ahab, by his paternal proximity, assumes for his own purposes. Invested with the dark truth of pagan bodies and black idiots, Ahab exalts his command with an image of unquestionable superiority and mystical revelation so true that it tolerates no dissent.[36]

Ahab eventually abandons Pip, causing the boy once more to feel adrift, as he did when Stubb, more concerned with the value of a whale than the value of a potential slave, sailed on, leaving him stranded in the immense loneliness of the sea. Yet the symbolic message Ahab wished to convey to the crew has been communicated. Besides fabricating an image of his judicious paternalism and his kinship with truth, Ahab uses Pip to allay the crew's fears about the political possession they are actually experiencing. Looking at Pip pleading with his captain "do ye but use poor me for your one lost leg; only tread upon me, sir," Ishmael's shipmates can assure themselves that, despite their consent to Ahab's hunt, they in no way suffer Pip's utter lack of autonomy (402). No matter how swayed the sailors are by Ahab's rituals, the crew can look at Pip and deny that they have resigned themselves to Ahab's control. It is Pip himself, however, who exposes the sailors' denial as a denial of the ritualistic situation that entraps each and all. As Pip approaches the doubloon after the mates and sailors mutter their interpretations of the coin, he says "I look, you look, he looks; we look, ye look, they look" (335). Though Stubb dismisses Pip's words as simple-minded drivel, the cabin boy's recitation does contain a germ of truth, just as, for Melville, Lear's mad despair probes a "vital truth." Pip's senseless conjugation hints at the homogeneity of each sailor's position, no matter what his interpretation: Pip serves, the Manxman serves, the mates serve, all serve Ahab's will equally.

A ritualized politics brimming with democratic enthusiasm and united passion catapults Ahab from captain to demagogue. However, this same ritualized politics distorted by a dehumanizing symbolism unmasks Ahab as yet another false demagogue. Prometheus falls under the weight of the political tyranny he has created in his perversion of the covenant. He is a tyrant not because he implements the covenant, but because he mystifies that covenant with a symbolism only he controls. Once laden with promise, Ahab's "frantic democracy" degenerates into antidemocratic practices upheld by the cultural persuasion of ritual (130). He preaches this shadowy covenant compellingly, encoding it within an undeniable ritual effected by a political vampirism that in its lust for the power of symbolism divests the pagan harpooners of their blood and their humanity. Exploitative symbolism, a political species of black magic, renders them citizen-ghouls, empty of signification and spirit; they are now at Ahab's disposal, ready to assume their roles as symbols in a publicly enacted ritual. Reifying man as a symbol, exploiting citizens' fears through the rituals of political demonology, the demagogue as a leader of the people transforms into a false leader who adulterates the democracy that authorized him.

SYMBOLIC RHETORIC AND POLITICAL FICTIONS OF THE NATION

Ishmael offers an alternative, more humane political vision to Ahab's command. Within his narrative, both in its content describing his friendship with Queequeg and in its form as a discursive democracy, people can interact politically without engaging in the exploitative symbolism Ahab uses. However, instances like "The Counterpane," in which Ishmael transcends prejudice to accept Queequeg's bridegroom embrace, vanish as the fascination with Ahab usurps control of the narration. The drama of democratic human interaction reappears only in isolated moments like "The Monkey-rope" and "A Squeeze of the Hand." Having dispersed his narrative authority among the crew, regardless of race or class, Ishmael presents the possibility of a political society that privileges, rather than obscures, the truth of each citizen's cultural difference. In turning from pistol and ball, in ceasing to loiter around coffin warehouses, Ishmael dedicates his narrative to what John Schaar calls "an ethic of action" in which each citizen is responsible for the tangible fulfillment of universal fraternity, in which it is incumbent upon every member to make the words of the Declaration of Independence come to life in the flesh of his or her companion.[37] Ishmael might succeed, too, if the false demagogue did not seize the narrative's polyphonic authority, wresting it away from this sea-going Anacharsis Clootz deputation to further a journey marked by an intended domination over nature, sultanlike command, expansion, and death. Pushing Ishmael aside, Ahab reduces the diverse potentialities of the crew into a uniform mission of vengeance. Once power and narrative are centralized, Ahab convincingly argues that the white whale—and closure—are in his grasp.[38]

Ahab's mastery expands as the narrative expands, absorbing Ishmael as his spokesman for his quest. What had once been the heterogeneous course of narrative, moving from anatomical discussion of leviathan to weighty metaphysical revelations, becomes the chronicle of reprisal and retaliation. Digressive and diversely grouped chapters, like the story of the *Jeroboam* followed by "The Monkey-rope" and then by "Stubb and Flask Kill a Right Whale," give way to the severe teleology of "The Chase—First Day," "The Chase—Second Day," and "The Chase—Third Day." Queequeg and Ishmael, as individuals wedded in "a joint stock company of two," in a universal fraternity, are lost amid the confusion and spray of the pursuit (253). Yet they both shoot to the surface once more. Pitched overboard, Ishmael avoids the vortex, finding salvation in the coffin / life buoy. Queequeg, however, is humanly absent, able to appear only symbolically via the coffin he prepared for his own death. His natural body sinks with the *Pequod*, but his alienated and figurative corpus rises to float upon the surface of the waters. Ishmael mentions the coffin without remembering the human, his bosom friend, to whom it belonged. Although carved with the same mystical designs tattooed upon Queequeg's body, the coffin does not impel Ishmael to assess the truth of this cannibal who taught him the value of human devotion and friendship. The essence of intercultural understanding and interracial fraternity contained in Queequeg's body has been hollowed out, made prone to carry some other meaning. The tattoos that "had written out on his body a complete theory of the heavens and the earth, and a mystical treatise on the art of attaining truth," remain undeciphered, now ignored by Ishmael (368). Perhaps only Pip, in his divine idiocy, could perceive the truth of Queequeg's human essence. Before the sinking of *Pequod*, Pip approaches Queequeg in his coffin, and implores him: "Seek out one Pip, who's now been missing long: I think he's in those far Antilles. If ye find him, then comfort him; for he must be very sad"—seek out and succor one Pip, the slave boy, whose value at auction Stubb estimates is thirty times less than that of a dead whale (367).

Ishmael forgets his bosom friend, dropping neither word nor tear to lament his disappearance. Why does Ishmael fail to recognize the type of politics Queequeg intuitively articulates with his body? To answer this question, we must reexamine Ishmael's role as narrator. Ishmael gives in to Ahab without a murmur, content to watch Ahab decipher and control the legendary symbolism of leviathan. Indeed, Ishmael seems somewhat complicit with his captain; his nonaction leads to a narrative repetition of Ahab's drama, duplicating the hunt for the white whale on a metaphysical level. Even after Ahab has gone down with the *Pequod* and can no longer enforce obedience, Ishmael still puts his narrative at his captain's disposal. Although aboard the ship, Ishmael the sailor may have been prevented from pursuing his friendship with Queequeg, in the text, Ishmael the narrator should be able to tell his tale under the auspices of his own authority. In fact, he nods toward Job in the epilogue to endow his position as an isolato storyteller with authority. Like Job, only Ishmael has "ESCAPED ALONE TO TELL THEE" (432). He seemingly acquires by default the authority to tell a narrative; no one lives who can dispute or amend or preface what he says. Yet even in the autonomy of memory, by at last narrating only the chase, Ishmael defers to Ahab, allowing his dead captain to structure the narrative of remembrance. Like Stubb, who pushes on in the chase and strands Pip, Ishmael abandons any counter-memories of Queequeg in which dignity and interracial community override the dictates of nationalism; he surrenders any narratives that depart from Ahab's impervious ends. In forfeiting his narrative authority to Ahab, Ishmael also forfeits his Job-like status of aloneness. He becomes part of an American community that has forgotten glimpses and memories of equality and fraternity.

As if the rituals of "The Quarter-Deck" and the electrical storm needed reaffirmation, Ishmael again agrees to Ahab's quest, now pursuing the white whale in narrative. Following Ahab's course, Ishmael is "rescued" by the discourse of American politics. It is the symbolic, politically demonized, spiritually empty coffin-body of Queequeg that buoys Ishmael. Ritual and symbolism, political practices that deny and exploit human beings, functioned as a principal mode of narrative and political discourse in antebellum America. Like Ahab, Ishmael floats upon the alienated body of blackness that is the coffin / life buoy, ignoring the human truth of Queequeg's body he once knew so intimately. He forgets the promise of "truth"—or democracy—encoded in the tattooed body by relinquishing his memory of Queequeg.

Willing to compromise the integrity of his former friendship, Ishmael finds many colleagues in the American political arena, where the adoption of the Compromise of 1850 subjected the founding fathers to the delusive memory of symbolism. Echoing Harvey Birch in *The Spy*, who produces from his shirt the name Washington as he prepares for death, echoing Ishmael as he finds salvation in Queequeg's coffin, Henry Clay dramatically ended his appeal for the Compromise Resolutions by drawing a symbolic talisman from his pocket. But unlike Birch, who eats the signature, Clay freely divulged his "precious relic":

> And what, Mr. President, do you suppose it is? It is a fragment of the coffin of Washington—a fragment of that coffin in which now repose in silence, in sleep, and speechless, all the earthly remains of the venerated Father of his Country. Was it portentous that it should have been thus presented to me? Was it a sad presage of what might happen to that fabric which Washington's virtue, patriotism, and valor established? No, sir, no. It was a warning voice, coming from the grave to the Congress now in session to beware, to pause, to reflect; before they lend themselves to any purpose which shall destroy the Union which was cemented by his exertions and example.[39]

Something of Ahab lingered in Clay, as it does in Ishmael. Clay adopted the role of political shaman, symbolically exploiting Washington in an effort to assuage disorienting ideological struggles. He conducted politics through symbolism, just as Ishmael performs his narrative act by relying on symbols; both employ symbols that hollow out the body and drag it into the political field as Foucault's body politic, where it has no memory of the promises it once signified.

Queequeg, we must remember, in Ishmael's "unconditional" democratic consciousness doubles as Washington. Not only does this cannibal bear a physical resemblance to the founding father, but he also functions in Ishmael's narrative as did Washington in American national narrative. Each man's corpus delivers a narrative to an ending. The coffin of Queequeg leads Ishmael away from the doomed ship, and the fragment from Washington's coffin carried the Compromise of 1850 that was supposed to heal the national schism between freedom and slavery. Although Queequeg and Washington instill the promise of closure, they are little more than political bandages that hopelessly attempt to save the ship of state from sinking. Given their equivalent uses of symbolic coffins, Ishmael and Clay seem to share the Ahabian tendency to practice a political sorcery that conspires to make human forms the vehicle for resolution and unity. Both speakers tell stories of survival that take bodies and transform them into Hobbes's "Artificiall Person," who represents the covenant and without whose authority civil society has neither foundation nor hope of preservation. Within these allusive bodies, patriotism and parricide converge: Clay's filial worship of fatherly relics segues into Ishmael's annihilating amnesia, his forgetting of Queequeg.

Even more resemblance between Ishmael and Clay as political actors appears when we remember that Melville gave voice to his narrator at the time of the debates surrounding the Compromise of 1850. I am not arguing for a one-to-one correspondence between Ishmael and Clay; instead, the discursive similarities between these two figures leads to an understanding of the disastrous course of an American politics that navigated the most profound of ideological struggles by appealing to symbolism.[40] We must not forget that *Moby-Dick*, whatever its allusions to real historical politics, is a work of fiction, and that, in contrast, Clay's Compromise speech, whatever its degree of fictional license, remains a work of politics. This is not to say, however, that *Moby-Dick* performed no political commentary; indeed, Ishmael's telling provided a critical truth about the American political scene. Yet it is to say that as opposed to Melville, who politicized his fiction in order to utter some snatches of covert truth here and there, Clay represented an American culture that practiced what is only a fiction of politics. He engaged in the symbolic rhetoric of an American politics that sought to efface the intense contradictions between democratic ideals and democratic institutions, between the commitment to freedom and the practice of slavery. Though it may seem Ishmael at last enters Ahab's tent of political symbolism and encounters Clay, through his mode of telling he approaches the Melville who yearned after truth in "Hawthorne and His Mosses." Recasting Clay's adulteration of Washington's memory as Ishmael's disregard for Queequeg and his coffin, *Moby-Dick* subtly implies how the fiction of politics spoken by antebellum America obscured and dishonored its noncitizens as well as its originary citizens. Just as Ishmael will never understand the "mystical treatise on the art of attaining truth" inscribed upon Queequeg's body, so, too, America was never to decipher the truth or "ruthless democracy" in Washington's legacy. Whereas the lie of Washington proclaimed that slavery, if not one of the cornerstone ideals of the founding fathers, was at least a favorable means to achieve those ideals, an unauthorized counter-memory of Washington's potential truth silently stood in a legacy of the forgotten apparition of freedom.

3

Monumental Culture

See the power of national emblems.
—Ralph Waldo Emerson, "The Poet"

STRANDED CITIZENS

Seized with an often monomaniacal desire to move faster and eclipse old transportation records and thus make history, steamship captains taxed their boilers to the point of devastating explosions. The people transported to the afterlife were certainly lamented by relatives and neighbors, but within the design of an expanding and progressing America, these individuals mattered little. Blessed with a cultural capacity to absorb calamities within a grand historical context, Americans did not severely bemoan the loss of individual life that accompanied national progress. In an 1852 editor's column introduced as "Victims of Progress," *Harper's* confidently forgot human tragedy by sacrificing citizens to a narrative of an advancing, industrial American civilization. Within an equally optimistic and federal vision, individual casualties of transportation disasters found resurrection as "martyrs of an ever-advancing, never-finished civilization,—they die that steamboats may be better built, that railroads may be better laid, that the speed of traveling, by land and sea, may be accelerated in a ratio which never becomes constant, and toward a maximum which is never to be attained." Barely a generation old, the nation, unlike its individual citizens, would endure, according to the filiopietism of the day, because of its own structural innocence, which ratified the outlook celebrated by *Harper's*, allowing for the pursuit of commercial and colonial expansion while thus appropriating even its graver consequences for those ends. An episode in William Wells Brown's *Clotel* portrays the nation's casual disregard for human life when measured against the grand spectacle of a steamboat race on the Mississippi. Amid the "wildest excitement" a boiler blows, causing "shrieks, groans, and cries" to fill the vessel. The dead and injured, however, do not weigh upon the collective conscience of the crew; they are "put on shore," and the steamboat is "soon again on its way."[1]

Brown christens these two steamships with resonant names from the arsenal of American mythic history—the *Patriot* and the *Columbia*. His critical representation thus encompasses more than the reckless character of slaveholding society. By naming the two vessels *Patriot* and *Columbia*, Brown suggests that what encourages an indifferent and even careless regard for passengers, citizens, and chattel is a myopic world view that depends upon uncritical configurations of the past. From boldly affirming representations of history, Americans are propelled not only to competitive achievements and national zeal, but also to amnesia. Within symbolic designations such as *Patriot*, individual victims and local considerations do not slow the course of American history.[2] This sketch from *Clotel* outlines the construction of national history in the post-Revolutionary period— powered by symbolic affiliations with the founding past, national narratives forged onward like Brown's steamships, committed to a course of remembering that often forgot individuals whose aberrant bodies and memories lay outside of national ends.

Americans proved themselves a fortunate people when they were able to intellectualize steamship sinkings as violent upheavals of history's progression. In the context of such technological disasters, the editor of *Harper's* asked:

> For what, after all, are a few lives, or a few hundred, or even a few thousand lives to the great cause of human advance! What is the individual, or any number of individuals, to the improvement of the race? and what is any amount of present or passing pain, to the triumph of ideas?
>
> Again—these sufferers by fire and flood, and steam furnish the occasion of advancing our knowledge of the physical laws—and there is much consolation surely in this. . . . At the cheap price of a hundred lives, we purchase the most useful knowledge that the elasticity, or expansive power of steam may exceed the cohesion of ill-wrought iron.

Sacrifice of the individual citizen to the indomitable, steam-driven advance of epistemological, technological, economic, or political progress was a common story: aboard the *Pequod*, the mad captain rejects Starbuck's prudence, disregarding ominous warnings that would have been apparent to any Puritan, to pursue the metaphysical mystery of a white whale; valuing a whale more than the market value of Pip, Stubb abandons the cabin boy upon the face of the waters; Ishmael loses himself while gazing into the furnaces of the industrial tryworks; and Queequeg, Tashtego, and Daggoo give up their lives to the possession of that political sorcerer, Ahab. As twin stories of technology and political rhetoric, *Moby-Dick* diagnoses a culture's monomania that had small regard for its individual crew members. Ahab's pursuit of the "unwonted magnitude" of the white whale replays the millennial fervor of mid-nineteenth-century America that carried forth the national mission into imperialism, dizzying industrial development, and expanding commerce.[3]

Queequeg, the passengers aboard the *Patriot*, the scarcely lamented crews in *Harper's*, all are abandoned and forgotten, not so much by the narrative of technology, which makes humans incidental, but by narratives of American history that obscured its citizens. In the first half of the nineteenth century, as America self-consciously articulated a national history, impressive artifacts of culture sprang up in painting, literature, architecture, and biography. The panoramas of the Hudson River School, the nativist mission of the Young America movement in literature, the memorial towers at Washington D.C., Baltimore, and Bunker Hill, all imagined a particularly American greatness of civilization and national unity. These expressions combined to form a national attitude of monumentalism whose very grandeur hailed America as an exceptional nation no longer dependent upon European civilization. Arising from the mighty cataracts, endless forests, and limitless vistas of a great continent destined to become the province of all Americans, the monumental stature of America was a peculiarly "natural" cultural concept. But while a monumental identity may have been a way to define all Americans at once, it posed serious consequences for individual citizens, whose desires to remember and exercise civic being have taken diverse and heterogeneous forms.

While the nation had real geographic borders and actual custom houses to police those borders, fictional constructs mobilized the *idea* of a nation that collects and regulates many different bodies, each with different memories. Lauren Berlant sees this array of fictional constructs as a "national fantasy" that organizes a mass identity.[4] In *The Anatomy of National Fantasy*, she argues that the vehicles of the "Na-

tional Symbolic"—images, narratives, icons, and monuments—
pervade the capillaries of the social body, transplanting and absorbing the local into the official site of national identity. Following Berlant, who derives the National Symbolic from the prototypical symbol
in American literature, the scarlet *A* that Hester Prynne wears on her
chest, I want to situate that examination of nationalism within popular
culture as a monumental narrative disseminated across a range of
expressive sites in the antebellum United States, including painting,
architecture, oratory, and fiction. Monumentalism stands forth as a
particular historical mode of articulating national culture, and this
specificity enables an understanding of how these varied discourses
intersected with the elaboration of the nation. Most importantly, monumentalism underscores the interstices between the fabrication of
historical consciousness and civic being. From *monere*, meaning not
simply "to remind" but also "to instruct" and "to say with authority,"
monumentalism suggests that remembering prompts more than independent musings on the past; rather, monumentalism narrates a
history exercised with power over citizens. It is indeed power that
shapes the history that defines people as citizens and collects them
in the construct of a nation.

As a critical term, monumentalism functions with both descriptive
and theoretical import, corresponding to an ability to act literally as
well as figuratively. On one level, as an analysis of the material
expressions of culture, monumentalism describes how similar narratives underlie different forms, from landscape painting, to the patriotic monument, to Transcendentalist manifestos. A painting of
Niagara Falls or an essay by Ralph Waldo Emerson each produces
within the viewing or reading subject an attitude of awe and reverence. Frederic Edwin Church's *Niagara* (1857), in an effort to reproduce the experience of the sublime, places the subject as a viewer
at the brink of the cataract, which is also the edge of the canvas. The
painting does not reinforce the subject's position as exterior to the
painting, but instead, drawn from the position of the viewer, and
poising the viewer at a commanding yet terrifying overlook, *Niagara*
situates the viewer within the sublime landscape (Figure 2). In the
same fashion, Emerson's *Nature* encourages the reader to enter the
environment of nature, which, like the text of *Nature*, "stretcheth out
her arms to embrace man, only let his thoughts be of equal greatness."
This sympathy for nature, however, is more than a passage into an

Fig. 2. Frederic Edwin Church, *Niagara*, 1857, oil on canvas, 42 1/2 × 90 1/2 in (107.95 × 229.87 cm.). In the Collection of the Corcoran Gallery of Art, Museum Purchase, Gallery Fund.

unmarked wilderness; Emerson's *Nature* and Church's sublime are political enclosures. At this other level, monumentalism indicates a discursive formation connected to nationalism. The Bunker Hill Monument observes the same aesthetic principles as an American landscape painter's or Emerson's representation of the sublime, and yet, as a nationalist expression, it narrativizes a political experience in which the citizen-subject undergoes incorporation, not into a natural scene, but into the national body.[5] Monumentalism refers not simply to various cultural artifacts of grand theme or dimension; it also delineates how the narratives encoded within these artifacts, whether literary text or architectural column, access the authority of *monere* to instruct people to enter the nation as citizens.

As a narrative form connected to the reminding of *monere*, monumentalism necessarily operates within the realm of history. Nietzsche's "On the Uses and Disadvantages of History for Life" underscores the connections between monumentalism and nationalism by asserting that without a "monumental history," national consciousness remains inert. He identifies the monumental mode as the historical sense best suited for action. Within monumental history resides the "great *stimuli*" of "mythical fiction" that can be unleashed to rally people around an exemplary figure who directs them toward a single purpose. Strength and potential inhere in the monumental

because as a construction of history it discards the restrictive particularities of the past so that the hero remembered will seem universal. As Nietzsche writes, if monumental history is "to produce
that mighty effect, how violently what is individual in it would have
to be forced into a universal mould and all its sharp corners and hard
outlines broken up in the interest of conformity." So powerful are the
discursive regularities emerging from monumentalism that historical representation sacrifices the memories and experiences that
would impede articulation of a homogeneous narrative. Details,
which have an unavoidably local character, must be transcended and
forgotten for monumentalism to make its broad, unifying appeal.
Calling monumental history "fiction," Nietzsche implicitly acknowledges its discursive nature, which privileges power over a regard for
"absolute veracity." Much as Ishmael's experiments in "Cetology"
communicate that truth is not the concern of authorized discourses
such as ethnology, Nietzsche's excavations of the monumental reveal that "approximations and generalities" are the disciplinary imperatives of nationalist historiography. Like any constructed story,
monumental history alters "facts" as it forgets others; monumental
history thus necessarily contains a thorough dosage of the "unhistorical," which Nietzsche understands as vital to any action. Constant and faithful remembrance stifles life, paralyzing humans with
tired precedents and stultifying anxieties that the present will never
bear any action that measures up to the examples of the past. Forgetfulness, in contrast, frees humans from a dependence on sluggish
rumination so that they can live, act, and create: "Forgetfulness,"
writes Nietzsche, "is essential to action of any kind." National history, as a source of "great *stimuli*" that animate citizens to unite and
act together, involves a remembering of the past that forsakes strict
accounting and casts off an obedience to factual accuracy. Once
committed to remembering unhistorically, a people can forge heroes,
icons, and myths that narrativize stories of a nation. "No painter will
paint his picture, no general achieve his victory, no people attain its
freedom without first having desired and striven for it in an unhistorical condition," asserts Nietzsche.[6]

Urging the completion of the Bunker Hill Monument (Figure 3),
Edward Everett reached similar conclusions—though he certainly
lacked Nietzsche's critical irony—when he described the interrelation
of monumental history and national identity: "The American who

Fig. 3. The Bunker Hill Monument, "a fit type of the national unity."

could look on it [the monument] with indifference, does not deserve the name of American." Instructing citizens in lessons of patriotic history, the monument was to act as a democratic narrator, disseminating the same story to all. From seemingly innate memories, a narrative was to emerge in which individuals would gather as Americans. Identity would not emanate from autobiography, but rather from a vague, self-justifying experience in which people, if they were Americans, would act and remember as Americans. In fact, the very structure of "the Bunker Hill Monument is a fit type of the national unity," emblematic of the virtues of incorporation: "Built in the form of a monolithic structure, but of such large proportions, and of such unique interior arrangement, as to compel the use of many separate blocks, it aptly illustrates, in its grandeur as a single object, and in the beautiful adaptation and harmony of its several parts, the national motto, '*E pluribus unum.*'" As an architectural structure the monument may be rooted on a patch of ground, but as a narrative invested with aesthetic codes of homogeneity, the monument casts off local geography, becoming authoritative and abstract. When Webster characterized the completed monument as a "plain shaft . . . that bears no inscriptions," he did not construe its specific textual paucity as a failure; instead, this blankness pointed to narratival plenitude, to encompassing meanings that did not recognize any non-national stories that would stand in the way of political universality. Although this monumental narrative is undoubtedly fixed in history, recalling the specific site where in 1775 American patriots fell in defense of political rights, the national identity that it gave the citizen was prone to forgetfulness and civic disinterest. Monumental history can supplant human action, dwarfing the crowd that gathers at its base. Alongside the great potentiality of monumentalism, Nietzsche notes the dangers of a swaggering history that can master those who erect and narrate it. Daniel Kemmis reframes this concern by identifying the growth of American nationalism as "the story of the eclipse of republicanism." History may have served as the foundation of nationalism, but within the course of empire, critical preservation of the past and responsible civic participation became castaways in the wake of cultural expressions and historical representations that were too grand to include the concerns or plight of the citizens they alienated. Monumentalism stands as an ambivalent force: it provides impetus for national unity and independence even as it poses dangers of disempowerment and political estrangement. The purpose of this chapter is to assess the oscillation of a citizenry united in a sublime, unified consciousness and a citizenry transformed, as Nietzsche puts it, into a "dancing mob" obsessed with a "half-understood monument to some great era of the past."[7]

THE "NATURAL" ORIGINS
OF THE CULTURE OF MONUMENTALISM

American monumentalism was exceptional from the start. Although other nations had erected colossal structures and had stretched across vast regions, America imagined itself to possess a natural innocence that distinguished its monuments from the swaggering productions of the Old World. The claim that American culture lacked antecedents bolstered the conception of antebellum politics, art, and literature as wholly original and American, capable of arising only from this nation. Who could equate the Bunker Hill Monument with the Pyramids, orators asked, if ancient Egypt lacked democratic forms of government? Nor did the Tower of Babel compare, for God had deemed that structure sinful and shattered that culture's prideful pretensions to unity. Though engaged in a similar project, antebellum America did not fear its grandiose expressions of unity would incur divine wrath. Whereas human arrogance built the Tower of Babel, nature cultivated American monumentalism. The vastness of the continent, its natural wonders, the richness of its resources, all bespoke a New World that dwarfed the tiny countries across the Atlantic. In *Notes on the State of Virginia*, Thomas Jefferson concluded that the ever expanding dominions of America provided ample likelihood for the existence of yet undiscovered mammoths that belittled diminutive European species. When Rembrandt Peale, best known for his portraits immortalizing George Washington, unearthed a mammoth skeleton, he seemed to have found an antediluvian record of America's destined monumental stature. The discovery of fossil traces convinced Jefferson that "the largest of all terrestrial beings" still roamed the aboriginal and unexplored territories of the western United States. Mammoths would be only a fitting complement to the already awesome topography of the New World that Jefferson found expressed by Virginia's Natural Bridge, "the most sublime of nature's works."[8]

Artists of the nativist Hudson River School painted "the most sublime" landscapes, where endless vistas lay just beyond towering mountain peaks. The works of Frederic Edwin Church, Jasper F. Cropsey, Asher B. Durand, and Thomas Cole depict an immensity of space out of which natural monuments arise. Certainly, European civilization had reared imposing cathedrals and castles, but such man-made expressions appeared as swaggering idols when placed next to the native innocence of American landscape. "You see no ruined tower to tell of outrage—no gorgeous temple to speak of ostentation; but freedom's offspring—peace, security, and happiness, dwell there, the spirits of the scene," wrote Thomas Cole in his "Essay on American Scenery" (1836). The pristine quality of the monumental produced a sense of nature that seemed innately American, unavailable to decaying countries of the Old World. Even the name, Hudson River School, fastened cultural expression to a particular non-European landscape, regardless of any similarities between American canvases and those from English artists such as J. W. M. Turner. Church "was immune to European influences, so at least it was believed," observes one critic. These nationalist associations coalesced into a tautological cultural logic: because the lakes of New Hampshire possess a character that, for Cole, was "truly and peculiarly American," they were sublime; and, because natural monuments preserved a homogeneous purity even within their grandeur, they deserved to be American. And because they were American, representations of nature transcended European creations; comparing the heavens of Italy and America, Cole declared: "For variety and magnificence American skies are unsurpassed."[9] Nationalism effects a series of metonomies in which an exceptional natural landscape substituted for America, an ideological configuration that was already heralded as transcendent. The sublime attributes of an undefiled cultural history were readily transferable to the "magnificence" of the natural world. The self-enclosed structure of this tautology, built entirely of domestic experiences, ratified American nationalism by making it the culmination of native, independent resources. Democracy, like Niagara or the Natural Bridge, was seemingly organic to the scene. No foreign influence, so liable to tarnish the view, was required.

Jasper Cropsey's canvases gather clouds and the rising mist from cascading waterfalls to suggest the terrible and forceful beauty—

terriblità—of an American nature capable of pulverizing matter into air. His *Niagara* (1856), in which spray rises above crushed rocks, stands among many views of the falls that, along with scenes of Virginia's Natural Bridge, were popular among antebellum patrons and critics. Both as tourist site and visual representation, Niagara Falls rushed forth as the single most consumed image in nineteenth-century America. Not uncoincidentally, only portraits of George Washington rivaled the popularity of Niagara's representations. That a single natural icon acquired this preeminence was instrumental to the imagining of a nation. The icon transmitted a vital lesson that stemmed from its dialectical properties of geographic uniqueness and democratic familiarity—unity. For a scattered people in a diverse territory, Niagara offered a common point of reference, a shared narrative of the nation as innocent, onrushing, inexhaustible. The metonymic structure of nationalism that substitutes and interchanges America, the sublime, and homogeneous purity encourages this lesson of federal unity, coordinating diverse aesthetic, political, and spiritual experiences around a single ideological axis. Paintings, lithographs, and tourist memories of such scenes amounted to an iconic currency in which the incredible volume of water flowing at the nation's border gave shape to a New World revealed after the Flood. The circulation and repetition of images permitted a distant mecca like Niagara to transcend the limitations of time, place, and context. What once seemed only a feature of upstate New York entered the contours of the nation. The particular environment became an icon whose lack of context and homogeneity enabled citizens to envision, in Benedict Anderson's terms, an "imagined community." Reproduced in visual representations and visited as part of what John Sears calls "one of the primary rituals of democratic life," Niagara conveyed a narrative of fecundity and power to a wide range of consumers and citizens, despite differences in class, background, or location. A Boston preacher in 1860 could thus exhort his congregation: "look at Niagara. What does it represent? Does it not resemble our country,— our vast immeasurable, unconquerable, inexplicable country?"; he knew that his listeners had of course seen paintings of the falls, had received the lithograph of Church's *Niagara*, then a fashionable wedding present, or had traveled there on a northern tour. He asked his countrymen to participate in a collective imagining that was in effect a journey from the specific to the federal, from nature to nation.[10]

Abraham Lincoln mused that the cataract's monumental stature and everlasting innocence made it an appropriate national beacon:

> Niagara-Falls! By what mysterious power is it that millions and millions, are drawn from all parts of the world, to gaze upon Niagara Falls? . . . When Columbus first sought this continent . . . nay, even, when Adam first came from the hand of his Maker—then as now, Niagara was roaring here. The eyes of that species of extinct giants, whose bones fill the mounds of America, have gazed on Niagara, as ours do now. Cotemporary with the whole race of men, and older than the first man, Niagara is strong, and fresh today as ten thousand years ago. The Mammoth and Mastodon—now so long dead, that fragments of their monstrous bones, alone testify, that they ever lived, have gazed on Niagara.[11]

Thinking of the falls and how they evoke "the indefinite past," Lincoln experiences the sublime primarily as a temporal wonder that commemorates human action even as it belittles the human historical record, exposing its inconsequential tenure and subordinate status. For American landscape painters, the sublime unveiled itself in the spatial dimensions of consciousness. In fact, for his painting, Church rejected traditional proportions, finding it necessary to enlarge the width in order to encompass the horizon of this national icon of Manifest Destiny. At the margins of Church's Romantic image of cosmic unity, human presence intrudes, only to be dwarfed by the incessant magnitude of the waters (see Figure 2). Lying prophetically within the arc of the rainbow of *Niagara* stands the United States border, with Terrapin Tower presiding over the scene. Only by using binoculars, as David Hunington notes, can the viewer who thus becomes the tourist at the falls glimpse the human figure on the tower's balcony. Diminutive figures also appear in Cole's *Niagara Falls* (1830), though with enough specificity to reveal they are Native Americans. One critic suggests that the Native Americans act as "surrogates" for the white viewer, but a more sinister economy is at work: their tragic and trivial aloneness—a convenient coincidence of Romantic aestheticism and Manifest Destiny—also presages their eventual and forced disappearance.[12] In each formulation, human subjects have a precarious toehold in representation: for Lincoln, human history is little more than a few seconds of natural history; for Cole and Church, the distinct triumph of New World grandeur remains connected to the marginal stature or inevitable effacement of individuals.

The object lesson of the preacher who asked his worshipers to "look at Niagara" was not to propel an examination of conscience; rather, the intent of the comparison was to acquaint people with an entity so large they could barely conceive it—not God, but a divine nation. In similar fashion, if Church's painting aimed to stir the individual's soul with the sublime, the quintessence of that experience was national. In *The Vagabond* (1859), Adam Badeau looked at Church's *Niagara* and recorded that its transcendent qualities emerged from its political representation of natural phenomena: "If it is inspired by Niagara, it is grand and sublime; it is natural to the nation. . . . it is a true development of the American mind; the result of democracy, of individuality, of the expansion of each, of the liberty allowed to all." Factoring the individual into an overarching unity is the goal of the sublime experience, whether emotional or political. Cole intended the depiction of a beautifully threatening environment to bow the viewer down before the colossal unity of nature: "In the terrible and the grand . . . when the mind is astonished, the eye does not dwell upon the minute but seizes the whole. In the forest, during an hour of tempest, it is not the bough playing in the wind, but the whole mass stooping to the blast that absorbs the attention: the detail, however fine, is comparatively unobserved." Showing human figures shrouded by a looming torrent of water and represented by little more than a touch of paint, artists of Niagara Falls sketched how the *terriblità* of national landscape was supposed to force citizens to ponder their own insignificance and abstract themselves from restrictive localities in the experience of the sublime. Aesthetic experience encoded the lessons and imperatives of rearing a nation-state.[13]

Elevated above the affairs of humans, the natural world was to impel the imagination toward a pure spirituality of the infinite. Overshadowed by natural immensity, the spectator experiencing the sublime at first senses his or her own ephemeral insignificance and then rises to a contemplation of divinity and creation. Unlike the haughty human project of the Tower of Babel, American monumentalism was properly reverential. "You involuntarily fall on your hands and feet, creep to the parapet, and peep over it," wrote Jefferson of the spectator's experience atop the Natural Bridge.[14] The dynamic of the sublime seems paradoxical: at one moment, its awesome magnificence reduces human beings to the posture described by Jefferson, and at the next, such transcendental power uplifts the meditative subject to the heights of Emerson's "transparent eyeball." Yet this apparent contradiction between degradation and transcendence actually inspires a harmonious metaphysics. Only by sensing one's insignificant relation to the rest of the universe can a human properly begin to conceive of a transcendental unity; only by understanding his or her position in the earthly world of nature and society could the nineteenth-century American, in Emerson's words, be "uplifted into infinite space" and shot through with "the currents of Universal Being" (*Nature*, 10).

Preachers and poets like Emerson, William Cullen Bryant, or even Henry David Thoreau helped popularize the sublime, suggesting that the realm of transcendence was egalitarian, equally the province of the farmer and the philosopher. Paintings and illustrations from the Hudson River School testify that art and literature attended the same classroom of nature. Thomas Cole painted scenes of steep crags and unearthly mists dwarfing savages and swooning women to accompany Cooper's *The Last of the Mohicans*. Cooper's Leatherstocking tales likewise draw detailed, painterly descriptions of the natural world, constructing a backdrop against which characters sense the interplay of their own insignificance and divine infinitude. Humans wait upon the landscape, offering their small stature as a measure of the grandeur of nature. The details in Cooper's novels function in the same manner as do the tiny, human particulars of nature in paintings of Niagara; as Cole said, the "minutest parts" are "subordinate and administrative" to the sublime. Durand's *Thanatopsis* commemorates William Cullen Bryant's famous paean by the same title, and his *Kindred Spirits* (1849) places Cole and Bryant in humble contemplation of a spectacular gorge and the airy horizon beyond it. Holding a short staff, the persona of Cole in the painting gestures toward the extending horizon, leading the viewer beyond an eventually insignificant foreground to the hazy distance. While the trees and gorge in *Kindred Spirits* envelop and embrace painter and poet, the background horizon and distant mountains claim the viewer's eye and subtly dominate the scene. If the fleeting horizon encourages contemplation of infinitude, then this aesthetic "truth" of Romantic harmony also supplies a national lesson: the eye searching after the painting's horizon enacts the imperatives of an expansionist discourse in which westward progress toward the setting sun and thoughts of greater unities outstrip the particularities of private, rooted localities.[15]

In its imaginative expanse, the sublimity of nature evolved into the sublimity of the nation. In *The Pioneers*, Natty Bumppo's lamentations over the destruction of game and forests describe how American monumentalism was only ephemerally located in nature. Monumentalism that once found a home in the imaginative conception of the natural sublime, in the resilient optimism of an American like Jefferson, who insisted that great mammoths must be out there somewhere, was developed and refined by a nation embarking upon the course of empire within its own borders. The change in addressee of Melville's prefaces from *Pierre*, dedicated to "the majestic mountain, Greylock," to *Israel Potter*, in which the Bunker Hill Monument dominates the textual landscape, charts the translation of the American sublime from the natural to the national. Not more than three years elapsed between these prefaces, and yet the change in referent from mountain to fabricated structure registers a significant evolution in the sublime. The nation's political legacies, not just its landscape and natural phenomena, were taken to originate as transcendent entities, innocent, pristine, and seamless. To be sure, within reproductions of Niagara, the panoramic landscape is not natural but a cultural representation of nature; however, with the articulation and expansion of American nationalism, the sublime ceased to take nature as its referent. To identify this desire for political transcendence is not to say that aesthetic representation in landscape painting does not relay a political code—indeed, the manner in which details give way to a whole synthetic representation of nature no doubt reenacts the imperatives of federalism and unity central to an incipient nation-state.[16] Instead, American culture, its institutions and historical narratives, became sublime. Cropsey's *Niagara* may have performed a political function and conveyed the nation's power and grandeur, but under this new configuration I am describing, the political realm itself becomes sublime. More specifically, the political history of the Revolutionary past is inscribed within the monumental mode as a magnificent narrative of homogeneity and unity. Memory becomes national.

The search for narratives of American national culture first began among literary nationalists. Sounding a call for literature to match the divine destiny of America and challenging the country's authors to facilitate the transition of the monumental from nature to culture, the *United States Magazine and Democratic Review* asked of American writers in 1859:

> When will they be inspired by the magnificent scenery of our own world, imbibe the fresh enthusiasm of a new heaven and a new earth, and soar upon the expanded wings of truth and liberty? Is not nature as original—her truths as captivating—her aspects as various, as lovely, as grand—her Promethean fire as glowing in this, our Western hemisphere, as in that of the East? . . . Why, then do our authors aim at no higher degree of merit, than a successful imitation of English writers of celebrity?

The emphasis this editorial places on literature as a central component of Manifest Destiny underscores the interconnections between nationalism and literature. The storied expanse of the American novel proffered a discursive territory where the nation could be imagined. *Moby-Dick*, for instance, brings together the "staid, steadfast" Starbuck as the exemplar of New England morality, the "easy, and careless" Stubb as the archetype of the jaunty Westerner, and the hot-blooded and "hereditarily" minded Flask as the Southerner always ready to fight a duel to defend a "point of honor." *The Spy* likewise spins a unifying tale in its final visions of Southerner and Northerner as kin who surmount differences in geography and ideology to battle the British. The novel, as Benedict Anderson contends, thus served the needs of protonationalism by allowing authors, readers, and citizens to imagine themselves as part of a single community in which the mortar of synchronicity and homogeneity is fictive.[17]

During the years called the American Renaissance, the national component of literature was by no means an unconscious drive or a latent ideology. Instead, the call for a literature to administer to the idea of the nation developed as a manifest duty for writers. A "native literature is essential to national patriotism—to the independence of the national mind," wrote Southern novelist William Gilmore Simms. Eminent literati complained of America's embarrassing indebtedness to European culture and urged literature to keep pace with the independence of the nation's political institutions. "Americanness" marked artistic originality and acted as the criteria of literary merit that faulted Melville's *Pierre* for its "Frenchified mode."

Writers and editors styling themselves Young America mandated the production of a national literature whose thematics and tone would distinguish it as a faithful aesthetic expression of the vast continent. Such literary nationalism paralleled the production of books with titles like *Behemoth: A Legend of the Mound-Builders* and *Big Abel and the Little Manhattan* or the writing of an epic sea voyage across the watery expanses in search of a monstrous leviathan named Moby Dick. According to Perry Miller, Young America operated under the "thesis . . . that we should automatically create a big literature because we were a big country." As an instrument of national culture, literature promised to surpass visual representations of the wilderness because it marked the refinement of a nation that had evolved beyond simply tapping metaphoric resources of the natural environment. Literature appeared as a more potent medium capable of transmitting biographies and legends that would make up a shared culture, capable of instilling a specifically American political morality and distinctness. Melville's review of Hawthorne captured this transition in its vision of an American literary genius in whose "deep and noble nature, you will hear the far roar of his Niagara." During his association with Young America, Melville prophesied the historicization of the sublime even as, in gestures of profound ambivalence, he doubted such national bravado and questioned if it was promise or threat to articulate national history as transcendent.[18]

THE HISTORICIZATION
OF THE SUBLIME

Nationalism most consciously engineered monumentalism within the limitless domain of popular historical representation. Compared with the Old World, whose traditions and customs stretched across centuries, America seemed a blank historical slate. Yet this very blankness opened up a virgin domain of history for America. Like the lands beyond the Mississippi, the unwritten history of America was ripe for discovery, exploration, and development. Jefferson's mammoth had more than biological interest; as an inhabitant of the American landscape, the anticipated mammoth announced a natural history predating the most ancient artifacts of European culture. This corollary between nature and history, however, simultaneously registered America's discomfort with its own historical virginity. "Our historical works are attempts, not achievements," confessed one critic of the American art scene, who then sought a more hopeful cultural vista: "But in landscapes the sky is brighter. . . . there is the inspiring theme."[19] And yet, the Edenic scenes produced by Durand or Church did little to allay this insecurity. No matter how monumental portraits of Niagara Falls may have seemed to the antebellum public, these scenes could never be properly monumental. The represented innocence of a garden wilderness shirked any sense of *monere*, of memory, reminding, restoring, and transmitting an instructive past to a younger generation. If anything, nineteenth-century landscape painting dedicated itself to advertising a memoryless tabula rasa, inviting the marks of settlement, inviting history, even as it forgot that the land had ever been populated by others. This incipient character of the national project marked America with an inexperience that, no matter how endearing, denoted a glaring lack of history necessary for foundations, continuity, and political ritual. To fill this void, filial America argued that it had lost its innocence in the trials of the Revolution.

The National Symbolic requires an official history; national culture can hardly be authoritative if it lacks the legitimation of the past. George Washington's death on the eve of the nineteenth-century provided one such source of legitimation, turning over a mythic ancestor to be embalmed by a collective imagination. Gilbert Stuart, the artist famous for his portraits of Washington taken from life, perceived the potential for profit when a culture saw him not simply as an artist, but as a living oracle of America's past. Working from "originals" he had painted of the deceased president, Stuart and his daughter turned out their *Washington*s and found a market eager for artifacts of national history. Until America found a new martyr in Lincoln, Washington remained the supremely popular topic for oratory and iconography, and the anniversary of his birth never failed to gather speakers to discuss his exemplary character or his sacred understanding of national union. As a monumental icon, the founding father inspired sublime lessons of citizenship; speaking on the centennial of his birth, Daniel Webster proclaimed that the name of Washington secured the *"unity of government which constitutes us one people."* All these gravediggers unearthed a mummified memory of Washington and made it part of a mythic culture. This translation and resurrection of Washington into "Washington," of lived body into mythic corpus, of natural body into a reified text, represented the most sublime moment of historical monumentalism. Thus, urging the preservation of Washington's home, one orator noted how Mount Vernon far exceeded "the sublime cataract of Niagara" because it is not a natural site, but a topos rich in the historical material of national narrative. With history, America ascended from the natural to the national.[20]

As a mythic-historical figure who dominated antebellum imagination, Washington relocated the sublime on a national scale. The private matters of his life did not remain mere details, but as with Cole's "minutest parts," which served to reinforce the "whole mass" of nature's unity, trivial memories of the founding father extended beyond the particular to represent America as an encompassing union. In Kirkland's *Memoirs of Washington*, even as Washington administers the federal government, he pays attention to local affairs at Mount Vernon: "not a broken fence or dilapidated negro hut but was repaired under his direction." Within the biography of the national father, even the most irregular particulars—such as human bondage—could be subsumed under the project of union. The dynamics of the sublime lent symmetry and order to a culture that contained potentially jarring social and institutional practices. Washington's simultaneous management of the nation and his plantation repeated the overall harmony of landscape paintings of Niagara Falls: particular sprays of water and jagged rocks give way to a larger scheme of a natural wonder that seems divine. As Kirkland puts it to her young readers, Washington's mind was expansive, able to encompass "now the shadow of an eyelash, now the perspective of Niagara."[21] As the founding father was allied with the most prominent image of grandeur and spiritual order, he translated and extended these themes of power and hierarchy to the ideological continuity of the United States.

A genealogy attempting to date the transformation of the natural sublime into a monumental historical culture might pinpoint Washington as the great man who, by an array of symbolic actions, most notably his own death, ushered America into history. A mezzotint engraving entitled *A Symbol of America* (Figure 4) graphically represents the symbolic interplay among nature, Washington, and history. Published in 1800, just after Washington had lost his natural body to acquire a corpus, this engraving centers upon the allegorical

Fig. 4.   Anonymous British artist, *A Symbol of America*, 1800, mezzotint engraving. Print Collection, Miriam and Ira D. Wallach Division of Art, Prints, and Photographs, The New York Public Library, Astor, Lenox, and Tilden Foundations.

representation of Columbia as a female figure holding the national banner. This figuration of America evokes the fertile nature of the continent via the ample body of a woman. Washington's tombstone lends support to her graceful attitude and gives rest to a crippled, despairing Native American. The posture of these figures, accented

by the downward slant of the branches, directing the spectator to the
site of remembrance, makes Washington's absence the source of an
extravagant historical symbolism. Inscribed with the bare facts of
biography, the monument in the engraving reveals the national history that has "naturally" evolved from the savage state of the de-
graded original inhabitant to the confident and civilized demeanor
of Columbia. Washington's iconographic presence, made possible
only by the memory of his absence, provides a solid foundation for
her emblematic being. Niagara Falls flows in the engraving's background as testimony that the inexhaustible splendor of the landscape
is found in the historical legacy. Although Elizabeth McKinsey points
to this image as "a moment when national and natural impulses came
together," the authority of writing—"To the Memory of Geo. Washington"—makes this union a relation of power in which historical
wonder overcomes natural splendor.[22] The engraving maps a predestined story of progression and development: the nation emerges
from an aboriginal, ahistorical context to acquire the dominant stability of a monument to its patriarchal sire.

A discordant note enters this family romance of legendary father,
mythic mother, and infant nation a year later, in 1801, when a variation of *A Symbol of America* replaces the humbled Native American
with a dejected black slave. Yet within the economy of the sublime
as national history, how disruptive is the presence of the slave? The
slave serves the allegory of this engraving, *America*, updating the
representation in the same way that the altered details of Columbia
(rustic hair style, simple sandals, and a liberty cap instead of a
diadem) more correctly identify the nation as an agrarian republic
rather than a classical polity (Figure 5). The slave—to use Kirkland's
formula—is "the shadow of the eyelash" whose reduced state con-
tributes to the overall "perspective of Niagara;" or, using Cole's
account of the sublime, the slave is "subordinate and administrative"
to the larger national narrative the engraving imparts. Just as the
speaker in "Self-Reliance" imagines himself dismissing the distrac-
tion of the "angry bigot [who] assumes this bountiful cause of Abolition, and comes to me with his last news from Barbadoes" in order
that he can better love those at home, in an analogous move in
America, the detail of the slave is subsumed by care shown to another
community—the whole of the United States ("Self-Reliance," 262).
Whereas Emerson prefers to pay attention to neighbors who fell

Fig. 5.   Anonymous British artist, *America*, 1801 mezzotint engraving.
McAlpin Collection, Miriam and Ira D. Wallach Division of
Art, Prints, and Photographs, The New York Public Library,
Astor, Lenox, and Tilden Foundations.

outside institutions, the allegory of *America* cherishes a country replete with institutions. The fact that *America* could accommodate this
forlorn racial body testifies to the triumph of the ideological con-
cordance of institutional practice, unique natural wonder, and the
unique historical personage, Washington, represented by the urn
and bas-relief. Union—as aesthetic principle and political imperative—dominates.[23]

Narrating a monumental history was at first analogous to painting
a portrait glorifying America's landscape. But these engravings indicate that the natural sublime was not the final vision, but a conduit
that invested icons with the power to narrate history. This transition
from pristine wilderness to written memorial, from nature to culture,
signified the triumph of an American project that created a historical
imagination as potent as the natural forces it displaced. Whereas the
Natural Bridge once humbled and then "elevated" Jefferson "up to
heaven," now history served as the vehicle of transcendence. The
foremost spokesman of monumental history, Emerson, outlines the
dynamics that inform a new sublime historical sense revolving
around participatory, temporal insights rather than geographic vistas: "all public facts are to be individualized, all private facts are to
be generalized. Then at once History becomes fluid and true, and
Biography deep and sublime," ("History," 246). Remembrance
promises to elevate the citizen to the height of democratic vistas,
where the subject becomes a "transparent eye-ball" and captures
sight of the universal. Not only does the spirit of the citizen's fellows
circulate through his or her body and being, but the mind domes-
ticates time and renders its barriers meaningless; the individual's
soul, according to Emerson, can worship across the centuries with the
soul of Plato or Pindar. When in his 1825 address delivered at the
laying of the cornerstone of the Bunker Hill Monument, Daniel
Webster said "we are among the sepulchres of our fathers," he hoped
the thousands of Americans gathered in front of him would disregard time and skip across the years to recover the storied viability
of democratic origins.[24]

Having harnessed the forces of the sublime, democracy became a
transcendental image. As an exalted political idea, however, antebellum democracy had more in common with Ahabian abstraction
than Melville's "ruthless democracy." Its constituency could only be
ideal: mid-nineteenth-century America attained an ascendant, self-

satisfying representation by dismissing enduring concerns over the political and social status of women, slaves, and those who held no property, all of whom were denied elective franchise, much in the same way that Emerson achieves self-reliance by shunning the "last news from Barbadoes." Still, a monumental culture assured of its own democratic principles demanded an illusion of vibrant civic participation, making history subjective, rather than making the individual subject to history. As Emerson understands the process: "The student is to read history actively and not passively; to esteem his own life the text, and books the commentary. All history becomes subjective; in other words there is properly no history, only biography" ("History," 239–40). In his schema, iconic symbols act as the nuts and bolts of monumental history, enabling the viewer to transcend his or her limited being as well as the material form of the symbol itself. Berlant notes the operation of a similar symbolic force in Hawthorne's representation of the American eagle outside the custom house as an icon that leads to the "transcendence of local history, narrative, and desire."[25] Governed by the metaphoric grammar of symbols, monumental history engenders the collective flowing together of citizens. The overwhelming crowds that gathered to inaugurate the Bunker Hill and Washington monuments dramatize the manner in which icons pervaded and shaped the culture's consciousness. Available to citizens of every class, symbols created an egalitarian outlook: as Emerson writes in "The Poet," "this universality of the symbolic language" caused "the distinctions which we make in events, and in affairs, of low and high, honest and base [to] disappear" (454). From the Greek *symbollein*, meaning "to throw together," symbols encouraged popular confluence around monumental historical icons—though, as we will see, that assemblage could bear alarming resemblance to Nietzsche's "dancing mob" that memorializes the forgetting of the past.

The symbol effects transcendence by rendering an event or person universally intelligible to the common mind through the stripping away of restrictive particulars—just as Ahab does in his demonological reification of the pagan harpooners. Historical events and people are subject to a similar Ahabian process of abstraction that prepares entry into national narrative. *Harper's* spelled out the criteria for determining what was qualified to be incorporated into the National Symbolic. For instance, to assess the symbolic resonance

of March 5, 1770, a citizen might ask: "What the masses were doing. . . . But even could this be ascertained it would not be history. On
that day the three millions of our land were engaged in the various
avocations connected with their ordinary life and ordinary inter-
ests." Hardly worth memorialization, the people are not the stuff of
history. Instead, history resides solely in the national. Thus March 5,
1770 has significance because, as the date of the Boston Massacre, it
"was *thought* by all, *felt* by all, and therefore became, for the time in
which it was thought and felt, the one common history of all." In the
same manner, for Washington to evolve as national symbol, for him
to be represented as *A Symbol of America*, the restrictive peculiarities
of his life had to be transformed and made "universally" significant.
"Oh no! give us his *private virtues*! In *these*, every youth is interested,
because in these every youth may become a Washington," exclaims
Parson Weems at the outset of his biography of the general, which
then magnifies to epic proportion childhood peccadilloes such as
chopping down a cherry tree.[26] Childhood transgression is elevated
to the height of a national myth. Antebellum historiography defies
distinctions between public and private to posit a universal memory
of the past common to all citizens; as Emerson's first sentence in
"History" asserts: "There is one mind common to all individual
men" ("History," 237).

　　Actualizing a monumental history with symbols thus necessarily
generates a degree of forgetfulness.[27] Monumental history is paradoxical; as a mode of history, it encourages a departure from the
materiality of facts to embrace what Nietzsche called "unhistorical"
representation. Only through forgetting could Washington be made
a historical symbol of national dimensions. Consider what happened
on a small scale when biography exhumed the body of Washington.
Besides ignoring a natural body subject to decay and restricted by
temporality, a biographer preparing the body of George Washington
for a monumental history visible from every corner of the republic
would necessarily reconstitute that body. Remembering the natural
body he never saw, Weems unabashedly writes: "It was at Bermuda
that George took the small-pox which marked him rather agreeably
than otherwise." In other biographical accounts, monumental history must forget the general's tactical blunders and sublimate them
as prudent military strategy. A national symbol can include neither
the history of public dissatisfaction with the Washington adminis-

tration's treaty with the British nor the subsequent denunciations of the president as a new King George. In fact, most popular nineteenth-century biographies of Washington tended to gloss over his eight years of presidency and remember the more glorious days of cannon fire and captured enemy colors. So when the 1855 edition of Jared Sparks's *Life of George Washington* admits to "omissions . . . mostly of a political or general nature," it can nevertheless insist that the essence of "the narrative [has] been preserved without change and nearly complete."[28] The generalized form of narrative—a story of youth achieving a heroic destiny—is what makes such omissions possible, even desired.

Lapses in memory underpin monumental history. Only forgetfulness can produce a sublime history in which specificities like smallpox scars or details of Washington's less than glorious foreign policy dissolve into a allegorical and repeatable pattern of national narrative. Lacking some amount of amnesia, antebellum historiography never could indulge in the unhistorical sense that invests icons and myths with a federal, unifying power. But even as Nietzsche declares that "it is altogether impossible to live at all without forgetting," he modifies this assertion with the caution that a zealous disregard for the past can become a "seductive" pursuit that tyrannizes a culture. Though Nietzsche warns us about "this kind of history in the hands and heads of gifted egoists and visionary scoundrels,"[29] neither Parson Weems nor Sparks fits this description. Instead, the threat of tyranny, the most severe danger to democratically inspired political and narrative representation, stems from a citizenry that actively, monomaniacally participates in national mythology.

SUBLIME DEMOCRACY AND THE INVISIBLE CITIZEN

Monumentalism, by the interplay of forgetting and colossal representation, sought to inspire people to muster around a symbol whose sublime qualities empowered it with the capacity to reflect a unified and directed national consciousness. But how are we to evaluate politically the narratives monumental history erected? Emerson, in *Nature*, like any one of the monumental emblems of national remembrance, the Washington Monument in Baltimore (1815–1829), the Bunker Hill Monument (1825–1843), or the Washington Monument (1848–1886) in the nation's capital, told the same story of democracy; it is an optimistic story, championing the democratic individual and his or her boon companion—national society.[30] Emerson's account of transcendence, culminating in the rapturous experience as "currents of the Universal Being circulate through me," introduces itself on a modest, yet resoundingly significant stage of "a bare common" (10). The individual reaches ecstatic unity at the mundane site of public space that denotes the New England township's commitment to democracy. Only by sensing a physical legacy of direct citizen participation can the individual encounter the landscape of sublime democracy. When the transcendence described in *Nature* solidifies into a historical monument, the importance of the individual's connection to a tangible democratic locus still remains. High above Boston or Washington, D.C., the monument cannot dismiss the "bare common" from which it ascends. The groundbreaking and final dedication ceremonies of these pillars occasioned mass gatherings of citizens collecting themselves into a common space where the individual could visibly see himself or herself as a constituent part of the public. On dates calculated to jog citizen memory, such as the fiftieth anniversary of the Battle of Bunker Hill or the Fourth of July, citizens gathered at these democratic temples to practice the rites of civil religion and publish their support for an architecture of national remembrance.

These lofty summits, it would seem, could not obscure the citizen even as they towered over him or her. Orators triumphed in interpretations decreeing that these monuments surpassed the wonders of antiquity because their design allowed for citizen participation on a previously unimaginable scale. Edward Everett, second as an orator only to Webster, wrote as part of an effort to boost popular support for the Bunker Hill Monument that whereas the "pyramids and obelisks of Egypt, the monumental columns of Trajan and Aurelius, have paid no tribute to the rights of feelings of man," the American memorial stood alone as an act of symbolic architecture courting the approval of the political "man." Staircases, even an elevator in the Washington Monument, invited the tourist to participate in the monumental and climb to the heights of the national sublime. So vital was the idea of participatory architecture that the "modern" designs of the Bunker Hill and Washington monuments eclipsed the already completed Baltimore Monument. A 15-foot statue of Washington presided atop the 160-foot column in Baltimore, deaf and indistinct to the populace below. In *Moby-Dick*, Ishmael suspiciously considers this iconic Washington who has lost contact with Emerson's "bare common": "Great Washington, too, stands high aloft on his towering main-mast in Baltimore, and like one of Hercules' pillars, his column marks that point of human grandeur beyond which few mortals will go. . . . [He never] will answer a single hail from below."[31] In contrast, the unified shape of the later monuments in which the entire structure, not just the pinnacle, represents the greatness of Washington, implied no such distance. The past, if isolated from human subjectivity, could decline into tyranny, as the populace, in Washington's towering eyes, degenerated into trivial, antlike beings. No conception of monumental history could be democratic if it forgot Emerson's reminder that the "Jerseys were handsome ground enough for Washington to tread" ("Heroism," 378).

Under this enactment of democratic architecture, the citizen could ascend the monumental icon without forsaking contact with the world. Like Antaeus, citizen and democratic icon located their powerful appeal in a bond with the earth, with the affairs of the "bare common." Atop these monuments, the visitor's eye embraced boundless geography rushing off to its Manifest Destiny, the metropolis of Baltimore bustling with commerce, and the edifices of the capitol's representative institutions presenting themselves with transparent austerity—in short, the individual intuitively sensed his or her connectedness and placement within the great democratic vastness of territorial expansion, capitalism, and governmental power. Enveloped by the political sublime, the citizen grasped an image of state power circulating through his or her civic being. A national impression rivaled the spectacle of nature's *terriblità* beheld by the painters of Niagara Falls. Just as outcroppings of rock, misty rainbows, and half-obscured figures contributed to the overall harmony of a single, nativist phenomenon, the monumental vision looked out over a complex unity of resources, development, and federal administration. Emerson's *Nature*, according to Pease, attempts to fulfill this vision by proposing the congruence of "the nation's principles" and "nature's laws."[32] The conception of something divine conjured up out of nature's magnificence was to give way to an equal, if not more powerful idea—the American nation. Aided by monuments of his own fabrication, the American was to overtake nature and move up the chain of being to manufacture a sociopolitical system whose grandeur would surpass the natural sublime because Americans themselves created that system. Struck by the extent of his or her view and the corresponding vista in the mind's eye, the citizen was to be awed by a capacity not only to conceive of America, but also to understand his or her connection to the larger democratic body.

Any icon, if it adheres to the Emersonian conception of a transcendent symbol, must guard as inseparable this unadorned connection to the common. Thus, as Weems set about fictionalizing Washington's boyhood, he portrays an unpretentious youth amid a humble scene. Prefiguring the legendary barefoot existence of Abe Lincoln, Weems reports that young George pondered God's bounty *"while with his little naked toes he scratched in the soft ground."* Similarly, both the Bunker Hill and Washington monuments reached their heights with the assistance of funds collected from the community at large. Edward Everett detailed the national vistas the citizen would behold from the monument's summit, only to suggest that this summit could not be completed without citizen participation: "The monument must be erected by the union of all the classes and members of society, and the smallest assistance, by contribution or encouragement, will aid in the great design." Echoing Emerson's description of the egalitarian monumentalism that "drive[s] men of every class to the use of emblems" ("The Poet," 454), Everett's circular pronounced a subjective history responsive to the actions of individuals who defined themselves as part of a pervasive, national community. Certificates given to contributors verified that the donor was not just an individual, but a national subject, someone who, through demonstrated reverence for the national historical narrative, had become an American. The 1833 certificate given to supporters of the Bunker Hill Monument, for example, imparted sublime lessons of the past: "The Law of Nature ordains equality among men in political rights and duties. The American Revolution established the dominion of the of this law, but at the cost of Valiant Patriots, who devoted their lives that future generations might rise to the dignity of Free Citizens. . . . The People of this day . . . unite in raising a monument on the field of battle."[33] Appeals for popular support converted financial

donations into a badge of citizenship; making a pledge to these designs confirmed one as a citizen who properly exercised a common
civic memory. Even the trivial action of contributing a single dollar
became sublime, instructing the citizen in the deeds of the fathers,
enrolling him or her in a "higher" national community.

A monumental history built in accord with democratic principles
narrates a story not only of great ancestors but of the everyday
patriots who make up the nation's fabric. The history erected around
George Washington and other fallen heroes includes a metanarrative
in which the architects of that history give an autobiographical performance of a community articulating itself as a unified body. Monumental history does not tell the story of a citizen's life, but rather
it pronounces the story of citizens sharing a common autobiography
that is coincident with the nation. When troubles with finances and
land mortgages stalled the work at Bunker Hill, the stoppage seemed
to indict the fidelity of the post-Revolutionary generation's memory:
"The whole community was in a false position, and it became absolutely necessary that the work should be finished," commented
one nineteenth-century historian about the 1840 cessation of the
project. The unfinished state of the Washington Monument during
the decades of constitutional crisis and civil war gave undeniable and
embarrassing proof that a unified people did not exist. Torn between
beliefs of freedom and practices of slavery, public construction became an impossibility. When the Washington Monument Society
warned in 1859 that "the completion of the Monument now in
progress is far more important to the fame of the American people
than to the fame of Washington," it hoped that a sublime history
could transcend vitriolic sectional oppositions and renew the national unity of a divinely chosen people. But by 1861, when the
society appealed for donations, the campaign for the year netted
$88.52, with Virginia and Mississippi making sarcastic pledges of
$.48 and $.15 (Figure 6).[34]

Communion around symbols of the monumental was supposed
to meld individuals into a structure much like Ahab's "indissoluble
league," affiliating them through a simultaneity of experience. Benedict Anderson identifies the novel and the newspaper as two modern
"forms of imagining" that have acted as key disseminators of such
temporal coincidence. Consumers of novels and newspapers receive
more than information; they ingest a temporal context in which

Fig. 6.   With construction stalled during the Civil War, the Washington Monument became a source of national embarrassment. Here lampooned as the Beef Depot Monument, this engraving records how the monument grounds were converted, perhaps all too appropriately, into a Union slaughterhouse during the war. Library of Congress.

events happen within an empty simultaneity that disregards the barriers of past, present, and future. As events happen across this simultaneity of time for readers of the morning newspaper, for instance, a cohesive consciousness develops. While this notion of "homogeneous, empty time" may describe a temporal attitude that

united Americans, even those not present at the Bunker Hill dedication ceremonies, those receiving the experience via the avenues of
print capitalism, this description of simultaneity fails to capture a
republican understanding of history that was central to national
imagination in the antebellum period. Republican remembrance enrolled citizens within a genealogical continuity linking the present to
the past. Overleaping temporal barriers, not to dismiss the notion of
a past, but to reestablish contact with the fathers, citizens insisted
upon the pastness, the historical depth, of their present. Rather than
"re-presenting" the imagined community, as Anderson puts it, republican remembrance of America historicized the present, making
it a recovery of the authority and legitimacy of ancestral founders.[35]
In genealogical terms, the sons maintained the past so that they could
follow in the footsteps of the fathers.

The Bunker Hill Monument thus supplied more than an observation tower surveying present horizons of territorial expansion. It
articulated a historical overlook that bore the citizen back to the
origins of American independence. Webster told the crowd of this
memorial's sublime communication with the monumental past: "Its
silent, but awful utterance . . . brings to our contemplation the 17th
of June, 1775, and the consequences which have resulted to us, to
our country, and to the world, from the events of that day, and
which we know must continue to rain influence on the destinies of
mankind to the end of time, the elevation with which it raises us
high above the ordinary feelings of life, surpass all." The column of
remembrance bound the citizen to a patriotic tradition in the same
way Emerson's understanding of subjective history catapulted him
to a region where conversation with Plato or Pindar seemed possible. The Washington Monument no less effectively doubled as a
time machine, recapturing instructive instances of Washington's
virtuous life and dignified public career. Monuments enabled a remembrance that was politically religious in the sense of *religare*, of
rearticulating the ligaments of the founding. Monumental architecture revealed the sublime moments of American history; it was a
catalyst for a healthy, republican remembrance that saw itself extending, back into the future, backward to the great deeds of the
fathers. Like a priest, Webster guided the civic mass back to the
martyrs who fell battling the British and did not end this historical

journey until the crowd returned to the fount of patriarchal authority—the founding father: "Washington! . . . The structure now
standing before us, by its uprightness, its solidity, its durability, is
no unfit emblem of his character. His public virtues and public
principles were as firm as the earth on which it stands; his personal
motives as pure as the serene heaven in which its summit is lost."[36]
Civil religion sanctified Washington as a vessel through which the
American public achieved a monumental stature rooted in the common ground of an ancestral legacy. Within the architectural incarnation of national narrative, monumental form was as vital as monumental content. While the manifest content of the Bunker Hill
Monument referred to the events of June 17, 1775, its structural
attributes provided emblematic expression of the persistent formal
qualities of antebellum historiography: coherence, directedness, and
unity. The present was to be no different from the past; indeed, the
future was to be its continuation. The monumental impelled the
citizen to a summit where civil religion held sway, where ligaments
between generations were fixed. Within these rites, a transcendental
vision operated, not just in space, but in time.

Visible to all as an iconographic marker in which citizens identified shared points of space and memory, as a discursive construction, monumentalism nevertheless took on sinister political implications. Although the expansive visibility of sublime iconography
represented an openness characteristic of democracy, manifest openness simultaneously functions as a primary pathway of power in
disciplinary society. Foucault can help diagnose the more effective
deployment of power onto individual bodies that occurs when discourses of knowledge, especially monumental narrative, become
more open and accessible. The transfer of punishment from hidden
spaces, such as dungeons and madhouses, to sites of acknowledged
and authorized disciplines, such as penal reform and psychology,
stands as a revolutionary reconceptualization of knowledge as a
more efficient, pervasive, and, in its frankness, scarcely noticeable
form of power. As Foucault observes of the Panopticon, "He who is
subjected to a field of visibility, and who knows it, assumes responsibility for the constraints of power; he makes them play spontane-
ously upon himself; he inscribes in himself the power relation in
which he simultaneously plays both roles; he becomes the principle

of his own subjection."[37] Power, by virtue of this insidious gaze, functions automatically and is exercised without effort; it is the individual who subjects the self to the self's own surveillance. In contrast to this panoptic power that places minute and ordinary details under constant vigilance, monumental vision overlooks differentiated aspects of the particular. Whereas disciplinary society enforces the visibility of the subject, American monumentalism propagates majestic affiliations and cosmic notions of community that obliterate the cultural differences of individuals as a meaningful political index.

But American monumentalism never transferred its visibility to the individual as self-induced observation. That is, American monumentalism by its blatant visibility rendered the citizen invisible. From the expansive height of cultural monumentalism, the citizen lost definition, forfeited distinctness, and melded into rituals of the democratic mass. In Foucault's account, panopticism regulates and normalizes a population because it breeds suspicions that people are the objects of a disciplinary vision; within monumentalism, an inverse relation was at work, however. Citizens entertained a fantasy of subjectivity, understanding themselves as agents who chose to look upon a single point of observation. Whereas panopticism implements multiple points of surveillance to codify diverse or aberrant individuals within a controlling system of knowledge, in monumentalism, diverse individuals all survey a common point that unifies them as sharers of the same historical vision, as citizens each equally versed in the narrative of the symbol. As Pease argues, in "antebellum America the masses were not homogeneous"; monumentalism was an attempt to render them so.[38]

In other words, moving from Foucault's model of panopticism to monumentalism involves a significant shift in the agency of the gaze. The panoptic regime looks out upon individuals; however, within expressions of American nationalism, individuals unified their gaze upon determined icons of remembrance. And yet, within each apparatus of vision, power bears a similar relation, grouping individuals in a systematized discipline of knowledge. Whether that system is penal reform or narratives of national remembrance makes little difference—the intent of each remains the inscription of individuals within a discourse. Choosing to view sublime moments of history, citizens no doubt experience themselves as free subjects, yet the singularity of that vision challenges notions of diversity, difference, and dissent that make citizens not only a visible, but a viable force. Underneath the harmony of Emerson's declaration that "there is one mind common to all individual men," the tension between narrative homogeneity and narrative difference emerges. National identity, as constructed in the antebellum era, ran the risk of effacing democracy.

One might argue, however, that the necessity of civic participation within American monumentalism dispelled any fears of tyrannous homogeneity. Neither Young America's call for a national literature nor popular support for national architecture were the results of coercion. As cultural productions, these literary and material narratives proudly attested to their creators' freely motivated and consensual accord; the design of the Bunker Hill Monument, Webster in 1843 affirmed, "rested on voluntary contributions, private munificence, and the general favor of the public."[39] Because active democratic participation powered the sublime textualization of key moments and figures of collective memory, these icons seemingly never could deteriorate into tyrannical structures. Washington and Bunker Hill adamantly symbolized the nascent democracy's resistance to despotic oppression, and their iconic memorializations arose from more elaborate and organized desires to preserve the legacy of that founding spirit. Yet citizens who consciously labored to produce a monumental culture came to resemble the residents within the panoptic regime who are "caught up in a power situation of which they are themselves the bearers"; each elaborated a structure within culture and consciousness that overshadowed them. That universal participation in the configuration of the monumental was not precluded, but actively solicited, recalls the democratic governance of the Panopticon: in Bentham's reformist vision, the observation tower is open to any member of the public, thereby preventing the possibility that "the panoptic machine may degenerate into tyranny; the disciplinary mechanism will be democratically controlled."[40] The frank visibility of monumentalism's openness provided a democratic foundation for America's towering expressions of sublime political unity; yet, it was a democracy fraught with ambivalence that descended from the earliest conflicts between Hamilton and Jefferson, centralization and localism, federal citizens and civic actors. These contradictory impulses produced a democracy unable to coordinate its vision between the fluctuating extremes and similarities of Emerson's "transparent eye-ball" and Foucault's eye of power.

MELVILLE'S CRITIQUE
OF TRANSCENDENTAL HISTORY

When, in March 1861, Herman Melville visited the nation's capital, he was received with reassuring familiarity. At the White House, he shook Abraham Lincoln's hand, noting a refreshingly common aura about the president: "He shook hands like a good fellow—working hard at it like a man sawing wood at so much per cord." The next afternoon, however, he made the pilgrimage to a monumental icon, only to report somewhat dejectedly: "I visited the Washington Monument. Huge tower some 160 feet high of white marble. Could not get inside. Nothing been done to it for long time."[41] What Melville experienced personally—greeted by the human representative of democracy and rebuffed by the reified memorial to democratic foundings—he had expressed as ironic critique in his 1855 novel, *Israel Potter: His Fifty Years of Exile.* In an effort to navigate a course for America between democratic candor and democratic repression, Melville resurrects forgotten history and argues for its placement within monumental culture even as he reveals the political pitfalls of figuring history within nationalist discourse. Melville's project is beleaguered by foundational American tensions between Federalists and Antifederalists, between the unity of individuals and the erasure of individuals, between national identity and anonymity. Caught within this dialectical ambivalence, *Israel Potter* embraces the transcendent power of democratically inspired monumental history only to employ the parricidal force of critical parody to renounce sublime national narrative. As self-conscious biographer, the narrator of *Israel Potter* aligns himself with Emerson and the monument builders and then reverses his position by the end of the novel, when the title character plummets from the illusive heights of democracy.

   Israel Potter thus appears as a case study of a history made sublime by its inclusion within the Revolutionary mythos. An Emersonian principle seems to inform the biographical project of *Israel Potter*, and its author might interrogate history as does Emerson to ask: "what food or experience or succor have they [dead, unindividualized facts] for the Esquimaux seal-hunter, for the Kanaka in his canoe, for the fisherman, the stevedore, the porter"—or for an American exile named Potter? ("History," 256). This biographer recalling the Revolution acts in concert with the transcendental thinker crossing "a bare common." Melville descends into the most common of circumstances to retrieve and elevate the life of this forgotten patriot. Browsing among the tatters of the "rag-pickers," the narrator stumbles across "a little narrative of . . . adventures, forlornly published on sleazy gray paper."[42] Out of "this blurred record" consigned to the dingy annals of obscurity, the narrator commemorates the life of a democratic hero who fought at Bunker Hill and humbly dedicates the resulting product to "His Highness the Bunker-Hill Monument" (425). Even though Israel dies impoverished and insignificant, when subjected to the elixir of democratic biography, he rises up, his story mingling with the architectural sublime of this monumental icon. The monument, a political echo of the "all" seen by Emerson's "transparent eye-ball," may "be deemed the Great Biographer" (426); it is through the influence of this lofty eminence that the almost forgotten Israel enters the currents of American national history. Melville imparts all this information in a preface dated June 17, 1854, the anniversary of American resistance to British forces on the heights above Boston. Monumental history once again works its democratic wonders of time, space, and status: barriers of time, centuries long, evaporate, and spatial divisions of low and high, common and noble, forgotten and remembered, dissipate in a sublime homogeneity of subject, biographer, and national history.

Just as orators held as indispensable the role of public desire in the erection of a monument, the design of *Israel Potter* emerged from Melville's anticipations of common readers. Although Melville lay his biography at the base of "His Highness," the popular mind guided the biographer. Aware that the novel was to appear serially in *Putnam's Monthly Magazine*, he wrote the editors: "I engage that the story shall contain nothing of any sort to shock the fastidious. There will be very little reflective writing in it; nothing weighty. It is adventure." The author who had declared his reluctance to write in accordance with the tastes of a widespread audience now, after the commercial failures of *Moby-Dick* and *Pierre*, took notice of the "bare common" and constructed a tale calculated to please a mass readership. He seems of the breed of vigorous intellectuals called forth by Emerson in "The American Scholar" who will "embrace the common . . . and explore and sit at the feet of the familiar, the low" (68–69); he agrees with the editorial position in *Harper's* that history "has presented us only with names of isolated pre-eminence. The time has come when we 'must change all that.'"[43] The authorial sovereign who killed off characters in *Mardi* with regal indifference and alienated readers with a belabored allegory experimented with democratic authority.

The popular dynamics informing Melville's narrative give birth to a democratic hero. Israel enacts his American story in a prose whose religious and political overtones replay the national history of revolution and liberation. Fleeing the oppressive conditions under his patriarchal roof, shunning "the tyranny of this father," Israel departs for new lands, the frontier, though this quest will eventually and ironically land him back to the fleshpots and prisons of the Old World (435). He enters a textual landscape marked by tenets of hard work and opportunity similar to the world described in *Letters from an American Farmer*; like Crèvecoeur's outcast immigrant from the Scottish Hebrides who achieves the American Dream, Israel collects his wages, purchases a tract of land, clears it, and establishes a homestead. But once seized by that unquiet American spirit, he lights out for the territories, becoming an Ishmael wandering in the wilderness as a surveyor, hunter, trapper, quick-witted peddler, and Nantucket harpooner. Israel stumbles across an American identity in his restlessness, falling into generic company with the archetypal Yankee folk hero, the jack-of-all-trades. The itinerant and changing nature of his commercial endeavors requires wit and native intelligence, characteristics to become embedded in the national folk fabric as American know-how and ingenuity. When the always pursued Israel outwits his captors by masquerading as a scarecrow or by intoxicating English sailors though remaining sober himself, he reveals his kinship with the "agile, jig-dancing, shrewd, talkative, humorous, flaxen-haired hero," Brother Jonathan of the early 1800s, who would evolve into Uncle Sam.[44]

The cultural distinctness of Israel's Americanisms leads to a notorious, though common, articulation of a politicized self that inevitably conflicts with the Old World mores of British culture. An original American son, Israel stands as independent from Europe as Jefferson's mammoths or as innocent as Cole's sketch of the United

States' historically virgin landscape. The young patriot naturally takes up arms at Bunker Hill, where his previous days in the woods shooting deer give him the marksman's skills to take exact aim "between the golden epaulettes" of the officers as though he were shooting "between the branching antlers" (440). Rustic talent with the rifle translates into monumental resistance to the legions of the British pharaoh. Israel, however, is taken prisoner at a later engagement and transported to England, beginning his fifty years of Babylonian captivity. Escaping from an English prison ship soon after, Israel nevertheless remains imprisoned within the confines of exile. Although he evades detection by disguising himself as a cripple, a ghost, a gardener in the king's garden, and a London brickmaker under the taskmasters of "the English Egypt," only with difficulty can Israel conceal his particularly American spirit (602). Unable to quell the distaste for patriarchal authority that first led him to "emancipat[e] himself from his sire," Israel cannot subdue his innate passion for independence: he fails, no matter how much he might try, to address his employer as "Sir John" and not "Mr. Millet"; he touches, but cannot bring himself to remove his hat when he bumps into King George along the walks of the garden; and he informs the monarch "firmly, but with deep respect, 'I have no king'" (434, 460). Politically as well as aesthetically, Israel springs up from humble origins to mature as a transcendent type in whom a community of nineteenth-century Americans would share a common cultural legacy. The calculated popularity of Israel's fictional figure transforms a forgotten soldier of Bunker Hill into a nationally recognized icon.

To say, however, that Melville inscribed himself as a writer of democracy simply because he considered what the popular mind would consume would be fallacious. Though he made his home in the democracy of nineteenth-century America, Melville thought himself as much an exile as Israel Potter. As Richard Brodhead observes, Melville's novels and correspondence often contained "brutal assaults on his readers and on American literary culture."[45] Melville found companionship only in his own forlorn fictional creation, Bartleby; both would "prefer not to" copy and write within the accepted forms of notation or narration. Bartleby's fate is well known; finding no place in society, he dies huddled at the base of a prison wall. Ishmael represented a more encouraging example for

Melville by overcoming alienation to outline a "ruthless democracy" in his friendship with a tattooed savage speaking broken English. Yet Melville could not enter into such a contractual agreement with the urbane and literate transcendental thinker of *Nature*. After hearing this popularizer of monumentalism give a lecture, Melville wrote: "I do not oscillate in Emerson's rainbow, but prefer rather to hang myself in mine own halter than swing any other man's swing."[46] And in "The Mast-Head" chapter of *Moby-Dick*, Ishmael effectively parodies Emerson's transcendental sublime, cautioning those who would swing from the top of an isolated eminence. Ishmael muses in an Emersonian strain, only to arrive at a grim reminder of the consequences of forgetting the self within transcendental currents:

> but lulled into such an opium-like listlessness of vacant, unconscious reverie is this absent-minded youth by the blending cadence of waves with thoughts, that at last he loses his identity, takes the mystic ocean at his feet for the visible image of that deep, blue, bottomless soul, pervading mankind and nature; and every strange half-seen, gliding, beautiful thing that eludes him . . . seems to him the embodiment of those elusive thoughts that only people the soul by continually flitting through it. In this enchanted mood, thy spirit ebbs away to whence it came; becomes diffused through time and space. . . . There is no life in thee, now, except that rocking life imparted by a gently rolling ship; by her, borrowed from the sea; by the sea, from the inscrutable tides of God. But while this sleep, this dream is on ye, move your foot or hand an inch; slip your hold at all; and your identity comes back in horror. Over Descartian vortices you hover. And perhaps, at mid-day, in the fairest weather, with one half-throttled shriek you drop through that transparent air into the summer sea, no more to rise for ever. Heed it well, ye Pantheists! (136)

Transcending to an elevated state where soul and cosmos become mutually transparent is not without its dangers. Unity, capable of expanding the individual to the scale of an empire, is also capable of effacing the individual in that expansion. Melville's quarrel with Emerson encompassed more than the ether of ontology, however; his comic imitation points to the blindness of the "transparent eyeball" and its destructive consequences for the citizen living within a political culture dedicated to monumentalism. Following the tastes of the American public and gratifying a culture pursuing the monumental may produce a paste-board mask of democracy, but not the "ruthless" substance of democracy necessary for the uniqueness of individual contribution and participation.

Despite its status as a memorial pillar to democracy, the Bunker Hill Monument obscured the patriot of democracy. When democracy became reified as a monumental structure, it loomed over the individual; when the representation of democracy achieved a grand scale, the individual forfeited political, local, biographical specificity in an exchange for a national identity that overrode and silenced the particular heroism as well as the personal tragedies of a common, exiled citizen such as Israel. Like much of nineteenth-century American culture, the April 1852 issue of *Harper's* could acknowledge the desirability of monumental modes of historical representation even as it affirmed without qualms that "national memory [or] . . . *public spirit* is often most blindly destructive of *private interest.*"[47] Stranded in England for a half century, Israel returns to the promised land of democracy on a day specifically designated for remembrance—the Fourth of July. He steps ashore in Boston and meets a mass celebration commemorating the heroes of Bunker Hill. In this sense, the monumental performs the key function of preserving the hero's fragile actions with a symbolic recollection. The monumental administers a civic memory, integral in instructing post-Revolutionary sons to remember the indispensable foundations laid by the American fathers. At the same time, however, Israel reaches "the Fortunate Isles of the Free" only to discover his exile remains intact (611). The patriotism enacted by Israel, now reified as public ritual, has no need for Israel: "the old man narrowly escaped being run over by a patriotic triumphal car in the procession, flying a broidered banner, inscribed with gilt letters:—'BUNKER-HILL. 1775. GLORY TO THE HEROES THAT FOUGHT!'" (613). The American fervor for monumental remembrance inadvertently tramples the citizen who, ironically, may have performed the very deeds that are being remembered. Although the public enthusiastically reaffirms the bravery of men like Israel, it has little space to commemorate Israel himself. America, able to articulate democracy only in monumental proportions, cannot construct a panegyric to a democratic individual and has no place for Israel; the former minuteman finds sanctuary only on Copp's Hill, a position occupied by British troops during the battle, to view the ceremonies at the "incipient monument" (613).

Undertones of monumentalism's pitfalls exist even within the ebullient dedication of *Israel Potter*. The narrator lavishes praise upon the patriotic column and concludes with a simile that yokes together Israel and the monument, but it is an uncomfortable union: "[I wish] summer's suns may shine as brightly on your brow as each winter snow shall lightly rest on the grave of Israel Potter" (426). The incongruities uneasily paralleling summer and winter, high and low, radiance and solemnity, all prevent the reassuring supposition of a sublime harmony that might raise up Israel out of his neglected grave. Even in death, Israel remains alienated, untouched by the impassive mode of the history reified by the Bunker Hill Monument. Unconcerned with Israel, unconcerned with the lost children of democracy, this "Great Biographer," whose intractable granite composition Melville emphasizes, stands above the subjects it honors. Under the aegis of monumental history, the political citizen is forgotten. This is not to say, however, that a sublime configuration of history could make no place for the individual. Just as the descending torrent in a painting of Niagara Falls diminishes the human figure, locating the individual as a minuscule element of the natural order, so, too, the historical sublime understood the individual as part of a greater historical process. Israel's life has meaning only insofar as it conforms to a national history too myopic to notice and avoid running him down with "a patriotic triumphal car." Under the gaze of "the Great Biographer," Israel becomes nameless and joins ranks with "the anonymous privates of June 17, 1775, who may never have received other requital than the solid reward of your [the Bunker Hill Monument's] granite" (426). Once enveloped by the iconic representation of the independence he defended, Israel forfeits the spirit of resistance he had faithfully preserved throughout his long years of exile and becomes dependent upon monumental history. Remembered as an anonymous patriot of Bunker Hill, Israel loses his identity as a sufferer exiled from America and achieves a new identity as an alienated subject marked by the nonmarkings of historical obscurity and political neurasthenia.[48]

Gathered up in the folds of a processional banner, Israel Potter as a human actor ceases to have significance. He forms an incidental part of the historical picture, just as the shrunken figures emphasize the natural order in a landscape portrait. Whether in the depiction of nature or the monumental representation of American history, a

mystified process subsumes the individual. Yet an important difference exists: whereas the "natural" need not embrace human action, American history and the politics it remembers is a discursive
space of human creation where individuals should be able to act and
appear to one another as citizens. What Hannah Arendt calls the
"space of appearance," where citizens speak and act to "reveal
actively their unique personal identities and thus make their appearance in the human world," dwindles and decays before a mammoth construction of history designed to be stable and immortal in
contradistinction to the fragility of human affairs. In short, the national architecture of monumental representation in the nineteenth
century invalidated politics. The discourse of American monumentalism held that monolithic iconic remembrance would supplant the
doddering and transitory memory of human deeds with a more
permanent icon of history. Although most dedications honored the
veterans of Bunker Hill who attended the 1825 groundbreaking
ceremonies, noting the "venerable men, the relics of a past generation, with emaciated frames, tottering limbs, and trembling voices,"
orators and writers mentioned these individual patriots only to gain
support for a less frail historical construction. By the time of the
monument's completion in 1843, Webster would stand before the
column and deny his own human agency as a participant in historical
discourse: the monument "is itself the orator of this occasion. It is not
from my lips, it could not be from any human lips, that that strain
of eloquence is this day to flow most competent to move and excite
the vast multitudes around me."[49]

Transcendent and unifying, the Bunker Hill Monument was the
sublime national icon. Webster's optimism that its lessons and history
would extend to "vast multitudes" depended upon monumentalism
in several ways. Its expansive, highly visible character allowed for the
enactment of democracy on a grand scale, but also imperative to the
perpetuation of Webster's democracy was an understanding of *monere* as an action of reminding and instructing Americans in examples
of civic virtue garnered from the past. Without *monere*, citizens would
lapse into forgetfulness of the founding principles. The monument,
however, was to guard against prodigal sons, becoming, as Webster
hoped, a ritual space of memory where "troops of ingenuous youth
shall be gathered . . . [and] there shall rise from every youthful breast
the ejaculation, "Thank God, I—I also—AM AN AMERICAN!" Yet ironically, in its triumph over time, Webster's version of the monumental

sacrifices the vital element of human responsibility and participation that characterizes a notion of republican remembrance best expressed by Lincoln in his 1838 address before the Young Men's Lyceum. Lincoln called for a *"political religion* of the nation" that, however improvident it may have seemed, could be located, lived, and experienced, only in subjects who would appear tenuous, ephemeral, and impermanent in comparison with the durability of the monumental. Rather than preserving history within a monolithic icon of remembrance, a diffused structure of republican memory had to be supported by "other pillars," whose rag-tag heterogeneity—"the old and the young, the rich and the poor, the grave and the gay, of all sexes and tongues, and colors and conditions"—defied the aesthetic and political principles of unified, enduring construction.[50] Like Webster, Lincoln acknowledged the imperative of preserving the founding legacy, but unlike Webster, he saw that democratic principles could be transmitted only by human beings. Icons, uninhabited by citizens, played no role in Lincoln's thinking. Whereas Webster preferred to trust the "Great Biographer," Lincoln understood that history, if it was to preserve an inheritance of participatory democracy, had to arise from human articulation.

Emerson also pronounced the death of politics, but little grief accompanied his announcement. In "Heroism" he writes: "Who that sees the meanness of our politics, but inly congratulates Washington that he is long already wrapped in his shroud, and for ever safe" (381). Death emerges as the supreme moment of historical transcendence, the summit where one forever escapes the obstacles that could sully the self with the physical dealings of the "bare common." Emerson's outlook emphatically opposed federal orderings, leading him to declare that "every actual State is corrupt" ("Politics," 563). What appeared in the void, perhaps unforeseen by Emerson, was not the ideal state founded on individual conscience, but the nation-state. The apex of politics was to be not involved in politics at all. Emerson represented the culmination of history as a sacrosanct realm that citizens enter only upon forfeiture of their lives, specific, full, and local. Advancing beyond Webster's understanding of the Bunker Hill Monument as a triumph over time, the Emerson of monumental culture posited the national historical icon as a triumph over life. Ishmael's parody of the transcendental dreamer atop the masthead— "There is no life in thee"—reads as the epitaph of Lincoln's republican citizen. In its sublime, transcendent configuration, monumental history stifled civic being; it resulted in the nihilistic slogan "Let the dead bury the living."[51]

The edifices towering over the Israels and Melvilles evoked what transpired within the culture of monumentalism as acting politically gave way to a fabricated remembrance that precluded the necessarily impermanent and unpredictable quality of action. The individual became a speck in the political landscape. Immediately after the speaker in *Nature* announces "I become a transparent eye-ball," material being fades, and he declares "I am nothing; I see all" (10). Despite the focus on "all," which may indicate ideals of brotherhood and community, Carolyn Porter states that within this passage the "rhetorical emphasis falls on the predicates, distracting us from the miraculous return in the second clause of the 'I' who has just been voided by the first. Swallowed up by its role as seer, the material self disappears."[52] This unsubstantial self can hardly participate in the materiality of daily life and the politics that emerge from life thus lived. Transcendence, although it may originate in the "bare common," severs the citizen from all the things—history, place, community, desire—that make him or her a citizen. Concern for a vital political community vanishes in an ethereal atmosphere: "The name of the nearest friend then sounds foreign and accidental: to be brothers, to be acquaintances, master or servant, is then a trifle and a disturbance" (*Nature*, 10). Politics are sublimated, as though the affairs of "street and village," the happenings that can occur only within public spaces, corrupt individuals. Emerson expands this view to affirm the value of a transcendent existence unconcerned with acting or speaking in the world, the sole ways to realize civic self-definition. He does not sing the praises of the political citizen; instead, he prefers the apolitical being whom he celebrates in "The Poet": "Thou shalt leave the world, and know the muse only. Thou shalt not know any longer the times, customs, graces, politics, or opinions of men, but shalt take all from the muse" (467). Monumental culture encouraged the purification of the individual, and it carried forth that process until any political sensibility was refined out of being.

CRITICAL MASS
AND CRITICAL HISTORY

Although the "Great Biographer" eventually conscripts Israel Potter to the forces of monumental historical progress, Melville preserves the vibrancy of human political action in writing *Israel Potter*. Turning to the subversive possibilities of irony and humor, Melville offers a strategy of biography calculated to undermine the monumentalism to which he pays tribute in his preface. Despite what appears to be the preface's abdication to the orthodox history of the iconic shaft, Melville safeguards the heroism of individual action, refusing to surrender his novel to the grand iconic moments and figures of American history. The narrator obsequiously approaches the Bunker Hill Monument, begging excuse for the slight changes he has made in the 1824 prototype of his tale, *Life and Remarkable Adventures of Israel R. Potter*: "Well aware that in your Highness' eyes the merit of the story must be in its general fidelity to the main drift of the original narrative, I forbore anywhere to mitigate the hard fortunes of my hero" or to retouch significantly the events described in that "tattered copy" (425). Melville, however, shared his hero's propensity for evasion and deception: just as Israel masquerades as a lowly beggar to escape notice, Melville adopted the disguise of a sycophant cowering before the icon of monumental historical narrative in order to tell another, properly human story. As a fugitive, Israel understands the potential risk "if he adhered to the strict truth" and thus cloaks his identity as an escaped Yankee (507). And as a novelist aware of his own fugitive dissent from a culture's passion for monumental historical representation, Melville discovered he too had to depart from any notion of "strict truth."[53]

While Melville's preface pledges historical faithfulness, his narrative betrays any confidence in the author's avowed regard for "general fidelity" to monumental history. Melville puffs up monumental history only to give it the exaggerated dimension needed for parody. He appears to revel in the grand stature of heroes like John Paul Jones or Benjamin Franklin, but this act of filial honor actually initiates the practice of parricidal criticism. That is, Melville enters the domain of monumental history as a subversive, employing parody to critique the iconic substance and construction of American national legacies. Parody as parricide attains its critical force by creating a disjunction in the patriarchal inheritance. Rewriting the history of the fathers in this ironic mode places the fathers at variance with themselves: at one moment they are unquestionable paragons of national virtue and at the next stifling buffoons. Parody indeed behaves as parricide, for it poses as a dutiful son and adopts a reverential attitude toward history, except that the posture becomes overblown, suggesting that the fathers expect too much deference and humility.[54]

In both the original narrative and Melville's refurbished version, Israel enjoys the honor of meeting Benjamin Franklin; however, in its sardonic portrayal of Franklin, Melville's biography commits far more than the "one or two shiftings" he apologizes for in the preface. Whereas the *Life and Remarkable Adventures of Israel R. Potter* succinctly wraps up the encounter with the venerable sage by saying "My interview with Dr. Franklin was a pleasing one—for nearly an hour he conversed with me in the most agreeable and instructive manner," Melville's story approaches this archetypal American at both great length and ironic distance.[55] He expands Potter's single sentence into four chapters, until the representation of Franklin collapses under its own weight. What begins as a scene where "stray bits of strange models in wood and metal" and books on "history, mechanics, diplomacy, agriculture, political economy, metaphysics, meteorology" attest to Franklin's prodigious mind soon degenerates into a caricature of an old man who employs dogmatic homilies to stifle the desires of youth (468). Although the visible signs of Franklin's intellect and maxims from *Poor Richard's Almanack* impress Israel, the exile feels constrained by the paradigmatic American who denies him brandy to substitute "white wine of the very oldest brand"—water—who discourages him from humor, counseling "never permit yourself to be jocose upon pecuniary matters. Never joke at funerals, or during business transactions," and who insists upon "business before pleasure" when Israel would rather explore the mysteries of Paris (475, 473, 474).

The narrator begs pardon for manifesting Franklin "in his far lesser lights; thrifty, domestic, dietarian, and, it may be didactically waggish" (479). Yet Melville intensifies the burlesque so that Franklin's insistence on "business before pleasure, my friend. You must absolutely remain in your room, just as if you were my prisoner," takes on an ominous and oppressive truth (474). Israel is trapped within an icon of American independence. Monumental culture, with all its patriarchal implications, afflicts Israel as he prepares for bed when Franklin enters the room, removes the cordials and pastries, and scolds his guest for flirting with the chambermaid. Franklin resembles Israel's father-tyrant who refuses to let his son marry the girl next door; the only difference is that Franklin's fatherly guidance is more insidious, insincere, and encompassing. Israel complains of this pervasive and prohibitive patriarch who insists upon dependence at each turn: "Every time he comes in he robs me . . . with an air all the time, too, as if he were making me presents. If he thinks me such a very sensible young man, why not let me take care of myself?" (486). Under the roof of an icon who does not see this wanderer as an individual, but as one indistinct part of the public addressed en masse in *Poor Richard*, Israel finds his goals and desires incarcerated—in short, he cannot act with independence. While patriarchal solicitude confines our hero in Franklin's lodging house, Melville escapes via the trapdoors of irony and satire. For instance, when the wise man confiscates the pleasures in Israel's room and warns him of the chambermaid, "an artful Ammonite," Franklin adds wantonly: "I think I had better convey your message to the girl forthwith" (485).

Recovering what is not included in the iconic—in this case the putative lechery of Franklin—Melville's revisionary history disables any projected leaps towards transcendence. Sublime lechers remain inescapably mired in the "bare common," hardly the stuff of patriotic lore. Wit and humor conspire to suggest an individualized space not authorized by the monumental figure of history. We might call this individualized space a story, as opposed to the generalized eminence of history, which tells the life of a hero who may possess no sublime qualities. Narrative, as Melville realized, is vitally political: narrative strategies can lead either to a story or to history, to heroes as human as Queequeg and Israel or to icons as lifeless and indifferent as Washington "aloft on his towering main-mast in Baltimore." *Israel Potter* makes a definite choice in this matter, resolutely following a failed story of a failed hero. Despite these bleak circumstances, *Israel Potter* reclaims an older inheritance in which the story reveals every human actor as a hero. The word *hero*, according to Arendt, in its earliest connotations implies particularity and difference. In Homer, "hero" indicated "no more than a name given each free man who participated in the Trojan enterprise and about whom a story could be told." Thus, while Israel certainly is, as Peter Bellis suggests, "a decidedly antiheroic figure, alienated from and dispossessed by history itself," Israel is also a hero because he falls outside the structures of history and is capable of being represented only in a novel constructed from discarded and repressed memory.[56]

Indistinct and indistinguishable from the forgotten mass, Israel nevertheless forms part of a critical mass. Foucault's sense of the panoptic regime identifies the individualized space of Israel's story as the most insidious reach of iconic repression, but elsewhere Foucault stresses that the local, regional spaces steeped with "popular knowledges" and "disqualified knowledges" are precisely where "criticism performs its work." Counter-memory appears in these stories saturated with nonauthoritative knowledges that can be used to articulate criticism of official forms of history. Berlant makes effective use of Foucault's notion of counter-memory in her study of Hawthorne. Even at sites infused with the discourses of official culture, such as the female body of Hester Prynne, counter-memory resides. If counter-memory, as Berlant states, is "a politically neutral category of knowledge and experience," it nevertheless contains the potential to evolve as a site of challenge, contestation, and criticism. Thus, the letter *A* signifies the inscription of the body with theocratic law, but the *A* also slips outside of this official codification. No longer dependent upon established regimes of thought, the *A* "circulates among the people, [and] becomes a vehicle for its imagination, a site on which a local collectivity emerges." From such sites, according to Foucault, the "local character of criticism" emerges as a "noncentralised kind of theoretical production"; for Berlant's reading of *The Scarlet Letter*, such theoretical work leads to the articulation of local heterotopias that effectively challenge the hegemonic structure of American nationalist discourse.[57]

One can locate similar instances of counter-memory embodied within *Israel Potter*. And, as Israel Potter becomes *Israel Potter*, as autobiography is reinscribed within the narrative strategy of Melville's biography, counter-memory evolves into critical history. The cross of saber scars on his chest provides an alternate memory to the unreflective puffery of patriotic history surrounding the Bunker Hill Monument. But in the end, counter-memory remains inert for Israel; as an instance of counter-memory, his story has "faded out of print—himself out of being—his name out of memory" (615). Melville, however, realized the potential dormant in Israel's counter-memory. Whereas Franklin addresses Israel as part of the uncritical mass in need of Poor Richard's wisdom, and whereas Israel understands himself as a nonpolitical entity dismissed by American history, within Melville's novel, Israel forms part of a critical mass productive of what Nietzsche calls critical history. Critical history offers more than the solace of resistance experienced within pockets of knowledge that have escaped incorporation into official discourse. While it may originate in a local situation, critical history moves beyond the local to examine grand, entrenched moments and monuments of history. In other words, critical history begins with counter-memory, but soon sloughs off its particularly local character to assess and even destroy seemingly implacable narratives of national history.

This distinction between counter-memory and critical history lies in the difference between Israel Potter and *Israel Potter*, between the politics of identity found in the autobiography of an oppressed Revolutionary soldier and the ironic practices found in a novelist's destabilizing historiography. Disgusted by the "riotous crowd" rallying around the Bunker Hill Monument, Israel returns to his rural birthplace in the Housatonic valley, futilely hoping to recapture local counter-memories that might identify him as his father's son and not the lost and forgotten son of America (613). *Israel Potter*, in contrast, practices critical history, reworking a national narrative as homogeneous as the uniform granite blocks of the Bunker Hill Monument so that it becomes disarticulated into a series of incomplete portraits and fractured histories. Israel's permanent exile—his homecoming leads to recognition of the tragic depth of his cultural abandonment—presents the biography of a nation whose sameness has become alienated in contradiction and irony. As a disjunctive repetition of the Revolution, Melville's novel fulfills Nietzsche's imperative that discourse must bring the past "before the tribunal, scrupulously examining it and finally condemning it." No matter how sublime the Bunker Hill Monument, no matter how revered the character of Dr. Franklin, *Israel Potter* resituates these fixed icons of national remembrance as ambivalent narratives doubtful of the nationalist project that those icons represent. As discourse, *Israel Potter* declares along with Nietzsche: "Every past . . . is worthy to be condemned."[58]

Melville had as little chance of eradicating a repressive, iconic Franklin from American cultural consciousness as he did of toppling the Bunker Hill Monument or even of forcing his way into the Washington Monument when it was closed. Yet Melville's purpose was not to destroy monumental history and make the American public an unhistorical herd, but to democratize implacable icons and make them subject to the participation of human interpretation. Rather than uproot Franklin, Melville intended to reinterpret such fixtures of monumental history as "spaces of appearance," as "bare commons" where citizens would not sublimate or transcend politics, but would appear as articulate political beings, revealing their human distinctness as they speak and act together. Melville's configuration of Franklin suggests abandoning docile reverence for what Nietzsche calls "Olympian laughter." It is "Olympian laughter" that allowed Melville to declare "that a thief in jail is as honorable as Gen. George Washington"; it is with the heroic humor of *Israel Potter* that Melville hurled the critical irony embedded within the "nobody" of this American Odysseus into the Cyclops eye of monumental history. Without such laughter, without such irony that smirks at the iconic representation of Franklin, criticizes the mode of history embodied by the "Great Biographer," and pillages Emerson's transcendental democracy to render it a space for parody, monumental culture engineers its own exile and imprisonment. As Nietzsche asks: what are the consequences "when the impotent and indolent take possession of it [monumental history] and employ it!" National narrative, no matter how many different democratic agents intone its promises, encourages representation founded upon the violence of political abstraction. Unless the citizen can reveal the iconic as ironic, the human endeavor of cultural remembrance becomes an unassailable representation of history.[59]

4

Monuments, Fathers, Slaves

Configurations of an Ironic History

*This is called the "land of the free, and home of the brave"; it
is called the "Asylum of the oppressed"; and some have been
foolish enough to call it the "Cradle of Liberty." If it is the
"cradle of liberty," they have rocked the child to death.*
— William Wells Brown, lecture delivered before
the Female Anti-Slavery Society of Salem at
Lyceum Hall, November 14, 1847

THE SEARCH FOR
NATIONAL LITERATURE

Literary nationalists looked across the expanse of the antebellum
landscape in hopes of sighting signs of a monumental author who
would place American letters on a map of literature still imprinted
with the claims of France and England. Herman Melville, taking up
the nativist banner of Young America, saw a race of cultural Titans
in America's future. "Believe me, my friends, that Shakespeares are
this day being born on the banks of the Ohio," he wrote in his
review of Hawthorne that simultaneously served as a reflection on
the state of American letters. More recently, Lauren Berlant has
suggested the interconnections between the desire to forge a homogeneous national space and citizens' impulses to produce art. "'The
American Renaissance,'" explains Berlant, "emerged under widespread pressure to develop a set of symbolic national references
whose possession would signify and realize the new political and
social order."[1] Art and politics should be bound in a sympathetic
union in which democratic literature would keep pace with democratic institutions. Literature would reach its most sublime moments
insofar as it was able to provide a national primer. Americans
searching for their nation did not look to the past, but sought literature as a guide to a future promised land, an outline of a New
World civilization. Shakespeares, emerging on a frontier horizon
already open to settlement, would one day mature as specimens of
national genius.

Separating their nation from the Old World, both geographically and politically, American reviewers, editors, and novelists conceived of the nation as a radical break from the previous accumulation of history. In the same breath that nationalists prophesied a Manifest Destiny, they forecast aesthetic originality as the dominant strain of national greatness. American civilization would be independent of Europe, just as its land mass was separate and its government was distinguished from all others by its democracy; it would belong to the future and not the past. John Louis O'Sullivan, the editorialist who coined the phrase "Manifest Destiny," declared cultural independence for the sons of the Revolution: "Our national birth was the beginning of a new history, the formation and progress of an untried political system, which separates us from the past and connects us with the future only. . . . we may confidently assume, that our country is destined to be *the great nation* of futurity."[2]

Melville prophesied the shape and scope of original American literature by turning to the future of the West, by turning to Manifest Destiny. Casting aside the urge to imitate European successes, the American writer would harness the bold power of a spectacular landscape, making his expression match a nation ever expanding its dominions. The "broad prairies are in his soul," wrote Melville of the American writer.[3] Literary nationalists evoked a literature undoubtedly "American" in spirit and origin, owing allegiance to no foreign model; it would be self-devised, arisen out of a Platonic conception of itself as American. Once imbued with an ineffable Americanness, national literature would act as a democratic medium for the inscription of the narrative defining a homogeneous people, collectively affirming with a single voice cherished traditions of freedom and equality.

Yet compared with the Jacksonian claims of an expanding democracy, burgeoning industrial development, and accumulating territorial possessions, the progress of American letters seemed sorely lagging. The sympathetic union between art and politics had not been realized. Assessing the intellectual climate at midcentury, Theodore Parker confessed his country's literary output was inferior to European productions. Parker identified a national literature by its distinctively embarrassing attributes; surveying the "permanent and instantial literature of America," he pronounced in 1849, the "individuality of the nation is not there, except in the cheap, gaudy binding of the work. The nationality of America is stamped on the lids, and vulgarly blazoned on the back." American books, laboring under what Melville called "literary flunkeyism," could never imprint individuality or any other national lesson. Armed with the legacies of Washington and Jefferson, democracy seemed unstoppable until it met up with "American Goldsmiths" and "American Miltons"—in Melville's disdainful comparison—whose aesthetic principles carried expression more appropriately suited to stuffy English society. Parker dejectedly characterized the American scene: "Our muse does not come down from an American Parnassus, with a new heaven in her eye. . . . [Instead] she has a little dwelling in the flat and close pent town, hard by the public street."[4] Impoverished in an era of unprecedented economic growth and political confidence, American literature partook of nothing sublime or monumental. Even so, within the cultural desert of this adolescent nation, Parker glimpsed a spot of originality. Unfortunately, these expressions of originality hardly enhanced America's cultural or political position among the nations of the world. And besides, he doubted whether this American-bred writing should even be considered literature:

> Yet, there is one portion of our permanent literature, if literature it may be called, which is wholly independent and original. The lives of the early martyrs and confessors are purely Christian, so are the legends of saints and other pious men; there was no thing like this in the Hebrew of heathen literature, cause and occasion were alike wanting for it. So we have one series of literary productions that could be written by none but Americans, and only here; I mean the lives of the Fugitive Slaves. But as these are not the work of men of superior culture they hardly help to pay the scholar's debt. Yet all the original romance of Americans is in them, not in the white man's novel.[5]

Parker's observation is undercut by his consideration that the slave narrative diminishes America's stature in two ways: the very existence of slave narratives indicts the principle of freedom that makes America a political pinnacle among nations of the world, and slave narratives, "not the work of men of superior culture," hardly represent monuments of national triumph for entry on the world literary stage. Narratives that reveal severely compromised democratic principles fail to provide foundations stable or patriotic enough for a

swaggering cultural monumentalism. Instead of signifying a cornu-
copia of originality—consistent with a limitless landscape or an un-
paralleled experiment in democracy—the testimony of fugitive
slaves demarcates the hollowness of freedom and the failure of white
American writers.

To safeguard the purity of national literature, Parker implies that
an insuperable gulf lies between the slave narrative and America, but
such a demarcation was false. Slavery pervaded nationalism as an
ever-present reminder of political sin, a repressed context always
threatening to return and rebel against the foundations of a monumental American culture. No matter how resolutely antebellum intellectuals might claim the Negro race and its contributions to be of
an inferior culture, not to be integrated in the proud monuments and
memories of history, Northern liberals demanded the inclusion of
slavery in any articulation of the American nation. Abolitionists cited
founding principles in their denunciations of political immorality.
Even slaves inscribed radical selves with appeals to the words and
actions of original American patriots, therefore assuring that racial
politics entered into dialogue with a legacy ironically authorized by
American history itself. In short, as Toni Morrison has insisted,
"miscegenation" informs, rather than detracts from, a sacred body
of American texts. Interpreters of texts, writes Morrison, have "made
wonderful work of some wonderful work," finding in the novels of
Melville, Twain, and others a pure aesthetic that transcends race,
culminating in a monument of "universal" literature. But an awareness of "miscegenation" argues against any conjured purity of literary tradition, reinvesting American literature with "unspeakable
things unspoken," suggesting how words, images, metaphors—in
short, meaning—derives from an African American presence that
has been repressed through the wonders of interpretation.[6]

Encouraging critics toward a "re-examination of founding literature in the United States," Morrison's strategy seems a not too
distant echo of mid-nineteenth-century works whose commitment to
republican theorizing reconceived the founding narratives of a nation. In sharp distinction to both abolitionists and proslavery thinkers
who equally employed the irony of juxtaposition to lament the
present as a degradation of a coherent past, republicans did not seek
to explain how an ordered past indicted the present. Republican
thinking did not accept the idea of an ordered or consistent past.

Rather, republicans understood that irony belied the moments of founding, that the meaning of American history was to be found in a legacy riddled with irony and inconsistency. Such thinking evaded the ideological consensus that Sacvan Bercovitch defines as inherent to dissenting jeremiads against the present in American culture. For Bercovitch, the criticism of America upholds the ideals of America; to "denounce American life," he writes, "was to endorse the national dream." Thus, although abolitionist jeremiads scathingly condemned 1850s America, these denunciations nonetheless reaffirmed national foundings by assailing slavery as a political and moral aberration from the principles of 1776. When William Lloyd Garrison prefaced Frederick Douglass's *Narrative* by reminding his audience that this fugitive slave is exposed to the risk of slavecatchers even "on the soil of the Pilgrim Fathers, among the descendants of revolutionary sires," he more than signals his outrage at current political variance with the past; he also rededicates his listeners to the foundations of the national mission.[7]

Bercovitch's analysis of how the "ritual of the jeremiad bespeaks an ideological consensus" certainly enables a compelling understanding of the particular resilience of the status quo and authorizing tenets of American culture.[8] Yet there is a risk that such an understanding can become too compelling, that the perception of ideological consensus can minimize republican acts that challenge the sacred past as well as the immoral present. No doubt Bercovitch is correct in suggesting the grim view of an inescapable American ideology in which citizens and noncitizens evoke national ideals to critique the nation. Ideology, Bercovitch contends, is flexible enough to contain this apparent contradiction. But not all those who decried the abuses of America did so by appealing to a sacred past. For some, that past was never sacred. Republican thinking, unlike the jeremiad, does not become misled in using an unquestionable past to excoriate current conditions; instead, it questions the past that had seemed beyond reproof or censure. William Wells Brown, Herman Melville, and Abraham Lincoln all act as republicans, not by ironically positioning nineteenth-century slavery against the legacy of 1776, but by reading slavery into that legacy. In the same way that Machiavelli in the *Discourses* writes a republican history by not shrinking from the origins of states stained with bloodshed and deceit, Brown's autobiographies, Melville's tale "The Bell-Tower," and Lincoln's most famous speeches all acknowledged the impurity and imperfection of American origins. Each reexamines the political traces of race within the foundations of America and discovers a set of national origins irresolvably disfigured by freedom coupled with slavery, by civic virtue cloaking political sin, and by a conception of liberty shot through with rapacity. Their critical approach does not simply bemoan the degeneration of the virtue of the past into the vice of the present; instead, the republican criticism of Brown, Melville, and Lincoln configures America's origins within a radical irony by juxtaposing founding history, not against the corrupt present, but against itself. These American republicans decry national origins that are also the nation's own moral aberration, a history at variance with its own sanctified authority.

THE INCONGRUITY OF RACE
IN WILLIAM WELLS BROWN'S HISTORY

Before pursuing these thinkers' ironic construction of the grand national past, it is first necessary to observe the racial dimensions, often repressed, of America's monumentalism. So imposing was the political and aesthetic unity of the monumental that the disjunctive element of race became a minor detail, in the same way that artistic representations of diminutive figures of Native Americans at the base of Niagara contribute to the overall splendor of the natural and national scene. This monumental vision enabled one orator to liken Washington's home at Mount Vernon to "the sublime cataract of Niagara," relying on the scale and purity of the natural landscape to uplift the domestic to the level of a national shrine while outstripping the baser associations of commerce and compulsion that were the mainstays of what was euphemistically called the "domestic institution." The monuments and icons of American culture represented a history untarnished by the tyranny, oppression, and serfdom that marred Europe's past. Thus, in the plantation romance *Moss-Side* (1857), the sons and daughters of the South make a pilgrimage to Niagara Falls to find innocence, if not absolution: "The spray dashed up to us, every now and then; and to our brows it was the baptism of Holy Mother Nature, purifying us for devotion in this, her most wondrous of cathedrals, from which volumes of incense arise unceasingly to heaven." Not even the abolitionist perspective could interject race into the monumental as an enduring disruption. The 1841 poem "The Fugitive Slave's Apostrophe to Niagara," though contemptuous of the roseate atmosphere of this Southern view of the falls, nonetheless shares the liberal optimism that monumental culture can forever sanctify the political innocence of America. The incongruities of American slavery dissolve before the grand harmony of transcendent nature, and the narrator finds in the "holy drops" of the cataract "the pure baptism of the chainless free."[9] Despite the disparity between proslavery romance and abolitionist lyric, these texts each adhere to a larger structure that requires affirmations of American exceptionalism and progress. National narrative, as relentless as the torrent of Niagara, permits no deviations of political contradiction or considerations of race that would impede its promised unfolding.

Could a different vantage point on Niagara, a different position in monumental culture, reposition the national horizon so that what once seemed a local discrepancy would metamorphose into a pervasive contradiction that could not be overlooked? When ex-slave Austin Steward stopped at the falls, he experienced, like Jefferson awed by the Natural Bridge, like vacationing Southerners, an inspirational contact with the *terriblità* of the sublime. Listening to "the ceaseless thundering of the cataract," Steward muses in *Twenty-Two Years a Slave* (1856), "how tame appear the works of art, and how insignificant the bearing of proud, puny man, compared with the awful grandeur of that natural curiosity." Although the natural power that dwarfs humans paradoxically elevates Steward to a conventional meditation on existence, his narrative reimplants itself in the social world to structure an accusation. Unlike Melville, who made the cataract a sign of literary talent, and unlike other citizens, who glimpsed in Niagara's mist the sublimity of American institutions and history, the noncitizen's thoughts contain no ether of national pride. Steward does not find himself impelled to a transcendental appreciation of republican institutions; instead, he returns to consider humanity in an even more debased manifestation:

> There [at Niagara Falls] you will find the idle, swaggering slaveholder blustering about in lordly style; boasting of his wealth; betting and gambling; ready to fight, if his slightest wish is not granted, and lavishing his cash on all who have the least claim upon him. Ah, well can he afford to be liberal,—well can he afford to spend thousands

yearly at our Northern watering places; he has plenty of human chattels at home toiling year after year for his benefit . . . and should
his extravagance lighten it [his purse] somewhat, he has only to order his brutal overseer to sell—soul and body—some poor creature; perchance a husband, or a wife, or a child, and forward him
the proceeds of the sale.

Once slavery entered the big house of monumentalism, a culture's
sublime pretensions revealed themselves vulnerable to contradiction
and dissemblance. Thus, Samuel Ringgold Ward, in his *Autobiography of a Fugitive Negro* (1855), witnessed at the country's border a sight
that disputed the supremacy of nature's nation: "the leap of a slave
from a boat to the Canadian shore . . . is far more sublime than the
plunge of the Niagara River."[10] In contrast with Ward's "sublimest
sight" of a transcendent bound that literally surpasses the United
States, Steward's slaveholder struts across the American ground of
the falls, sullying its greatness, leading the citizen, not to a rhapsodic
tribute to Washington or the nation, but to a more archaic history that
supposedly had been left in the Old World among dissolute aristo-
crats. Steward's slaveholder shows embarrassing continuity with a
tradition of seigneurial dependence that America believed it had
escaped forever in 1776.

Concerned with attacking business rivals and the political imbro-
glios of a settlement of escaped slaves in Canada, Steward does not
elaborate his portrait of an American sublime whose magnificent
splendor harbors licentious tyranny. Monumentalism met with a
much more extended and severe critique in the lectures, memoirs,
and fictions of William Wells Brown. The sublime, for Brown, could
never transcend slavery. Even though the virgin character of the
landscape seemingly invested national history with a similar innocence, Brown saw that both the land and the patriarchal mythos
suffered the corruptions of race slavery. Drawing upon that common
image of the sublime, Brown asked in an 1848 verse entitled "Jefferson's Daughter":

> Can the tide of Niagara wipe out the stain?
> No! Jefferson's child has been bartered for gold.

In the same way that Emerson in "The American Scholar" pursues
"the sublime presence of the highest spiritual cause lurking" in the
"one design [that] unites and animates the farthest pinnacle and the

lowest trench," so, too, Brown conjoins the lofty cataract with a mundane newspaper notice informing that Thomas Jefferson's slave daughter fetched a thousand dollars at a New Orleans auction.[11] Whereas Emerson uncovers an underlying principle of unity, Brown's conjunction only emphasizes the disjunction within American monumentalism. The "tide of Niagara," though it inspired sublime paintings from the Hudson River School, was ineffectual in returning America to innocence.

Brown's insistence that the monumental cannot wipe out discordant stains has profound effects for historical imaginings of America. His refocusing of the icons of national transcendence skews perspectives so that the disparate details that prefigure transcendence stand out, defiant of aesthetic incorporation or political assimilation. In this recalibrated vision that looks at rumors of the sexual and at mundane business transactions—"Jefferson's child"—and is unmoved by myths of the national—"the tide of Niagara"—a different story, one possessing no self-assured coherence or conclusion, one contradictorily rife with "unspeakable things unspoken," emerges. Rejecting the distant national horizon to concentrate on bodies overlooked by such an expansive vista, Brown's narrative dissolves harmonious ideological unity. The docile slave who sits sandwiched between Columbia, Washington's tomb, and Niagara Falls in the engraving *America* (see Figure 5) may now serve other, unforeseen functions. His own potentially disruptive presence is no longer subjugated to a sublime economy of unity. Within Brown's methodology of looking at the sublime, the slave in this engraving is not merely placed among foundational icons, but is himself a founding figure whose presence throws into question the generative processes of nationalism so aptly symbolized by Columbia as mythic mother and Washington as historical father. As prominent figures restored to the family portrait, "Jefferson's Daughter" and the slave of *America* instigate a genealogy speaking in tones other than the regularities of filiopietism.

Like Steward, Brown fled North to freedom, and when the passage of the Fugitive Slave Law threatened to return him to bondage, he traveled to England. The irony of the journey was not lost on Brown: the imperial power that had resisted American independence seventy years before now offered a freedom that the United States denied. Both in oratory and writing, Brown argued against slavery and racial prejudice, not by appealing to religious tenets as many white abolitionists and slave narrators did, but by manipulating the discourses of American politics and history. His slave narrative and memoirs rival Douglass's classic autobiography, recalling how he bribed white schoolboys with candy to teach him to read, thus linking, as did Douglass, literacy and freedom. Finding his name prohibited when his master's nephew, also named William, joined the family, and refusing to accept the surname of the white master who fathered him, Brown writes of his flight to the North: "So I was not only hunting for my liberty, but also hunting for a name." Brown continued to improve his literacy, producing histories of blacks' cultural contributions, and with the publication of *Clotel; or, The President's Daughter* (1853), he became the first African American novelist. Soon after his escape from slavery, Brown emerged as a powerful and articulate spokesman for black emancipation, suggesting that just as white revolutionaries fought for liberty in 1776, so, too, would black patriots demand theirs. Hesitant to cater to the complacent pacifism of many Northern whites, Brown played upon American founding principles to advocate violent overthrow of the slave power. In *St. Domingo: Its Revolutions and its Patriots* (1855), he no doubt alternately thrilled and shocked audiences with graphic scenes of Haitian blacks killing so many whites that "the waters [were] dyed with the blood of the slain." He concluded the work by forecasting a similar scene south of the Mason-Dixon line:

> Who knows but that a Toussaint . . . may some day appear in the Southern States of this Union? That they are there, no one will doubt. That their souls are thirsting for liberty, all will admit. The spirit that caused the blacks to take up arms, and to shed their blood in the American revolutionary war, is still amongst the slaves of the south; and, if we are not mistaken, the day is not far distant when the revolution of St. Domingo will be reenacted in South Carolina and Louisiana.[12]

While these not so subtle whisperings of slave rebellion assailed the present by exploiting recurrent white fears of Babo-like patriots armed with cunning and razors, Brown also staged an insurrection against the monumental past. He pledged himself to civic religion, but without paralyzing himself with docile enactments of ideological consensus. He understood the lesson also inscribed in Melville's

Israel Potter, that a citizen had to interrogate actively America's monumental legacy if civic ideals of participation and independence were to be preserved. Yet, unlike Israel, who took up arms in the name of American independence and had a memory of his actions on a battlefield sanctified by the Bunker Hill Monument, Brown had no legacy of the founding fathers within his constitution. The fact that his father "was a white man, a relative of my master, and connected with some of the first families of Kentucky," circulates only as rumor, as a spurious form of history.[13] Genealogy, for the slave, conferred little more than an illegitimate legacy. Denied his birthright of history, Brown nevertheless authorized himself as a historical subject able to comment upon the history of the nation that denied him history from the outset.

Brown's autobiographical prefaces to *Clotel* and *The Black Man: His Antecedents, His Genius, and His Achievements* (1863) accord him a personal history, authorizing him to construct fiction and history about slavery and the position of blacks in the United States. Although nineteenth-century literary conventions demanded narratives adhere to the truth, a concern that led to doubts about the veracity and authenticity of slave narratives, Brown's autobiographical sketches serve a greater function than merely answering a readership's demands for accuracy. In constructing his own past, Brown figures national history as a construction as well, perceiving how shibboleths of monumentalism validate racial injustice. Details vary in Brown's memoirs of slavery and his escape to freedom; for instance, he records three different birthrates and gives varying accounts of his family genealogy, one claiming his mother was Daniel Boone's daughter.[14] The various narratives highlight different scenes from Brown's life in slavery and afterward. *The Narrative of William W. Brown* records the author's quest for freedom and a name; the autobiographical preface to *Clotel* shifts the drama to focus on a fugitive slave bribing children to teach him how to read; the memoir of the author introducing *The Black Man* documents the slave's ingenuity to survive and his greater ingenuity to escape. These diverse autobiographical accounts do not so much constitute a complete life, inviolable in the authority of its own experiences, as they subtly deconstitute history, implying its mutable and selective aspects.

Having formulated an autobiographical narrative from privileged instances of memory, Brown intimates that a similar logic of construction permeates narratives of American history. *The Black Man* devotes a chapter to Crispus Attucks, "the first martyr to American liberty," who ignited a crowd and emboldened resistance to British soldiers in a riot memorialized as the Boston Massacre. This episode, remembering a different national past, concludes by censuring the present, whose faculty of memory is impaired by an ethic of historical construction that resists incorporation of nonwhite elements:

> No monument has yet been erected to him. An effort was made in the legislature of Massachusetts a few years since, but without success. Five generations of accumulated prejudice against the negro had excluded from the American mind all inclination to do justice to one of her bravest sons. When negro slavery shall be abolished in our land, then we may hope to see a monument raised to commemorate the heroism of Crispus Attucks.[15]

Brown practices a strategy that pits monumental history against itself, disrupting the narratives it tells. That monumental history touches up or omits segments of the past Brown was not the first to discover. Nor is his perception that such alterations follow a color-blind logic particularly revolutionary. Rather, the comments of this fugitive slave are critically republican, articulating a counternarrative to historical monumentalism from within. Even as he issues what may seem a typical jeremiad that rails against contemporary antebellum society, Brown's criticism also evades the trap of ideological consensus: his comments push beyond denunciation of the present to evaluate the underpinnings of national history.

A sly addition from the mouth of a fugitive slave can dispel the sublime sanctity of tradition. While Brown complains of Crispus Attucks's omission from monumental history, he elsewhere refills the American heroic tradition with instructive touches of irony:

> Some years since, while standing under the shade of the monument erected to the memory of the brave Americans who fell at the storming of Fort Griswold, Connecticut, I felt a degree of pride as I beheld the names of two Africans who had fallen in the fight, yet I was grieved but not surprised to find their names colonized off, and a line drawn between them and the whites. This was in keeping with American historical injustice to its colored heroes.[16]

Brown repeats his criticism of a legacy that denigrates blacks either by exclusion, as in the case of Crispus Attucks, or here, by grudging inclusion. Still more significantly, this passage unearths the ideological foundations of America's projects to fabricate a monumental history. Brown's use of the word "colonized" reveals how a consideration of race wrests America's monumental history from its nativist innocence and situates it within another, unacknowledged and destabilizing past. Two different connotations reside within "colonized," echoing the oppositions that constitute the monument as well as monumental history. On the one hand, within the context of Revolutionary remembrance, "colonized" elicits the colonies' struggle for independence. On the other hand, in the antebellum period, to "colonize" meant not simply to settle a new land in quest of greater freedom, but to separate, and was applied to the "Negro question" when discussing plans to transport emancipated blacks to Africa.[17] Brown mocks the staggering mass of the monument, pointing to subtle fractures that threaten the coherent narrative it encodes. In Brown's representation, the monument's double meanings—its promise of inclusive freedom and its practice of exclusive injustice— bear a mutinous relation to the narrative it presents. Foundational origins, in the hands of the fugitive slave, suffer the insurrection of rhetorical civil war.

Just as Brown's search for freedom caused him to flee for England, so, too, his search for a foundational history that would be not blindly monumental, but critical, sent him abroad. In London, Brown visited Nelson's column, which represents a heroic black man at the admiral's side, and reflects: "How different, thought I, was the position assigned to the colored man on similar monuments in the United States." That a comparison to English public monuments prompted his analysis was especially damaging to America's intentional efforts to remember a national history unconnected and superior to the traditions of the Old World. The irony inadvertently inscribed within the Fort Griswold monument discredits the historical narrative and reinforces the provincial state of national culture that Theodore Parker and Young America sought to amend. Placed in the context of a European past, American historical consciousness remains a colonial production as well as a "colonized" narrative. In fact, for Brown, a consideration of the narratives encoded on ancient Roman monuments further illustrates the irony of American historical construction: "I once stood upon the walls of an English city, built by enslaved Britons when Julius Caesar was their master. The image of

the ancestors of President Lincoln and Montgomery Blair, as represented in Britain, was carved upon monuments of Rome, where they
may still be seen in their chains. Ancestry is something the white
American should not speak of, unless with his lips to the dust."
Brown prefaces these conclusions with an ironic apology: "I am sorry
that Mr. Lincoln came from such a low origin."[18] Such conclusions
effectively question nationalist exceptionalism, which basked in declarations of America as the stage of a new historical era, a *novus ordo
seclorum*. The history of the fugitive slave here denies that any rupture has ever occurred, and within the restored continuity Brown
uncovers a foundational history of an older republic, Rome. His
archaeological endeavor overturns the myopic American construction of history by resituating national origins within a larger historical context that reveals the American citizen to be descended from
slaves.

Brown thus challenges not the past that America remembers, but
the ways in which it remembers that past. Like Nietzsche, he sees that
forgetfulness inevitably accompanies the monument's admonition to
remember. He resists this amnesiac tendency, not by recovering lost
episodes of the Revolutionary past, but by supplying his own autobiographical history as a postscript to national history. Near the
close of his 1848 autobiography, he reflects: "While the people of the
United States boast of their freedom, they at the same time keep three
millions of their own citizens in chains; and while I am seated here
in sight of Bunker Hill Monument, writing this narrative, I am a slave,
and no law, not even in Massachusetts, can protect me from the
slave-holder."[19] Here, *The Narrative of William W. Brown* rebels
against the narrative of American history. The series of clauses following the statement "I am seated here in sight of Bunker Hill
Monument" imply syntactically the fugitive slave's attitude toward
monumental history: each clause qualifies the original statement,
throwing the reader back to the contradiction that structures not
simply the sentence, but the fugitive slave's tenuous hold upon
freedom. At first glance, "writing this narrative" further defines the
position of the "I" relative to that icon of freedom, the Bunker Hill
Monument; yet his act of "writing this narrative" is also an act of
historical remembering sharply opposed to the mode of history embodied by the monument. Though he can see Bunker Hill, clauses
and reservations keep Brown colonized off from the securities that

the memorial symbolically promises. Refusing simply to deplore his segregation from monumental history, Brown makes his segregation part of the American narrative; he divisively integrates his autobiography into the legacy encoded by the Bunker Hill Monument, Melville's "Great Biographer" of American history. Inscribing his separation into the architecture of the past, Brown makes inequality and ironic contradiction part of America's monumental history. National narratives rise up triumphantly, only to be discredited by an unmasking of the chain of inconsistencies and exclusionary clauses feebly supporting the structure.

REVERBERATIONS OF
RACIAL INCONGRUITY

Although Brown critically evaluated how racial politics fractured monumentalism's configuration of history, not all post-Revolutionary sons were perceptive—or ideologically motivated—enough to note the fissures in the past. While Brown juxtaposed American foundations with his own slave history and artifacts from classical antiquity, George Lippard published a lengthy, patriotic volume, *The Legends of the American Revolution, 1776; or, Washington and His Generals* (1847). As Brown did repeatedly throughout his career, Lippard briefly inscribed a black figure into the Revolutionary past. He tells the story of Black Sampson, who comes upon "that hideous object among the embers," the burned body of his master, and swears vengeance against the British regimentals who committed the murder. Further incensed by the rape of his young mistress, Sampson takes up his scythe, calls his faithful dog, and wreaks havoc among the British lines at Brandywine: "The British soldiers saw him come—his broad black chest gleaming in the sun—his strange weapon glittering overhead—his white dog yelling by his side, and as they looked they felt their hearts grow cold, and turned from his path with fear."[20]

Lippard understood that the inclusion of a black figure into the sacred history of the Revolution might have appeared inappropriate and shocking to his audience. He advises the reader: "Start not when I tell you, that this hero was—a Negro!" Although Black Sampson fights for the memory of white patriarchy and the honor of white womanhood, the narrator fears the miscegenation of a slave within a tradition of freedom might blemish the patriotic legacy and call attention to the political contradictions of the present. Nor does the invocation of racist physiology making Black Sampson a "white Negro" descended from African kings allay these fears of historical anarchy: "A Negro, without the peculiar conformation which marks whole tribes of his race. Neither thick lips, flat nose, receding chin or forehead are his." A direct and lengthy address from the author dispelling any unintentional lingerings of subversive connotations is needed:

> Do not mistake me. I am no factionist, vowed to the madness of treason, under the sounding name of—Humanity. I have no sympathy—no scorn—nothing but pity for those miserable deluded men, who in order to free the African race, would lay unholy hands upon the American Union.
>
> That American Union is a holy thing to me. It was baptized some seventy years ago, in a river of sacred blood. No one can count the tears, the prayers, the lives that have sanctified this American Union, making it an eternal bond of brotherhood for innumerable millions, an altar forever sacred to the Rights of Man. For seventy years and more, the Smile of God has beamed upon it. The man that for any pretence, would lay a finger upon one of its pillars, not only blasphemes the memory of the dead, but invokes upon his name the Curse of all ages yet to come. . . .
>
> So the American Union may be the object of honest differences of opinion; it may be liable to misinterpretation, or be darkened by the smoke of conflicting creeds; yes it may shelter black slavery in the South, and white slavery in the north. Would *you* therefore destroy it?[21]

This authorial intrusion seeks to guard against a racial fracturing of America's monumental narrative by colonizing off with a series of apologies and explanations any trace of blackness within the Revolutionary legacy. Sensing that his introduction of Black Sampson into the "sacred" and "sanctified" Union may inadvertently perpetrate a subversive irony, Lippard fortifies his narration by appealing to the Union as a transcendental entity. Convinced that race slavery is unjust, his narrator nevertheless refuses to urge its abolition and jeopardize the "baptized" body politic. The memory of the fathers in the legend of Black Sampson narrates a foundational structure stable enough to contain sectional crisis. Yet this same span of temporal continuity between 1776 and the 1850s degenerates into an unbridgeable gap of temporal alienation. What Lippard omits is that the "seventy years and more" that linked a people to its legacy also acted to divide a people from its legacy.

Although Lippard convinced himself this address to the reader had warded off the specter of "feverish philanthropy," making it safe to proceed with the narrative of Black Sampson, he nevertheless calls attention to the fractures he has covered with rhetoric and patriotic zeal. In the background of his denunciation against those who would repeat "the leprosy of Arnold's Treason," is the voice of more militant proponents of abolition who held the patriotic legacy as a mere shibboleth. In 1844, William Lloyd Garrison pronounced a sentiment that must have sounded as blasphemy in Lippard's ears:

> If the American Union cannot be maintained, except by immolating human freedom upon the altar of tyranny, then let the American Union be consumed by a living thunderbolt, and no tear be shed over its ashes. If the Republic must be blotted out from the roll of nations, by proclaiming liberty to the captives, then let the Republic sink beneath the waves of oblivion, and a shout of joy, louder than the voice of many waters, fill the universe at its extinction.

In contrast to Lippard, Garrison could not proceed with the narrative of American Union. Whereas God told Lippard to honor the creation of thy fathers at all costs and contradictions, Garrison received the word to slay the unfaithful. The range between these two passages alarmingly illustrates how God, like William Wells Brown, could also speak with an irony inimical to historical continuity. While some Americans like Lippard ritually reaffirmed the Puritan promise of a blessed community, others, perhaps not all as extreme as Garrison in his call for heavenly retribution, looked at the present and doubted the future the American legacy had promised. Or, as Lincoln looked at America in 1861, he saw an "almost chosen people."[22]

THE PARENTHETICAL CONFIGURATION OF HISTORY

The divine narrative of America, born to conquer a New Canaan, now ironically promised to unravel. One response was to make the antebellum present seem an exception, a political and moral aberration. In terms of rhetoric, we can understand this aberration within

the national narrative by the trope of parenthesis.[23] Finding its promises tainted by its sinful ways, and unwilling to deem its whole
history corrupt, American narrative placed the contaminated elements in the quarantine of parenthesis, thereby insulating the purity
of the founding origins and divine future. In *The Estrangement of the
Past*, Anthony Kemp describes parenthesis as a temporal consciousness in which the immediate past is placed as an abyss between the
distant past and the present. Examining Protestant foundations,
Kemp shows how Luther, and later, Puritan historian John Foxe,
cordoned off the innovations of the Catholic Church in order to
overleap its corruptions and return to the purity of the primitive
Church. Characteristics of this historical consciousness emigrated to
America in the Puritan conviction that the preceding centuries of
European history formed a moral aberration in the eschatological
journey from Canaan to New Canaan that deservedly fell into the
brackets of parenthesis. In the Puritan settlement, growing evidence
that interpretation of the social world might not readily reveal a
divine plan reflected political schisms uninterpretable within the
system of divine typology. In John Winthrop's words, "God no
longer gives the interpretation." Kemp argues that the increasing
difficulty of applying a secure typology to the interpretation of the
world produced for the Puritans a sense of temporal estrangement.
Rather than leading toward a promised land, human history, removed from the irrevocable pastness of God's acts, initiated a dynamic of supercession as generation replaced generation with no
sense of spiritual advancement.[24] Although the seventeenth-century
theocracy of Boston had passed, 1850s America still lingered in the
shadow of Puritan culture, as studies from Hawthorne's *Scarlet Letter*
to Bercovitch's *American Jeremiad* show, and its national narratives
retained spiritual overtones promising a pure, originary tradition.
The structure of parenthesis thus also describes the political logic of
American historical narrative. Skipping over the aristocratic dissolution of the recent European past, a community could unite with the
republican foundation of Rome. Washington became the American
Cincinattus, refusing, like the fabled Roman general, the temptation
of dictatorship, wishing only to return his plow. Representations of
Washington draped in a toga allowed America to place Europe
within parenthesis and remember itself as the inheritor of a classical

republican tradition. America styled itself as the *novus ordo seclorum*, the new Rome described by Virgil.

1776 became the pure, originary past, allowing America to remain in continual temporal and ideological harmony with its own genesis. Throughout much of the antebellum period, this continuum seemed visible and intact. During his presidency, James Monroe used to appear on ceremonial occasions dressed in his Revolutionary War uniform, even though the heroic days of 1776 had been past for nearly a half century.[25] So close was that unassailable past, a citizen could count with certainty back to the moment of founding, as Lincoln did at Gettysburg: "Fourscore and seven years ago our fathers brought forth on this continent a new nation, conceived in liberty." Yet in the context of increasing talk of disunion, unity with the past of 1776 seemed illusory; 1776 ceased to form part of the recent past, retreating into an era as mythically pure and remote as the foundations of Rome or the genesis of the primitive Church. The past preserved itself as sacrosanct, in contrast to the splintering, impure present. It was not 1776 that belonged in parenthesis; on the contrary, parenthesis encircled the present as though it was a historical epoch as corrupt as the profligate era of the Catholic Church or as politically profane as the European centuries of aristocratic privilege. Parenthesis cordoned off the factional, slaveholding present, ensuring that the contaminated 1850s did not infect either the past or the future of America. "Fourscore and seven years ago" indicated a connection with the past, but it also marked the dimensions of the temporal abyss.

Parenthesis asserts that the origins remain pure because it places the present in an ideological and temporal quarantine. Parenthesis deems the past virtuous and the present politically impure; America supposes itself a political virgin, refusing to see that its origins had spawned an ignoble present. Despite this assumption that the unalloyed past bears no genealogical connection to the present, the fractious antebellum present really does originate in that past; unruly post-Revolutionary sons were not the product of spontaneous generation, but descended from fathers who trafficked in political sin and inconsistency. Parenthesis masks these affiliations by writing a narrative in which past and present splinter into dissimilar historical epochs lacking the genealogical resemblances usually evident between a generation and its descendants. Post-Revolutionary sons confessed their own political shortcomings; even so, they knew nothing incriminating about their fathers, pillars of virtue and egalitarian faith that they were. Here, parenthesis resonates with a classical connotation of irony, that is, as ignorance purposefully affected. Bred with careful regard for their legacy, social reformers decried the incongruity of a nation at odds with its own foundings.

Few critics, however, evaluated how scorn and outrage over present practices acted as an ideological buffer insulating the founding ideals from censure. The present absorbed all of the abolitionists' contempt; the present became a scapegoat in order to preserve the unsullied reputation of 1776. In this sense, then, criticism of the present merely reinforced the foundations of America; or, as Bercovitch has written, dissent actually acted as consent. Yet Brown, Melville, and Lincoln, as critical republicans, dissent from the foundings, not simply from the present. Their acts of dissent evade the containment of the dissent/consent relation that Bercovitch finds so pervasive. Brown's *Clotel* as its premise a situation explicitly linked to 1776 in order to reestablish the genealogical affiliations that parenthesis seeks to deny: "Thus closed a negro sale, at which two daughters of Thomas Jefferson, the writer of the Declaration of American Independence and one of the presidents of the great republic, were disposed of to the highest bidder!"[26] And both Melville and Lincoln not only perceive how proclaiming a disjunction between past and present safeguard the past, they also make their way beyond an ideological dissemblance that centers all dissent on the present, engaging instead in an interrogation of American foundings.

In their return to patriarchal and national origins, fugitive slave, novelist, and statesman question the governing framework of American narrative. Certainly, Brown, Melville, and Lincoln challenge the content of national narrative as they vilify slavery in varying degrees. As Bercovitch argues, however, such opposition is subsumed by a controlling orthodoxy of American liberalism that privileges moments of dissent as confirmations of national reform and progress. The underlying structures authorizing American society have been the same, for those who consent as well as for those who contest social institutions and practices. Though abolition assailed an America that condoned slavery, as a type of responsible, liberal social activism, abolition worked to "confirm the sanctity both of law in general and the Constitution in particular." Or, in the case of Hester Prynne, the wearer of the scarlet *A* signifies at once a transgressor of the law and a citizen brought back within the letter of the law. According to Bercovitch, literary production of the American Renaissance operates within this structure of containment and even in its most vehement moments of dissent upholds America.[27] But Brown, Lincoln, and Melville do more than criticize the slaveholding content of America: they also question the *form*, the narrative strategies, that the antebellum generation used to construct an affirmative national history.

MELVILLE'S "THE BELL-TOWER" AND INCONGRUOUS HISTORY

While Brown's sketches of American monumentalism critique the present's remembering of the past and not the past itself, Melville's short story "The Bell-Tower" resolutely examines the origins from which monumentalism erected itself. Just as Brown implies that the colonizing off of black patriots on a revolutionary battle monument is inconsistent with the ideals they died for, Melville begins his story within a disjunction between pretensions of monumental grandeur and their frequently-narrated sequel: "In the south of Europe, nigh a once-frescoed capital, now with a dank mould cankering its bloom, central in a plain, stands what, at a distance, seems the black mossed stump of some immeasurable pine, fallen, in forgotten days, with Anak and the Titan."[28] In addition to its content, depicting decline and ruin, the structure of the sentence parallels the image of the crumbling tower. The sentence falls from "once" to "now," with an empty, poisonous gulf separating the two eras. Lincoln repeatedly adopts this structure in his address before the Young Men's Lyceum of January 27, 1838 to forecast the imminent erosion of America's political foundation. He tells his audience that the foundational principles "are a legacy bequeathed us, by a *once* hardy, brave, and patriotic, but *now* lamented and departed race of ancestors."[29] The echoes of Titanic greatness on the Italian plain that Melville imagines dwindle to a castrated stump, and for Lincoln, a vigorous patriotic presence lapses into absence. In each instance, the parenthesis of the present forms a vacuum of incongruity and intervenes between the "once" and the "now."

This incongruity, however, performs an instructive political function as an admonition to recuperate a vanishing past. Lincoln hoped to rededicate his audience to his ancestor's republican faith; for example, consideration of Washington's greatness could lead to the act of *monere*, of reminding the present generation not to backslide into civic forgetfulness. Although not designated as a monument, the bell tower of Melville's story similarly returns the narrator from the present state of decay to the resplendent acme of a small Italian republic's history. Imbued with an air of magical realism and anchored by political allusions to Melville's America, the story promises to deliver a satirical allegory reminiscent of *Mardi*. Just as *Mardi*'s narrator Taji witnesses the severe contradictions of the liberty-loving nation Vivenza that enslaves the tribe of Hamo, "The Bell-Tower" transmits a critique of a republic that authorizes the erection of an overtopping edifice adorned with a mechanical slave named Haman.[30] But rather than shuttling between past principles and the present monumental project, Melville keeps his attention focused upon the moments of foundings, refusing to sidetrack his interrogation of the past with a denunciation of the present. That is, Melville does not succumb to the dissembling nature of parenthesis; he does not adopt a purposefully affected ignorance about the foundings as a means to conserve the sanctity of their legacy.

First published in August 1855, Melville's story narrates the prideful demise of the architect Bannadonna. Commissioned to construct "the noblest Bell-Tower in Italy," Bannadonna watches the edifice rise, resolving to "surpass all that had gone before" (819, 821). He devises a mechanical figure representing a manacled slave to advance along a track and strike the bell every hour. On the consecration day of the tower, absorbed in some final adjustments to the bell, Bannadonna forgets the time, and at one o'clock, when the slave advances to strike the hour, he smites and kills the artist-creator instead. This homicide echoes an earlier murder in the narrative of the monument. As further proof of his ingenuity, Bannadonna creates a "great statebell" destined for the top of the tower; the narrator thus designates him a "founder," accenting his dual role as one who establishes the foundation of the republic's tower and as one who melts the metals and casts the bell (820).[31] Yet at the moment of founding, a murderous taint infects the design: "The unleashed metals bayed like hounds. The workmen shrunk. Through their fright, fatal harm to the bell was dreaded. Fearless as Shadrach, Bannadonna, rushing through the glow, smote the chief culprit with his ponderous ladle. From the smitten part, a splinter was dashed into the seething mass, and at once was melted in" (821). From this original sin, a host of other offenses against the spirit of republicanism emerge. Not wishing to compromise the glory the great bell will bring to the republic, the magistrates and citizens ignore the homicide. Once the bell is finished, the civil authorities grow anxious, pressing Bannadonna to determine the day when the republic can baptize the tower in a public ceremony. The magistrate tells the architect the city officials are "anxious to be assured of your success. The people, too,—why, they are shouting now. Say the exact hour when you will be ready." (824) The republic shares in the guilt of the founder's crime as well as in the glory of his creation. It forgets the scandal of the past to triumph in the rituals of the present. Caught up in a narrative of denial, the republic ineluctably continues to erase the flaws within its history; it accords the murderer-founder a state funeral, while under the cover of night, it hustles the rebellious mechanical slave out of its dominions and sinks it in the depths of the ocean. The republic, intent upon conserving noble foundations that were never noble, effaces the blemishes in its representation of the past. Indeed it literally re-presents the past, altering its composition and structure, exiling unpleasant memories to the realm of amnesia by repairing the ruined tower and recasting the defective bell.

Melville's story acts against the body politic and records the genealogy of sin that the American populace sought to deny through specious historical constructions. Wishing to overleap Bannadonna's crimes as well as its own complicity, the public casts off uncomfortable memories into the abyss of purposeful amnesia; it declares it knows nothing about any crimes in order to fabricate an unadulterated legacy. Yet the narrator counteracts the community's irony of dissembling and exposes the bad faith of feigned amnesia. While the republic pretends ignorance about the past, the narrative manipulates the incongruity to sketch a repressed connection between the "once" and the "now," illuminating how the republican pomp of the city-state stems from the "cankering" bloom of Bannadonna's tyrannical license. Restored to its problematic integrity, history ruptures, as an incongruity imposed by the narrator reveals his readers' dissemblance, laying bare how they, like the magistrates and citizens

in the story, have placed the sins of their own history in the parenthesis of forgetfulness to deny a temporal continuity that would
indict their state.

The community's fraudulent representation of history coincides
with Bannadonna's fraud to conceal a defect in the composition of
the bell. The fragment from the murderous ladle thrown into the
molten mass spawns a hardly noticeable but defective inconsistency
in the bell's composition: "Next day a portion of the work was
heedfully uncovered. All seemed right. . . . At length, like some old
Theban king, the whole cooled casting was disinterred. All was fair
except in one strange spot. But as he [Bannadonna] suffered no one
to attend him in these inspections, he concealed the blemish by some
preparation which none knew better to devise" (821). Bannadonna
certainly acts in his own self-interest, and at the same time, he
performs a civic duty by insulating the community from any memory
of the homicide they have condoned. Using "some unknown com-
pound," the architect smooths over his defective founding, forging
a monumental history whose key element is forgetfulness (833).
Standing on the Florentine plain, the tower promises to acquire
symbolic prominence, to serve as an icon of republican openness.
This promise, however, is as false as Bannadonna's bell is imperfect.
Although the great state bell perched atop the campanile could serve
as a monument and recall the past laced with the flaw of the slain
artisan, Bannadonna forestalls the act of *monere*. The republic sees no
reminder of breached justice in the bell, but only confirmation of its
own affluence. The narrator works against Bannadonna's and the
republic's construction and again insists on temporal continuity,
even though that continuity jeopardizes ideological cohesion. A legacy of violence resonates within a tradition of republican glory.
Although Melville asserts continuity, linking the splintering of the
bell with the homicidal splintering of the ladle, the community resolves to place history in an alembic and refine away any impurities.
Soon the campanile requires repair, but rather than follow Bannadonna and dissemble the defect, the republic improves upon his
methods and refounds the bell as though nothing—not the artisan's
murder, the architect's "accidental death," or the mechanical slave's
revolt—had taken place: "The remolten metal soon reässumed its
place in the tower's repaired superstructure" (833).

We can better understand the significance of "The Bell-Tower" for the American republic if we restore the story's contiguity to the antebellum era and trace its allusive import. The defective bell evokes the memorial icon of public freedom, the Liberty Bell.[32] Like Bannadonna's creation, the state-house bell in Philadelphia cracked during its founding, was recast, and then, according to tradition, irreparably fractured as it tolled on Washington's birthday, February 22, 1846.[33] Even though the crack in the bell could suggest on some metaphoric level the distance between the founding father's generation and its descendants, for much of antebellum America the bell served as a relic of a patriotic legacy, clasping together the fathers and sons in a paternal embrace. The same volume containing the story of Black Sampson, Lippard's *Legends of the American Revolution*, initiates a sacramental status for the Liberty Bell by narrating a story that would be construed as fact by thousands of Americans.[34] Lippard's most famous legend begins when on July 4, 1776 an old bell ringer tries to make out the inscription on the bell of the Philadelphia State House. His tired eyes fail him, so he calls "Come here, my boy; you are a rich man's child. You can read. Spell me those words, and I'll bless ye, my good child!" Reading the chiseled verse from Leviticus, "Proclaim liberty to all the land and the inhabitants thereof," the boy invokes a democratic spirit that levels the class distinctions between himself and his elder. The bell ringer requests another favor from the youth, asking him to wait in the street and listen for the decision of the congress debating the resolution for independence. As though he were part of the expectant citizen mob described in Bannadonna's republic, the old man waits anxiously, doubting that the boy has remembered his promise: "Moments passed, yet still he came not. The crowds gathered more darkly along the pavement and over the lawn, yet still the boy came not. 'Ah!' groaned the old man, 'he has forgotten me! These old limbs will have to totter down the State House stairs, and climb up again, all on account of that child.'" Like Lincoln in his speech to the Young Men's Lyceum, the bell ringer distrusts the sons, suspecting a weakness in their civil faith that would cause them to become distracted by the present and ignore the obligations to the past. The stakes of this legend are enormous; the communication of liberty would be jeopardized if gaps were to arise between generations. As Lincoln put it in 1838, if America were to forget the "task of gratitude to our fathers, justice to ourselves, duty to posterity," then the national fabric of founding principles could well unravel.[35]

Since Lippard was more fortunate than Lincoln and could rely upon the convention of narrative closure to dispel the threat of amnesia, the rich man's son, of course, dutifully awaits the outcome of the congress's deliberations. Hearing the acceptance of the Declaration of Independence, the boy, "swelling his little chest . . . raised himself on tip-toe, and shouted a single word—'RING!'" Only a reverential civic memory can realize the verse inscribed upon the Liberty Bell. Later versions of Lippard's tale, which after discovering a blood relation between the boy and the old man culminate in the cry "Ring! Grandpa, ring!" stress the importance of genealogical continuity for antebellum America. The boy's shout disproves Lincoln's admonition "that the scenes of the revolution . . . [are] like every thing else, they must fade upon the memory of the world, and grow more and more dim by the lapse of time." As the old man translates the boy's "RING!" into the "terrible poetry in the sound of the State House Bell," his body is rejuvenated with the honest Yankee resilience of independence.[36] Liberty does not fall into the abyss of forgetfulness, but is rescued by a tenacious link between the bell ringer and the boy, between the fathers and the post-Revolutionary sons. Liberty is renewed, made eternal, forever young as the fathers were in their heroic youth:

> Do you see that old man's eye fire? Do you see that arm so suddenly bared to the shoulder, do you see that withered hand, grasping the Iron Tongue of the Bell? The old man is young again; his veins are filled with new life. Backward and forward, with sturdy strokes, he swings the Tongue. The bell speaks out! The crowd in the street hear it, and burst forth in one long shout![37]

In contrast, "The Bell-Tower" hardly acquiesces to the tone of republican renewal ensured by the genealogical continuity that Lippard's legend evokes. Although the republic refurbishes the tower and remelts the bell, the renewal lasts only until the first anniversary of the tower's completion, when an earthquake reduces the edifice to an impotent stump. The campanile does not resonate with the lusty sounds of liberty that echo through the Philadelphia State House; instead, Bannadonna's death muffles the peal, emitting only "a dull, mangled sound—naught ringing in it; scarcely audible, indeed, to the outer circles of the people—that dull sound dropped heavily from the belfry" (827). The orchestrated ritual to inaugurate the bell tower merely renews the cycle of violence begun out of Bannadonna's "esthetic passion" that took the life of the workman (821). It is not the slave who deadens the sound; he faithfully performs his office. The founder, Bannadonna, impedes with his own skull the ringing of the bell he has forged. The monumental history of the fathers slays itself in its own contradictions. Absorbed in concealing the murderous flaw in the bell of liberty, the founder forgets to watch his back, and looks up to see his slave bludgeon him. Intimations of slave insurrection dropped by Brown reappear in Melville's tale; and, yet, the rebellion staged is not simply one of slave against master, but of founder against himself. Melville adopts the logic of the fugitive slave: like Brown's use of ironic contradictions to subvert the battle monument's narrative at Fort Griswold, "The Bell-Tower" discloses the fissures that belie monumental representations of republican foundings. In the hands of the narrator, the trope of parenthesis no longer protects the past. The infectious present is not bracketed off from the past, nor does the decayed state of the narrator's current surroundings lead to idylls of a once glorious founding. Instead, "The Bell-Tower" insists on the continuity of political history even if that historical view uncovers atrocities within sacred origins. The fissures, canker, and ruin that mark the present state of the tower are nothing new; murder, fraud, and contradiction disfigure the very inception of the republic's self-representation. Melville's skeptical reexamination of the past removes national origins from their dignified and unassailable foundation and regrounds the noble republic in foundations continually undercut by ironies of deception and forgery. Such ironic historiography cripples monumental narrative, for a generation cannot inherit a coherent legacy if that legacy was never coherent in its origin.

''A NEW BIRTH''
OF INCONGRUOUS HISTORY

Within a culture erected upon incongruous foundations, only forgetting can fashion a narrative stable or coherent enough to support the accumulated layers of history stretching from the origins to the present. The citizens of "The Bell-Tower" contract to remember the past, but—desirous of erecting a monumental body politic—they also contract to forget the past. In the *Second Treatise of Government*, John Locke acknowledges the necessity of political memory: citizens "begin to look after the history of their founders and search into their original, when they have outlived the memory of it." Lincoln echoes this stance in his speech to the Young Men's Lyceum, registering how America sat befuddled at the historical crossroads of memory and forgetting. Whereas the previous generation once embodied "a *living history*" in the memories of those patriots who stood as a "forest of giant oaks" and witnessed the triumphs of the Revolution, the post-Revolutionary sons now were finding their historic forebears dead and gone and the exemplary "forest" destroyed by time, "the all-resistless hurricane has swept over them, and left only, here and there, a lonely trunk, despoiled of its verdure, shorn of its foliage; unshading and unshaded, to murmur in a few more gentle breezes, and to combat with its mutilated limbs, a few more ruder storms, then to sink, and be no more."[38] Memory replaces "living history," but it may be only a paltry substitute. Memory cannot resurrect the fathers; it can only cherish their legacy. Yet as Lincoln looks around antebellum America, he notices mob violence and racial bigotry, indications that memory failed to adhere to the revolutionary legacy. Lincoln hopes to stave off an apocalypse called forth by this amnesia, imploring the current generation to restore its weakening legacy with sober reverence for the Declaration of Independence and the Constitution designed to protect it.

After describing the search for origins, Locke issues a caution deflating any enthusiasm about the search he has just outlined: citizens "would do well not to search too much into the original of governments" or else they might exhume a foundation whose secrets and instabilities would little authorize their current political legitimacy.[39] But unlike Locke, Lincoln does not include a measure of amnesia in his political faith. Lincoln insists on remembering the foundations of liberty even if uncovered ironies make that liberty appear contradictory and incongruous; he does not defer to a strategy of bad faith in which the citizens of a republic can overlook the flaws in the founding just so they can proceed to erect a bell tower or state that will "surpass all that had gone before." Objecting to the small print of Locke's contract that sanctions amnesia within the project of memory, Lincoln resembles the narrator of "The Bell-Tower," retelling the history of a republic, including events and rumors the magistrates and citizens would rather sink in the sea with the rebellious slave. Each renounces a parenthetical version of republican memory that would forget the political sins of the past by concentrating on the "dank mould" of the present. While many opposed to slavery decried America's prodigal disregard for its sacred origins, both Lincoln and the narrator of "The Bell-Tower" unflinchingly question the sacredness of the past. Surveying the history of the ruined capital, the narrator does not shrink from representing a founding contaminated by murder, fraud, and slavery, but undertakes a genealogical investigation bearing him back to the origins. And Lincoln, examining the history of a prosperous republic, steadfastly confronts the principles of the founding fathers. Acknowledging that the origins of American republicanism contain sanctified principles, Lincoln nevertheless understands that many of these principles, despite their unassailable status, were, in fact, flawed. Imperfection resides within the tradition of liberty begun in 1776; a genealogy of sinful discontinuity, not political virtue, links the "once" and the "now."

Even as a figure invested in the workings of the American political system, much more so than Brown or Melville, Lincoln maintained a critical ambivalence toward national genealogy that often led him to distrust the patriarchal metaphors governing the crucial debates of his culture. He often phrased his filial dissent cautiously, as if to belie its radical, parricidal import. In a speech at the Cooper Institute in 1860, as he ritualistically invoked "our fathers that framed the Constitution" in the conviction that their wisdom would resolve the crisis over slavery, Lincoln admitted the possibility, if not the necessity, of filial disobedience: "I do not mean to say we are bound to follow implicitly in whatever our fathers did."[40] Any understanding of Lincoln as a republican or critical genealogist, however, first needs to remember that Lincoln himself would soon occupy a prominent niche in the national genealogy. If Washington was the father of his country, Lincoln became, in the words of one historian, "everybody's grandfather." Not "everybody" assented to this atavism; Frederick Douglass detected a difference that thwarted this legacy of inclusive patriarchy and suggested that African Americans bear a much more attenuated relation to Lincoln: "You are the children of Abraham

Lincoln. We are at best only his step-children, children by adoption, children by force of circumstances and necessity." Douglass emphasizes this lack of a blood connection as well as the gulf between "you" and "we" to signal his own distance from the prevailing mythos of 1876 America that monumentalized Lincoln—Douglass was speaking at the dedication of the Freedmen's Monument—in an uncomplicated tradition as the "great emancipator." His aloofness springs from his memory of Lincoln as "the white man's President"—an epithet that challenges a more universal and unprejudiced designation, preserving the profound contradictions and vacillations that marked Lincoln's course in restoring the Union and destroying slavery.[41]

The inconsistencies Lincoln noted in the foundings would reappear in his own administration. Just as the fathers' freedom remained tarnished by slavery, the emancipation Lincoln secured was subverted by his support of colonization, hesitation to insist upon political and social equality for ex-slaves, and commitment to the Union above all else. Nowhere does this undercutting appear more deeply than in the document that Lincoln called "the greatest event of the nineteenth century"—the Emancipation Proclamation. The greatest irony surrounded this "greatest event": as a document of freedom, it did not free a single slave. The people Lincoln declared "thenceforward, and forever free" included only those slaves held by rebel states; all others, slaves in regions controlled by the Union army and slaves who had fled across Confederate lines, were legally unaffected by the resolution. As Benjamin Quarles writes, "In the South the only areas in which the proclamation could be publicly celebrated were those to which it did not apply—those under the federal flag."[42] This inconsistency nevertheless formed a key element of the union Lincoln was waging war to preserve. The edict of January 1, 1863 announced itself as a stratagem to suppress the "rebellion against the United States"; the desire for an undivided national union, not freedom, was the source of the proclamation. This ascendancy of union over freedom—little different than the compromises initiated by the fathers Lincoln found it necessary to revise—again inscribed freedom as contested, always frustrated, within the national narrative.

Amid his own ambiguous decrees, Lincoln articulated some of the most significant commentaries on the originary fractures within the American political tradition. Speaking in Baltimore on April 18, 1864,

Lincoln praised the soldiers passing through the city and observed "that three years ago, the same soldiers could not so much as pass through Baltimore." Lincoln's words connote a structure of parenthesis in which the immediate past of Union military debacles is colonized off from both the present and the distant days of antebellum harmony. Parenthesis would render the war a bad memory, a hiatus better forgotten in a temporal quarantine protecting the purity of the past. Lincoln, however, undercuts this parenthesis by subtly betraying America's complicity with its past: "But we can see the past, though we may not claim to have directed it." Despite the present republic's predilection for affecting innocence about the cultural chaos that once transpired, Lincoln's ironic remark exposes the desire to deny temporal continuity (and thus ideological responsibility). Foreclosing the possibility of a reassuring parenthesis, he discourages a reverential view of an untouchable past and announces his findings even though they unsettle hallowed foundations. His representation of the past discovers a founding like Bannadonna's, inherently fractured in its origins:

> The world has never had a good definition of the word liberty, and the American people, just now, are much in want of one. We all declare for liberty; but in using the same *word* we do not all mean the same *thing*. With some the word liberty may mean for each man to do as he pleases with himself, and the product of his labor; while with others the same word may mean for some men to do as they please with other men, and the product of other men's labor. Here are two, not only different, but incompatible things, called by the same name—liberty.[43]

Never, even within its origins, has America been able to wield a seamless definition of liberty. Authorizing the domination of men over men, liberty always has been divided against itself, engendering an inconsistent narrative that nevertheless has lapsed into forgetfulness in order to guarantee a smooth, coherent telos for the nation. In the same way that "The Bell-Tower" erects a history ruptured by the incongruities and dissembling ironies it houses, Lincoln's America rests upon a cornerstone marked with lines of fracture. Though heralded as a sacred new order with a unified ideological foundation, America, as Lincoln reveals, is always politically schizophrenic, always marked by an element of the "incompatible," always in debate about its fundamental, authorizing principles.

Acknowledging the inconsistencies of founding narratives can radically alter the conception of national history. Lincoln opens the Gettysburg Address by remembering the birth of the American republic: "a new nation, conceived in liberty, and dedicated to the proposition that all men are created equal." The origins seem whole, immaculately conceived in a liberty that Lincoln does not mark as inherently fractured or prone to contradiction. Still, Lincoln does not call for a rebirth of this liberty; instead, he resolves that America "shall have a new birth of freedom." Though subtle, the difference between a rebirth and a "new birth" implies that citizens should not strive to replicate the past. Nor is the project to restore and refurbish the past as the citizens of "The Bell-Tower" do, devising a strategy even more effective at concealing the murderous crack in the bell. A "new birth" would not establish itself as pure and uncontaminated or invent ways to forget and recast imperfection as perfection; it would devote itself to its own memory, even though that memory may record division and contradiction. This strain of antifoundational thinking aligns Lincoln with Douglass, who more than a decade earlier had proclaimed that he was "for starting afresh under a new and higher light than our piratical fathers saw."[44] For each speaker, the past is no longer an infallible standard, but is as tainted and as perfectible as any human creation, whether those humans are patriot forefathers or pirates. It is perhaps in this uneasy commonality, which links the political theorizing of president and ex-slave, that freedom can be imagined outside of tired precepts and faded men.

Without memory, any founding has as little legitimate authority as Bannadonna's design for a mechanical slave, which, upon prescribed command, kills its creator at the precise moment of public affirmation. Without memory, any conception of liberty will accrue as much suspicion as the liberty achieved by Babo in "Benito Cereno." Murder infects Bannadonna's founding as much as a history of bloodshed stains the liberty formulated by Babo aboard the *San Dominick*. The political message encoded within each story shows that once authority effaces its past, it can only be ironic, subject to the debilitating mistrust of all citizens, even ones as obtuse as Amasa Delano or as blindly patriotic as the populace of "The Bell-Tower." Like the situation in the foundry of the Italian republic or on the deceptive decks of the *San Dominick*, the "new birth" of liberty at Gettysburg emerged from the violent origins of a Civil War battlefield that claimed close to fifty thousand killed or wounded. Lincoln articulated this "new birth" at a cemetery, a grisly site of memory, ensuring that the liberty engendered engaged in none of the historical evasions and cover-ups characteristic of the Italian republic or Babo. A "new birth" of liberty could have none of the parenthetical bad faith that would characterize a rebirth of liberty. Melville could not conceive of a "new birth" of liberty; he could see only monstrous rebirths in which the recessive traits of violence became more dominant with each generation. Political hope for a severely tested republicanism did appear in Lincoln's understanding of the solemn moments of Gettysburg. From a memory of cultural conflict and "incompatible" ideologies, he brought forth a sketch of civic faith committed to a narrative of foundations that, ironically, may be inconsistent, incongruous, even bloody. Such a narrative remembers the founder George Washington alongside the founder Bannadonna and acknowledges the blood of the father in the face of the son, even if the son is a slave, even if that blood stains the parricidal son's hands.

5

Discursive Passing and
African American Literature

A traditionary freedom will not save you.
— William Wells Brown, *Clotel*

*Mimesis allows the absences of national history to
speak in the ambivalent, ragbag narrative.*
— Homi K. Bhabha, "DissemiNation"

INCONGRUITIES OF FREEDOM

The name Washington is discarded by the fugitive slave narrator of
Narrative of the Life of Frederick Douglass. Born Frederick Augustus
Washington Bailey, Douglass states that he "dispensed with the two
middle names" well before he undertook his flight for freedom.
Drawing upon Sir Walter Scott's *Lady of the Lake*, Doulgass claims a
new, expressly literate identity, but this renaming also suggests a
rejection of cultural precedents. Excising the reference to Augustus,
Douglass declines association with the imperial domination of the
Caesars, and deleting the name Washington, he repudiates affiliation
with the patriarchal authority that denotes not just founding fathers,
but slave masters as well. With the publication of "The Heroic Slave"
(1853), however, Douglass reclaims Washington for his hero's name
and then proceeds to have this slave rebel defend black male violence
with the explanation that "if we are murderers, so were they [the
founding fathers]."[1] Douglass's changing attitudes do not so much
represent an acceptance of the national legacy as they indicate the
development among nineteenth-century African Americans of a narrative strategy that repeats history in order to deform it.

While the plot of "The Heroic Slave," in which slaves mutiny and
kill white authority figures, may have alienated more timid readers,
especially those adhering to abolitionist platforms of nonviolence,
Douglass's recuperation of a violent historical legacy found kindred
expression within the parricidal tensions of the white filial generation

of the American Renaissance. The slave's desire to resist and overthrow the plantation patriarch compares with the parricidal urges
that marked the worlds of Melville, Lincoln, Emerson, and Cooper
with political guilt and the trauma of historical denial. Various studies have documented how pious white sons complained of tiring
cultural precedents as their historical necks chafed under the yoke
imposed by the cult of legendary fathers that maintained a hold upon
the antebellum generation. Even in their desire to stage an Oedipal
rebellion against the patriarchal mythos that oversaw political, cultural, and social life, America's post-Revolutionary sons were stymied by their own guilt indicting them as parricides. Genealogical
ambivalence frustrated the sons of the American Renaissance, who
at one moment cherished a filial identity that confirmed them as the
inheritors of freedom and at the next rejected the deferential posture
of patriarchal retrospection. "We are among the sepulchres of our
fathers," Daniel Webster told an estimated hundred thousand Americans gathered at the Bunker Hill Monument to pay ritual reverence
to the founding past, even as Emerson criticized the confining precedents of his age that "builds the sepulchres of the fathers" and
asked "Why should we grope among the dry bones of the past?"[2]

This convergence of Emerson and Webster at the monuments of
the patriarchal past declined into divergences of awe and respect
versus critical interrogation. In the years leading up to the Civil War,
Americans invoked Mount Vernon, the Washington Monument, and
the Bunker Hill Monument as literal embodiments of the topoi in
classical rhetoric—a mnemonic technique that remembers a text or
idea through associations to an image of place. An actor thus visits
an image of Hercules in a niche of his "memory theater" in order to
be reminded of examples of cunning and strength.[3] But not everyone
remembered the same lessons when they looked at the monumental
topoi of the nation. Douglass's vacillating responses to the founding
father recurred even among those whose descent and patriotism
should have guaranteed a less disturbed relationship to the Union.
When abolitionist and slaveholder meet across Washington's tomb
in the proslavery novel *Aunt Phillis's Cabin* (1852), they find "a
melancholy fascination in this hollow, deserted grave" that echoes
the distance between two sets of national sons. Mount Vernon provided for some Americans didactic recollections of "the spot where
he [Washington] sat for a whole morning carefully timing the de-

liberate labors of his negro Carpenters as they consulted and planned, and sawed and hewed their logs, in order to compare what amount of labor he might require on a daily task, without being severe or exacting." Other visitors to this New World Bethlehem did not encounter memories of industry or fairness, but instead found a history saddled with shame. In *The Liberty Bell* of 1852, the abolitionist pilgrim who recounted his horror at meeting outside Washington's tomb a slave trader leading three manacled men also recorded that slavery had made Washington's lands barren. After giving vent to to his staccato laments, "Alas! . . . for the Ancient Dominion—the land of Washington!—her soil worn out—her children led away captive—surely a curse has fallen upon her," he can only ask "why is it so?"[4]

The despairing impotence of this unanswerable query reveals how ruptures in authority made impossible a national narrative in which ancestors would clearly point the way to a destiny secured by unambiguous moral principle. Like the retrospective traveler who reaches Mount Vernon but finds the moral closure of "Washington" unattainable, the antebellum sons failed to arrive at a critical theory of freedom because freedom, so dependent upon the examples of the fathers, did not legitimate criticism of those fathers. The incongruity of patriarchal servitude within national memory—both as filial obedience to the founding legacy and more viscerally as race slavery—paralyzed a generation attempting to restore and preserve a freedom it never had or practiced. What the sons of the American Renaissance failed to understand was that incongruity is fundamental to narratives of freedom, and that freedom itself is dependent upon recognition of the disjunctions in the national legacy. This understanding of the contradictory necessity of freedom could be expressed only by those whose lives and texts marked the incomplete and aberrant quality of the founding promise. Enslaved by the legal coding of maternal genealogy, not free to claim the authority of paternal genealogy, and considered a problem in the national genealogy, only ex-slaves had the experience to theorize the hybrid, contested line of freedom.

It remains to be asked, then, what narratives of political freedom prevailed among those sons born without an inheritance other than illegitimacy and bondage. Slavery certainly erupted as a disruptive codicil to a generation's political and cultural inheritance, but how did that inheritance figure for those whose enslaved bodies were the source of conflict within national narrative? Could those held in bondage by both the founding fathers themselves and the discourse of founding fathers nevertheless appeal to national ancestors in their struggles for freedom? In other words, does a legacy of freedom exist within a history of enslavement? Can a legacy of freedom exist without a history of enslavement? To investigate these questions, I intend to read slave narratives, plus two works of fiction authored by fugitive slaves, William Wells Brown's *Clotel; or, The President's Daughter* and Frederick Douglass's "The Heroic Slave," as highly ambivalent instances where competing senses of genealogy combine. These authors all unavoidably situate their texts within the genealogical metaphors of national narrative that delineate political continuity between generations, and yet each ex-slave writes from the memory of a more peculiar historical context in which continuity between fathers and sons was ignored, even outlawed. From this disjunction, from the gap between national genealogy and the slave's illicit genealogy, a critical historiography of genealogy emerges revealing the inherent deformations and contradictions within the narrative of American freedom. Considering the all too typical condition of the slave narrator, the abolitionist editor of *The Narrative of William W. Brown* (1848) exclaims "A father—alas! slaves have no father"; however, in a lecture appended to his narrative, Brown identifies with national patriarchal discourse and wonders "I might carry the audience back to the time when your fathers were struggling for liberty in 1776. When they went forth upon the battle-field and laid down their bones, and moistened the soil with their blood, that their children might enjoy liberty. What was it for?"[5] As the lack of personal genealogy confronted the plenitude of national history, African Americans writing in the mid-nineteenth century intensified the ambivalent articulations of national narrative, but they saw no reason to deplore this ambivalence. Instead, texts by ex-slaves prohibit the restoration of any genealogical line, suggesting that only in the discontinuity and disorder of bastard histories does remembering properly construct freedom.

DISCURSIVE PASSING

The fact that eight years after the appearance of his *Narrative*, Douglass retrieved the patronym Washington for "The Heroic Slave" in no way indicates that he made peace with the associations of a contested legacy. Rather, for Douglass and other ex-slaves, subscription to national narrative produced a hybrid narrative in which black rebels resemble white patriots even as they differ from them. This disjunctive tension of resemblance and difference takes on particular resonance given the use of passing as a strategy of resistance within the slaveholding South and the prejudiced North. In passing, the slave mimicked the appearance of white ancestors only in some way to remain dissimilar to those he or she resembled. What seems innocuous sameness was only a deception laden with subversive potential. The action of passing encompassed more than the fair-skinned slave who exploited and confounded the liberatory identity of the white, enfranchised citizen. Passing is more than an action; it is also an intervention in the cultural authority of language.

Passing offers an explanation of how enslaved and oppositional discourses repeat authorized discourses without becoming identical to or subsumed by that authority. Ex-slaves reiterate stories of the founding fathers, but passing maintains a loophole of textual escape through which narrators ironize and make different the national narratives they mimic. Such mimicry is rife with an ambivalence that disrupts even the most settled and authoritative configurations of power. Although the genealogical African who passes with a white mask perhaps acknowledges the supremacy of white culture, and the ex-slave who repeats the names of founding fathers may appear accepting of the nation that enslaved him, these seemingly co-optive mirrorings, repetitions, and emulations always lack perfect duplication. This moment of lack, this unassimilable remainder, undoes exact repetition, and this inexactness becomes the site of visual discrepancy, narrative variation, and possible resistance. The colonial subject who visibly repeats the dominant authority of the empire enacts a subversive strategy that Homi Bhabha calls a *"difference that is almost the same but not quite"*—a difference that is *"almost the same but not white."*[6] Passing—in both its literal and discursive uses—signifies a comforting sameness, another reaffirming repetition of the white father's biological and political ancestry, even as it harbors a racial difference that interrupts and unsettles white patriarchy and its accompanying control over national imagining.

The slave who passed set in motion an ambiguous play of differences visually coded as resemblances. The presence of people legally defined by the slavocracy as black slaves whose appearance may have been no different than that of white landowners signaled a rupture within the fabric of social and political boundaries. The status of white and free, upheld by a complex cultural apparatus, could bleed into the category of black and slave. Even though slave and citizen might be indistinguishable, the slave code contended that an ineffable, essential difference must exist. What ensued was a disjunction: what is the same is not the same. Artful legal determinations no doubt denied freedom and dignity to many held as chattel, but this same insistence upon difference proved instrumental to ex-slaves who crossed the boundaries of white, literate discourse. Difference remained the mark of the slave narrator. Invoking Washington, as might any antebellum white son, the slave narrator failed to duplicate perfectly the rituals of filial obeisance. Some tinge of difference—an unlooked-for irony, an uncertain intention, a discordant inflection—persisted. A differential history always lingers: ex-slaves' autobiographies, stories, and novels appear to consent to national ideology and to be fodder for national narrative—but are not. In other words, to adapt a seminal concept from Henry Louis Gates, Jr., ex-slaves' repetition of national narrative conjures up the rhetorical play of "signifyin(g)," in which black texts bear an intertextual and revisionary relation to the more "original" texts they follow and supplement. Although Gates's theory concerns manipulations of *"homo rhetoricus Africanus,"* who signifies upon other black writers, his suggestion that "black formal repetition always repeats with a difference" applies to a simultaneous imitation and transformation that occurs when national narrative is spoken by those who have been denied historical speech.[7]

Writing of the rebellious slave in *My Bondage and My Freedom* (1855), Douglass makes aggressive use of this power, which we might call "discursive passing": "If he kills his master, he imitates only the heroes of the revolution." Despite its incendiary directness, Douglass's statement is laced with cultural and historical residues that render dark and murky any distinctions between heroes and oppressors. This confusion filters across several identifications, most prominent of which is the rebellious slave who "passes" as revolutionary patriarch. Douglass's hypothetical violence aligns founding fathers and slaves through a sort of historical doubling that transcends racial markings. Yet most of antebellum America was loath to discard visible identifications of race and enter a rhetorical space like Douglass's, where distinctions blur between white patriots and black rebels. Few citizens would see black slaves as offspring of white Revolutionary heroes; rather, stronger connections appeared between the white skin of the men of 1776 and the white skin of the slaveholding sons of the 1850s. Ironic undercuttings surround Douglass's equation of slave and patriot because this affiliation occurred within a cultural situation that more readily recognized the slaveholder as the descendent of founding fathers. Indeed, in the year following the publication of Douglass's declaration in *My Bondage and My Freedom*, Chief Justice Roger Taney juxtaposed slaves and these same heroes of American history, not to argue the legitimacy of blacks' efforts to achieve freedom, but to reaffirm the foundations of black servitude. In his rejection of a suit for freedom made by Dred Scott, Taney cited "the conduct of the distinguished men who framed the Declaration of Independence," and comparing this legacy with the present conduct of antebellum institutions, he discovered no disparity, finding only ample precedent and justification for race slavery. Holding other beings in bondage, he declared, the slaveholder "imitates only the heroes of revolution."[8]

The comparison of slaves and patriots proves an uneasy association in which dominant rhetoric threatens to dispel Douglass's incendiary suggestion by containing it within traditional patriarchal readings saturated with the precedents and practices of race slavery. Or does the sanctified narrative of the founding fathers serve as an ironic frame, a disguise that allows for the subversive articulation of black, male violence? This uncertainty arose from the conflicted circumstances and ironic strategies—black violence against whites, illegitimate and muddled genealogies, and passing—that surrounded the slave's quest for freedom. At the level of narrative, not just the slave's narrative, but the discursive space where an ex-slave interacts with the historical narratives already embedded in the culture, these conflicts elucidate how in America freedom as a foundational narrative is written and authorized. Whether or not Douglass's use of the founding fathers is a moment of acquiescence or subversion seems endlessly debatable, and it is in fact a skewing of a larger question. Rather than asking how mention of the founding fathers affects Douglass, we can ask how in their articulations of national history Douglass and other ex-slaves alter the manner in which America narrativizes freedom as a coherent, seamless, and unambiguous story. Writings by ex-slaves make discontinuous and incongruous a narrative of freedom that was so unquestioningly consistent. But for that to happen, slave narrators had to first pass into the rhetoric, myth, and history that emplots freedom in America.

Douglass's career as a slave narrator provides a glimpse into the difficulties of writing the slave's story with biographies and recollections reserved for white patriotic discourse. The conscription of resisting slaves into the ranks of American patriots that occurs in *My Bondage and My Freedom* reverses subtle trends voiced first in Douglass's previous autobiography, *Narrative of the Life of Frederick Douglass* (1845). The *Narrative* timorously approaches history, representing resistance to tyranny only through apology and evasion and placing this resistance within the American revolutionary mythos only after prefatory documents of white abolitionists draw the bulk of historical parallels. As a composite text mediated by white editors, his *Narrative* removes its central narrator from the panoply of American history. What Douglass narrates is his personal history, and he begins with an acute sense of an inability to write his life with the dates and facts that make up the grist of history. Shakily grounded in "no accurate knowledge" and "opinion," dubiously supported by statements such as "I do not remember" and "the nearest estimate I can make," this slave narrator, like virtually all others, speaks from a historical void. Sketchy of his own history, the slave author has little authority to suggest intersections between his *Narrative* and American historical narrative.[9]

The text looks to white editors and abolitionists to provide access to discourses capable of a more extensive and critical historical commentary. From the introductory letters of Garrison and Phillips, which suggest resemblances between a slave son and the founding fathers, the *Narrative* finds a critical impetus by mingling with broadly construed discourses of religion and American history; and yet, such moves often seem engineered by those elements of the *Narrative* with explicit white textual overseers invested with the authority of race and genealogy to invoke dates like 1776 and names like Patrick Henry. When Douglass states in chapter 10 that "we did more than Patrick Henry, when he resolved upon liberty or death," he does not access American historical narrative so much as he echoes Garrison's prefatory authentification, which first situates the

Narrative in the context of Patrick Henry and other heroes of the Revolution. A similar situation hounded Douglass on the Garrisonian lecture platform, where white abolitionists encouraged the fugitive slave to keep within the bounds of personal narrative and to refrain from accessing larger cultural narratives. "Give us the facts," the general agent of the Massachusetts Anti-Slavery Society told Douglass, "we will take care of the philosophy." Garrison seconded this caution, encouraging his protégé to "repeat the same old story month after month" and not to move beyond the mediated confines of the slave's autobiography.[10] No doubt Douglass wrote his own narrative, but the critical potential of subscribing to national narrative remained cordoned off, guarded, however kindly, by philanthropy and charitable advice, as a discursive arena not to be assimilated to the slave's voice.

Upon his break with the Garrisonians, Douglass cast off this hesitation to connect the slave's history to sacrosanct narratives of American history. This change charts Douglass's increasing literary self-reliance and creative independence, but it also forms a part of a significant tendency in antebellum African American discourse to encode lives, memories, and political struggles with dominant narratives of American history.[11] Blurring distinctions between slave murderers and revolutionary patriots, Douglass amalgamated illicit black rebellion to nationally authorized history; in effect, he disguised potentially alarming aspects of black discourse with the plots, characters, and signifiers of American narrative.[12] Much like the strategy whereby light-skinned mulatto slaves passed as white citizens in order to attain freedom, ex-slave narrators and authors in the decade before the Civil War made figurative use of American Revolutionary history as a means to pass off a political theory of black freedom. Exploring the connections between black slaves who passed as whites and black rebels who cloaked themselves in the history of white "fathers" allows for a reevaluation of confused identities and ambivalent national constructs. Just as literal passing frustrates rigid distinctions between races, a figurative, discursive passing in which marginalized narrative passes as dominant narrative ironizes once seemingly clear and unadulterated narratives of freedom.

Upstart colonists once likened themselves to slaves suffering under the political oppression of the king, and a generation later, fugitive slaves cast themselves as the adopted descendants of heroic patriots.

In defense of his participation in Nat Turner's revolt (originally planned for July 4), a slave in *Clotel* declares: "You tell me that I am to be put to death for violating the laws of the land. Did not the American revolutionists violate the laws when they struck for liberty?" He justifies his attempt to secure freedom by appealing to foundings that saw the importation of slaves to Jamestown and the *Mayflower* refitted as a slaver; he sanctifies his rebellion by looking to a national narrative that remembered George Washington not solely as a liberator but also as the industrious employer of Mount Vernon who made certain his human chattel were not consumed by idleness.[13] The politics of searching out freedom within this paradoxical context reveals the ambivalent genealogy of freedom itself, caught within an equivocal patrimony that acknowledges the masters' sons' claims to the promises of American history even as it disavows the same legacy to those "children" it enslaved and even fathered.

William Andrews, Hazel Carby, Henry Louis Gates, Jr., Valerie Smith, and Robert Stepto among others have made significant contributions to the study of slave narrative and African American fiction, demonstrating its rhetorical, cultural, performative and deconstructive aspects.[14] Still, critics have little assessed the complex, "signifyin(g)" interstices between ex-slave writings and national narrative. Such an association goes beyond suggesting that slave narratives contain political elements such as resistance or the acquisition of literacy, however. Autobiographies and fictions by ex-slaves form a necessary supplement to the corpus of foundational documents and legacies that define and constitute national narrative. But these supplements hardly shore up that narrative. Invested with the visual and discursive havoc of passing, slave narratives throw into confusion the genealogical metaphors used to delineate freedom in antebellum America. The preface achieves its most parricidal articulation in the slave narrative. Coming after the originary texts of patriarchal history, the slave narrative bears a filial relation to American national culture, but its preface to the founding legacy is discordant, a chronological homage that is in actuality a wholesale disclaimer. Though fatherly codes would never view its author as a legitimate descendant, the slave narrative insists on textual kinship with the fathers' history so that it can occupy a critical position and repeat—though differently—what the father has said. Slave narratives ambiguate national narratives, performing the critical work of genealogy by focusing upon the interruptions and gaps within history to assess, expose, and question the discursive configuration of American freedom.

Ex-slave writings form a history that mut(il)ates as it repeats founding narratives; African American texts supply what Foucault calls an "effective history" that counters accepted patterns and dominant codes in order to "uproot . . . traditional foundations and relentlessly disrupt . . . pretended continuity." The slave's "effective history" lacks a totalizing account; it tells the story of the nation—but not exactly. Tethered to the representation of the slave as founding father is a narrative of the slave's genealogy that does not match the nation's genealogy: this discrepancy within sameness, this repetition that remains different, calls attention to what Bhabha terms a "minus-in-origin" that questions the basic story of America—freedom.[15] Emerging from the slave's uncertain family history, discursive passing exposes the incongruities of a national narrative that delimited freedom by employing a mythos that recognized only the avowed sons of the fathers. The slave's genealogy—both as personal history and as national critique—does not declare freedom null and void so much as it recontextualizes freedom from plenitude and promise to a narrative of lack and deferral. Freedom, like the legally delineated slave visibly inscribed as white, like the slave passing as a free citizen, like the noncitizen speaking the legacy of citizens, appears as a contradiction and an inconsistency, forever chained to the slave discourse it would repress without return.

PASSING FROM AHISTORICAL CHATTEL TO FATHERED CITIZEN

Although slave narrators' strategic use of the patriotic legacy constitutes a remarkable configuration of history, even more complex is the slaves' appeal to history when their identities, families, and experiences were deprived of history. An authorized genealogy remained inaccessible to many slaves. "My father was a white man, and he would not let me be called by his name," remembered ex-slave Aunt Jane Lee in the Reconstruction volume *The House of Bondage* (1890).[16] Octavia V. Rogers Albert, who interviewed residents of an ex-slave community in Louisiana, titled her story "A Touching Incident," referring to the maternal embrace rejoining mother and son separated by slavery that concludes the collection. A healing touch reconnects blood that had been sold, though forever prohibited is contact with the white father who could authenticate (and manumit) his blood. Slave codes privileged a history that had no privilege: the legal formulation decreeing "the condition of the child follows that of the mother" left slaves with a genealogy that bespoke only servitude. Certainly, a genealogy of black matriarchy could function as a powerful locus of family solidarity. Despite evidence of matriarchal resistance in works like Harriet Jacobs's *Incidents in the Life of a Slave Girl* or Lucy Delaney's *Struggle for Freedom*, the absence of a recognized patriarchy placed slaves within a genealogical void. Under the Southern legal system, black women were the bearers of chattel, not people generative of historical subjectivity. The slave child followed no history of a father's rights and duties of citizenship; instead, the slave issued forth not from a woman, but from a matrix of nonhistory, from a textual-sexual space that signified emptiness and absence, illegitimacy and silence. Whereas the title character of Melville's *Pierre*, like Melville himself, is anchored by his "double Revolutionary descent," the slave received no birthright but a mess of pottage containing, in the words of Orlando Patterson, nothing more than "natal alienation and genealogical isolation."[17]

The act of resistance encoded within the slave narrative did not always liberate the slave from the genealogical void imposed by the master class. Consider John Thompson, who remembers his mother and father as field hands who raised a family of seven, but nonetheless begins his narrative by recording the genealogy of the white family he served. This history of the black self acquires no autonomy, remaining dependent upon the authorizing line of the plantation's paterfamilias. Solomon Northup's *Twelve Years a Slave* (1853) represents a rare exception to the genealogical anonymity of the slave's condition. This narrative, recounting the kidnapping of a free black and his sale to the Deep South, attains freedom in the confirming facts of an identifiable patriarchy. In the final sentence of his tribulations, Northup states: "Chastened and subdued in spirit by the sufferings I have borne, and thankful to that good Being through whose mercy I have been restored to happiness and liberty, I hope henceforward to lead an upright though lowly life, and rest at last in the church yard where my father sleeps."[18] Freedom and fatherhood provide closure to narrative. One assures the other: because he is raised in freedom, he can reclaim a pastoral image of the land where his fathers died; because he can remember his father, he can re-achieve the freedom he so tragically lost. Northup's closing formula, positing a certain equivalence between freedom and fatherhood, hardly would seem unfamiliar to America's post-Revolutionary sons. After all, as they constantly reminded themselves, the heroic deeds of their fathers forged a freedom to be transmitted through the generations. Northup's memory of his father and his "paternal counsels" provides him with a poetic impulse to struggle for freedom; yet it is white fatherhood that legally returns this kidnapped son back into the fold of freedom. Only through the efforts of the white Northups does the legal machinery move to emancipate him. As with Thompson's narrative, which initiates a history out of white genealogy, Northup's narrative resolves itself with a return to the same originary fount, inheriting freedom from a culturally acknowledged patriarchy.

"What is there for him in past history?" asks Samuel Ringgold Ward as he considers the "American Negro" in his *Autobiography of a Fugitive Negro*. Within the practices of antebellum domination, history fathered a narrative that excluded the memory of black slaves. Ward's one-word answer—"slavery"—encapsulates the dearth of historical material in formulating a liberatory African American consciousness. Whereas William Wells Brown's survey of monumental America shows how a black patriarchy of national proportion was colonized off in the country's memory, white fathers were characterized by a plenitude of tradition and copious rituals of remembering. White patriarchy indicated more than a social organization ordered around the supremacy of the father's genealogical line; it signified the origin of freedom and acted as the reference for the self's national identity. Without white fathers—or at least white fathers whom slaves could acknowledge as kin—slaves had no connections to the lines of freedom. Patriarchy fathers freedom: it represents a masculine capacity to create dependents whose very dependency confirms the ascendancy, autonomy, and centrality of the father. Inverting the Declaration of Independence, one proslavery essayist asserted: "all men are born absolutely dependent, and utterly devoid of freedom." More extensive than the biological implications of fatherhood, patriarchy spawns others—children, wives, and slaves—who possess no independence and whose inability to claim political freedom constantly reiterates the father's freedom. In other words, patriarchy fathers freedom for itself because it fathers slavery and dependency for others. *The Narrative of James Roberts* (1858) dramatizes how the fulfillment of Revolutionary independence for the fathers translated into increased servile dependence for slave sons. Though he helped Washington's armies to capture Cornwallis at Yorktown, Roberts realized he fought for a freedom that was summarily capitulated to men who, with that newly found freedom, caused the "chains of slavery to be bound tighter around the necks of my people than they were before."[19]

Deprived of a recognized genealogical author of his or her being, denied the historical mooring necessary for political identity, the slave self and the slave's text suffers gaps and absences. Fugitive slave James Pennington reached a conclusion, shared by many slaves, that slavery "throws his [the slave's] family history into utter confusion, and leaves him without a single record to which he may appeal in vindication of his character, or honor."[20] Compare this absence of an authorized legacy with the benefits that more regularly descended sons of the American Renaissance received as their inheritance. Although Melville's Pierre Glendinning encounters repressive traces of his paternal ancestors, national tradition still predicts for him a powerful position in society and history. Looking back at ancestral relations, Pierre sees a past laden with precedents promising an inheritance of renown and esteem. Likewise, the boy Henry Adams surveys his family line and concludes that he will one day claim the White House. Both family history and knowledge of past distinguished deeds lead these sons to embark upon the world with confidence. Their births figure as extensions of lives begun by their forefathers, lives that prompt them to assume destinies from respectable merchant to president. And though these sons eventually witness their inheritance dissipating in the harshness of urban capitalism and technology, that inheritance defines and consecrates the self with a genealogy as authoritative as national history because the story of the Adamses or of Pierre's grandfathers is the hallowed story of America.

In contrast, the slave enters the world from a historical void, with no inheritance other than the legal determination that he or she is to be inherited by the master's legitimate descendants. "In antebellum America," writes Henry Louis Gates, Jr., "it was the deprivation of time in the life of the slave that first signaled his or her status as a piece of property." Lacking patriarchal genealogy, slaves had no claim upon the masculine ordering of time, rectilinear, originary, and historical. Slaves seemed fettered within the nonauthoritative rhythms of biological time generated by the slave mother's blood, which under the codes of slavocracy transmitted racial servitude. Defined by the nonmarkings of historical anonymity and genealogical absence, the slave received only a birthright of dependence and nonpersonhood, what Orlando Patterson calls "social death."[21] Recalling life under the peculiar institution, Silvia Dubois remembered of slave masters: "They didn't no more keep the date of a young nigger than they did of a calf or a colt; the young niggers were born in the Fall or in the Spring, in the Summer or the Winter, in cabbage time or when cherries were ripe, when they were planting corn or when they were husking corn, and that's the way they talked about a nigger's age."[22] Denied to the slave was any sense of advancement; time existed in a circular void deficient in either progress or development. Whereas pious republican sons enjoyed a defined mission, to recover the examples of the fathers, the unacknowledged black sons, in the eyes of slaveholders, could only repeat maternal and enslaved origins. The white sons' mission was to move linearly across history and space and bring the fathers' freedom to California and Mexico; in contrast, according to one proslavery thinker, blacks were subject "to the empire of the white man's will," trapped within a closed destiny that "was plainly written on the heavens during our Revolutionary war."[23] Though originating from vastly different subjectivities, the words of the slave and the apologist each record how the history lived by citizens deprived others of a ratifying past.

Not only did slaves seem to originate without male descendants from the nothingness of predestined servitude, they themselves often lacked a fixed point of origin. Unable to assert a birth date, many slaves could not summon a lived historical subjectivity as a reference point to found and order a past. Exclusion from historical subjectivity denoted the more pervasive segregation of the slave, a segregation from humanness. The conventional opening for many slave narratives, "I was born . . . ," responds to the sentence of historical deprivation by asserting an origin for the slave through the act of narrative. Yet, too often, the narrator fails to achieve any certainty about his birth date or family history—an ironic strategy that authorized the speaker, not with the historical facts available to honorable white citizens, but with the deployment of the gaps and rumors of a slave's history. "It is quite a truism that 'a nigger never knows when he was born,'" stated John Brown in his 1855 narrative. "For though he may be quite certain of the year, and might swear to it blindfold, he must say he is just as old as his master chooses to bid him do, or he will have to take the consequences."[24] Personal and familial history, integral to the articulation of self within American culture, served the slave owner.

Why, after all, would slaveholding culture admit the slave into the domain of history, when it is history that makes an animal into human being, when it is history that extends legitimacy to the self? The men who carved plantations from the wilderness saw themselves as founders originating resplendent patriarchies. Writing from eighteenth-century Virginia, William Byrd declared: "Like one of the Patriarchs, I have my Flocks and my Herds, my Bond-men and Bond-women, and every Soart of Trade amongst my own Servants, so that I live in a kind of Independence on everyone but Providence."[25] Within this scriptural metaphor of founding, any history the slave possessed originated with and descended from the father of the plantation. Ex-slave James Roberts, who, like Melville's Israel Potter, had memories of heroism upon the revolutionary battlefield, found himself stripped even of those traces of freedom. Instead of redeeming the promise of freedom framed by the thirty-nine signers of the Constitution, Roberts received the "nine-and-thirty lashes" that marked his career as a slave. Presented before his new master, Roberts must forfeit the historical signs identifying him as a participant in founding American narrative:

> And now will commence the statement of the payment of wages, for all my fighting and suffering in the Revolutionary War for the liberty of this ungrateful, illiberal country, to me and my race.... He [my master] took from me all my clothes which I had worn in Philadelphia, and some of my regimentals which I wished to keep as memorials of revolutionary times, and gave me instead a bare breechclout, and sent me into the field to work.[26]

In a most literal way, Robert's master senses how history unsettles enforced docility by providing the slave with a residue of freedom and impetus for rebellion against tyrannical rule. The master thus strips Roberts of the institutional registers of freedom, shrouding him instead in garments that signify only genealogical alienation and the drudgery of ahistorical existence. Without the sanction of the patriarchal institution, freedom fails to be preserved and recognized by history.

The denial of history at the most elemental level—the self—kept the slave alienated in bondage.[27] This alienation was physical as well as discursive: the slave qua slave could exact no claim upon genealogical metaphors that order self, community, and nation. Fathers, dates, ages, historical fact, chronology, all the signs of the patriarchal ordering of time into legitimate forms of memory, substantiate larger affiliations and confirm the self within a web of relations that bestow identity, origin, and belonging. Virtually all slave narratives recount at some point how the codes of the peculiar institution refused rudimentary historical inscriptions and thereby atomized the self within his or her own bondage. The slave might find solace of continuity and identity in family associations, but inevitably, a mistress's whimsy, economic necessity, or slave auctions could make tenuous and sever genealogical history. Or, if ancestral markers at first seemed more authorized—say, in the person of a white father— that history remained unutterable, inaccessible to the slave. Douglass, for instance, can only repeat a nonauthorized history when speaking of patriarchal origins: "The opinion was also whispered that my master was my father; but of the correctness of this opinion, I know nothing; the means of knowing withheld from me."[28] Cut off from kin, ancestors, even their own memories, slaves were not simply alienated, but discursively isolated. Slavery in this manner prohibits James Roberts from claiming any affiliation between personal history and national history; he is forbidden access to a larger cultural narrative that would identify him not as an object of drudgery, but as a human connected to other humans through the ties of family and collective memory of the nation. Slaveholding society set racial restrictions upon the patriarchal history that embraced white sons as citizens qualified to claim both an economic and a cultural inheritance while it bridled slaves with an interpretation of matriarchal history that defined and delimited illegitimate sons and daughters as slaves whose role was not to inherit but to be inherited.

Passing, however, provided ways for slaves to circumvent these prohibitions and to practice subversively a recognized patriarchal

history. The light skin of the antebellum mulatto signifies a genealogical history of freedom that, despite being unrecognized by the
peculiar institution, could not be recognized as different. In passing,
difference passes itself off as sameness, and the result is that difference suddenly has access to an arsenal of representation, rhetoric,
and freedom. The slave's literal passing as white soon opened up a
larger figurative field in which the slave moved from troping upon
visual ambiguity to a discursive troping upon white patriarchal
history and the national ideals it included. The 1860 slave narrative
Running a Thousand Miles for Freedom illustrates how visual passing
quickly led to subversive historical inscriptions of political freedom.
William Craft recounts his sensational escape with his wife, Ellen,
who both pass by exploiting an unauthorized version of white fatherhood. That version is Ellen herself. Her master's daughter, Ellen
is "almost white," and she and her husband signify upon the historical trace of the white father to rewrite themselves. Husband and
wife enact a gender and racial masquerade in which Ellen passes as
a Spanish gentleman and her husband, darker than his wife, becomes
"his" loyal manservant. The Crafts don new clothing and new roles,
becoming "master" and slave, and escape from a Georgia plantation.
Visual passing soon escalates, granting the slaves access into narratives reserved exclusively for whites. At a crucial point in their
flight, master and servant are refused tickets to board a northbound
steamer. But seeing the white face of Ellen, a drunken Southerner not
only supposes her to be white and a man, but grants her the privileges
of identity and family that invest patriarchal history. "I know his kin
(friends) like a book," the Southerner swears, giving her a legitimate
genealogy, and the fugitives receive permission to travel across the
Mason-Dixon line. The brandy-enhanced formulation of the Southerner reveals the authoritative status of white patriarchy; like a
written document, an acknowledged genealogy carries the legitimacy to pass into freedom.[29]

    Running a Thousand Miles for Freedom opens with Craft's descrip-
tion of his and his wife's isolation from the larger cultural narratives
of American politics and religion:

> Having heard while in Slavery that "God made of one blood all
> nations of men," and also that the American Declaration of Indepen-
> dence says, that "We hold these truths to be self-evident, that all
> men are created equal; that they are endowed by their Creator with

certain inalienable Rights; that among these, are Life, Liberty, and
the pursuit of Happiness"; we could not understand by what right
we were held as "chattels."

Like James Roberts, who had to forfeit his Revolutionary mementos
and memories, William and Ellen Craft must relinquish the history
of the Revolution and the founding fathers, for they have no recognized fathers, and after Nat Turner's 1831 uprising, planters had little
intention of permitting talk of "Revolution" among their slaves.
Patrolling the borders of patriotic discourse, one proslavery pamphlet thus asserted: "The celebration of the Fourth of July belongs
exclusively to the white population of the United States." Adopting
a similar perspective, the Supreme Court determined that the phrases
from the Declaration that Craft cites in the first paragraph of his
narrative do not "embrace the whole human family. . . . the enslaved
African race were not intended to be included, and formed no part
of the people who framed and adopted this Declaration." *Running
a Thousand Miles for Freedom* confronts these taboos and seizes history,
amalgamating dominant white discourse to black political purposes.
Craft refers back to the title of his narrative to tell how far he and his
wife would travel to break out of their discursive isolation: "we felt
perfectly justified in undertaking the dangerous and exciting task of
'running a thousand miles' in order to obtain these rights which are
so vividly set forth in the Declaration."[30] In the first sentences of this
narrative, Craft refers equally to American history and to his own
and his wife's history as slaves. He quotes from the Declaration and
then mingles discourses by quoting from his own narrative in the
next sentence. One historical narrative passes into the other, allowing
not just for the visual paradox of the black slave who appears as a
white citizen, but for the discursive paradox of silenced "chattels"
who intone the documents of freedom.

    The genealogy of freedom for which the light skin of the mulatto
stood was thus inconsistent—the slave with free blood, the ahistorical chattel marked with the history of citizen fathers—and these
contradictions had the power to disrupt dominant understandings of
patriarchal identification in antebellum America. As an "almost
white" woman held in bondage, Ellen Craft poses the possibility of
a confused narrative whose ambiguity threatens the cozy, seamless-
ness of Southern domesticity. *Running a Thousand Miles for Freedom*

details how the inescapable sameness of Ellen's light skin unsettles order and appearance in the master's family: "Ellen is almost white—in fact, she is so nearly so that the tyrannical old lady to whom she first belonged became so annoyed, at finding her frequently mistaken for a child of the family, that she gave her when eleven years of age to a daughter, as a wedding present." And in her adult life, the unstable narrative implied by Ellen's visible being jeopardizes the genealogical respectability and purity so central to the plantation patriarch. In one of the most ironic scenes of the Craft's narrative, Ellen, disguised as a white gentleman, receives an invitation to call upon a "good old Virginian gentleman" to further an acquaintance with the man's marriageable daughters.[31] The genteel rituals of courting, designed to keep spotless the blood of the first families, prove ineffective before the ambiguous trope of passing. The father's effort to preserve the sanctity of family history flirts with an interracial lesbian affair.

Sensitive to such sexual embarrassment and genealogical danger, slaveholders interpreted the ambiguous narrative of the mulatto with a severity intended to eradicate any confused and contradictory inscriptions of history. For this reason, illegitimate traces of white patriarchy resulted not always in freedom, but in greater subjection and cruelty. What represented political legitimacy for the acknowledged white child was anathema to the slave. Moses Roper's unsolicited and invalid patriarchy that spoke freedom's genealogy thus threatened to make slavery more than mere social death:

> As soon as my father's wife heard of my birth, she sent one of my mother's sisters to see whether I was white or black, and when my aunt had seen me, she returned back as soon as she could, and told her mistress that I was white, and resembled Mr. Roper very much. Mr. R's wife being not pleased with this report, she got a large club stick and knife, and hastened to the place in which my mother was confined. She went into my mother's room with full intention to murder me with her knife and club.

Southern legal codes identified the signs of patriarchal freedom as contraband when manifested in the physical aspect of the slave. The law permitted slaveowners to rehistoricize the slave's body, even by the most brutal means. Masters could alter the slave's body in an effort to nullify any traces of white genealogy. In the appendix to

Brown's *Narrative*, an account from a Southern newspaper details an incident in which an "almost white" slave was "branded in the face with the words, 'A slave for life.'" Other masters preferred more subtle methods: *Clotel* paints a portrait of a mistress who sentences her husband's near-white daughter to labor in the "broiling rays" of the sun, causing her "fair complexion" and its attendant signs of freedom to disappear.[32]

PARRICIDAL PATRIOTS

William Wells Brown's *Clotel* and Frederick Douglass's "The Heroic Slave" offer reasons for plantation patriarchs' vehement reaction to the possibilities of passing. In these literary crosses that mix slave narrative, fiction, and national history, Brown and Douglass feature not just slaves who pass as white men, but heroes who, as they resist and even kill whites, pass themselves off with the valor and rhetoric of white founding fathers.[33] Passing is an exercise of critical authorship in which the slave narrator usurps a legitimate history of freedom and whiteness and rewrites the self with the rights and privileges of historical presence, countering institutional injunctions that rendered the slave a blank historical cipher. The radical doubling and subversive appropriation of American patriarchal history that occurs in each of these fictions first evolved from the slave's contested subscription to literary fatherhood. Even before outcast daughters and sons such as Clotel Jefferson and Madison Washington steal into the ranks of patriarchy and inherit the justifications of founding narrative, Brown and Douglass write themselves as authors, as progenitors of the written word. Given the prejudiced assumptions surrounding race and writing that denied the slave originality, the ability to name, and textual authority, the metaphoric associations linking authorship and patriarchy seemed outside the reach and scope of the slave pen.

    Although born out of a fugitive's life, slave narratives hardly appeared to the public as autonomous efforts. Slave narratives frequently open with prefaces from white editors who authenticated the slave's account, either compromising the text by revealing the presence of an amanuensis or affirming that the slave did indeed write his or her own narrative. Once again, the preface is parricidal, though the racial dynamics are now inverted. Whereas black slaves impede the transmission of fatherly authority in biographies of Washington, here, a white figure interrupts articulations of black textual independence. Literary fatherhood originates in an already established editor who protects and oversees the fledging work's entry into the world. Further impairing the fugitive's adoption of a cultural patriarchy, skeptics held that literary talents were not self-generated, but descended from white fathers. Newspaper accounts attributed Brown's eloquence to a species of biological ventriloquism, denying the African American self any participation in aesthetic procreation: "Mr. Brown is a gentleman of pleasing appearance and good address. He is far removed from the black race, being just the 'color of mahogany,' and his distinct enunciation evidently showed that a white man 'spoke' within, although the words were uttered by the lips of a redeemed slave." Wit, charisma, intelligence, in short, anything distinguishing the slave as a man, supposedly derived from a white legacy that had managed to show through the slave's more "essential" illegitimacy. The slave's accomplishments were not viewed as his own property, but as the illicit fruits of white patriarchy. As an English newspaper reported in 1857, "The remarks and anecdotes of Mr. Brown, who is a bright and handsome mulatto, were exceedingly eloquent, humorous and interesting, showing clearly the white blood of his father."[34] Genealogical determinations prevented the authorship of a self-devised black patrimony, absorbing black cultural achievements within a white tradition or classifying blacks as a lawless breed.

Douglass and Brown freed themselves from this cultural vise by authoring literary texts uncompromised by white editorial control. After his break with the Garrisonians to start his own newspaper, Douglass expanded his autobiography as *My Bondage and My Freedom*, prefaced, not by a white editor, but by the black abolitionist James McCune Smith. Smith paid tribute to Douglass for slipping out of the fatherly "embrace of the Garrisonians." Three years earlier, Douglass had recognized this situation of discursive constraint and confided about Garrison: "I stand in relation to him something like that of a child to a parent." The parent soon sought to reprimand his rebellious child. By the time of the publication of *My Bondage and My Freedom*, Garrison had removed Douglass's newspaper from the *Liberator*'s list of approved antislavery publications, and as Eric Sundquist notes, this white editor and abolitionist began reprinting

Doulgass's articles under a column entitled "Refuge of Oppression," where proslavery pieces usually appeared.[35] In the latter segment of this autobiography, entitled "Life as a Freeman," Douglass now narrated the life of a self no longer under a master's ownership and subscribed himself to a text not under the guidance of a white editor. Like so many American sons, Douglass had left the paternal roof. Brown similarly played the literary father by penning a number of autobiographical selves in prefaces to the histories, novels, and travel narratives he authored. Brown's repeated use of his own autobiographical slave narrative as preface and introduction declared that literary output descended neither from a white editor nor slave master, but from a self conceived out of a newly acquired literacy.

Douglass's revised autobiography and Brown's texts willingly engender prefaces as signs of their narrative power. Evidence of this creative and procreative capacity echoes the gendered aspects inherent in the preface-text relation, but attention to race in antebellum America lends Derrida's account of the preface historical depth. The text's "mastering" here appears as part of repressive cultural context upheld by an elaborate apparatus of bondage. *My Bondage and My Freedom* and *Clotel* avoid parricidal subversion from Smith's introduction and Brown's prefatory autobiographical sketch because within a scenario of white editors and black authors, textual mastery and resistance are cast in terms of the racial specifics of bondage and freedom in the United States, and these specifics shift Smith's preface from a relationship of domination and subversion to one of cooperation. Smith does not abjure a filial relation in his tribute to Douglass, but he claims for each an identity as his mother's son, not his father's: "The son of a self-emancipated bond-woman, I feel joy in introducing to you my brother." Sharing this maternal identification, Smith and Douglass have the same cultural positioning—sons of an African American mother—and parricide does not become a factor because their discursive relationship is not one of fatherly hierarchy but of fraternal equality based on a common legacy of maternally derived servitude. Instead, its supplemental potential is reserved for the white patriarchal authority that underwrites the larger cultural narratives encompassing nineteenth-century politics.

The fictions of Douglass and Brown figure as ascending acts of literacy through which the ex-slave then begins to acquire a patriarchal identity and its attendant freedom. Sundquist sees Douglass's

"The Heroic Slave" as an "act of self-fathering" precisely because it is a fictional narrative. Freedom accompanies the inscription of textual authority. The conclusion of *Clotel* concedes that its plots have been fashioned from the tales told by other fugitives. But what may seem a confession actually points to Brown's authority to adopt others' stories—what he calls his "free use" of narrative—which he associates with the privileges of authorship.[36] Douglass and Brown depart from strict accounts of life under the peculiar institution to experiment with fiction, signing themselves as creators of historical narrative. In doing so, they realized not how fiction is opposed to history, but how the "factual" discourse of history is itself a fabricated domain forged from the authority of patriarchal nationalism. Yet even as they sabotage history and free themselves from white editorial control, Douglass and Brown reinscribe themselves within a patriarchal legacy once held by founding fathers and passed down to sons who included respectable slaveholders.

In *Clotel* and "The Heroic Slave," each author regains a cultural inheritance never allowed to him, recuperating a legacy marked by men who generations earlier had dictated black enslavement. Remembering founding fathers, the slave no doubt refers to an oppressive national narrative, but the slave also passes into a discourse that provides a rhetorical framework for freedom. In the same way that the Crafts transform the circumstances of amalgamation and resituate the illicit history of the mulatto's face, Douglass and Brown critically recontextualize the legacy of the founding fathers so that it resists univocal interpretation and reads as an amalgamated story of freedom and enslavement. In other words, the history and ideology of slavery pass as a narrative of freedom. This confusion, stemming from the slave's irony, radically contests the presumed moral clarity and political virtue of founding principle. This appeal to the legacy of freedom by two ex-slaves contains all the disruptive ambivalence of difference passing as sameness; their histories acknowledge and rebuke ancestors who legislated independence even as they secured the slave system. Like the mixed blood of the mulatto child, and like the mixed practices of freedom and enslavement, the ambivalence of a hybrid national genealogy remembers blood sons who were excluded from the political family of citizens. The nation's heritage appears undermined by its own contradictions and ironies, which reveal legally sanctioned bondage as the undeniable twin of freedom.

To understand this more complete genealogy of American freedom, it is helpful to consider briefly freedom's often ambivalent origins. Colonial Virginia emerged as the breeding ground of the struggle against British tyranny, not in spite of, but because of the peculiar institution's hold upon the land. The presence of people totally deprived of freedom and dependent upon a patriarch warned planters not to suffer a similar relation of subservience to their king. Orlando Patterson places this dynamic between freedom and enslavement in a transcultural context to identify slavery not only as the twin of freedom, but as its point of origin: "And so it was that freedom came into the world. Before slavery people simply could not have conceived of the thing we call freedom." Douglass and Brown participate in this sort of disruptive and revisionary genealogy even though they were born in absence, amputated from genealogical trees. Remembering themselves in the context of the founding legacy, Douglass and Brown do not simply recover the silent facts of their own political identity; instead, they outline a more complete genealogy of American freedom, inclusive of its unacknowledged kin, even, as Patterson suggests, its disgraceful father.[37] This fuller genealogy elides the distinctions between freedom and slavery—just as the mulatto Ellen Craft passes as a white man, frustrating the boundaries of master and slave.

The first novel written by an African American, Brown's *Clotel* dramatizes an unabridged genealogy. Originating from whispers that Thomas Jefferson kept a slave mistress, *Clotel* fathers a biography of the daughter of the Declaration of Independence sold upon the auction block. At the text's climax, Clotel escapes from the slave pen and rushes through the streets of Washington, D.C., close by "the President's house," hoping to hide in the woods on the southern side of the Potomac. Freedom does not reside in the nation's capital, and having no sanctuary, Clotel darts along the Long Bridge that carries her back to the slaveholding South. Yet at the end of the bridge, on Virginia soil, a refuge seems to stand, sanctified by its line of descent from the progenitor of American freedom, George Washington. For Clotel, freedom is so close: "It is not a great distance from the prison to the Long Bridge, which passes from the lower part of the city across the Potomac, to the extensive forests and woodlands of the celebrated Arlington Place, occupied by the distinguished relative and descendant of the immortal Washington, Mr. George W. Custis.

Thither the poor fugitive directed her flight."[38] Although Brown's description geographically orients the reader, his characters unsettle and confuse the signs of freedom: Clotel, the blood daughter of Jefferson, is powerless to make any claim upon an inheritance of freedom, whereas Custis, only an adopted relation of Washington, has full use of the republican patrimony. The names of Jefferson and Washington no longer serve as unequivocal or unadulterated signs of freedom. Embodied within the illegitimate person of the quadroon, Jefferson's legacy of freedom must flee to find security in a false descendant lacking any direct genealogical affiliation with the originary freedom of the founding fathers. Jefferson's name degenerates into a confused sign of freedom tinged with the blood of enslavement, and in the same manner, Washington's, reduced to the single initial in Custis's name, forfeits any fatherly power to signify freedom, appearing only as a severely attenuated link to the blood of patriarchy's freedom. The search for freedom in *Clotel* is deferred, becoming as hopeless and as contradictory as Clotel's tragic flight across the Potomac that seeks sanctuary in the Old Dominion of slavery.

From Clotel's story, authored by Brown but first engendered as rumor by Jefferson, a host of tainted associations are born, not the least of which are the mulatto characters who figure centrally in the novel. In fact, it is the si(g)n of miscegenation that disrupts once inviolate signs of freedom. The mulatto characters, however, do not succumb to this instability; rather, they manipulate a prohibited patrimony to pass as white. The trickster's ease with which they cross the boundary between freedom and slavery undermines the distinction and threatens a racial hierarchy based upon the inevitable "facts" of descent. Not only do Brown's mulattos pass as respectable white gentlemen, but they also assert their right to the patriarchal legacy with a vengeance. After the execution of the last of Nat Turner's insurgents, one rebel, George Green, remains confined in prison, even though the visible signs—"his eyes blue, nose prominent, lips thin, his head well formed, forehead high and prominent"—hardly identify him, in the minds of antebellum readers, as a likely participant in the slave uprising. A bastard son of "an American statesman," George dismisses the refusal to grant black sons an inheritance and worships a political commitment to revolution that the nation's ancestors successfully and—in the eyes of America—justifiably implemented against British tyranny: "I will tell you why I joined the revolted Negroes. I have heard my master read in the Declaration of Independence 'that all men are created free and equal,' and this caused me to inquire of myself why I was a slave. . . . The grievances of which your fathers complained, were trifling in comparison with the wrongs and sufferings of those who were engaged in the late revolt." It is George who declares: "You tell me that I am to be put to death for violating the laws of the land. Did not the American revolutionists violate the laws when they struck for liberty?"[39]

An amalgamated politics of patriotism arises from George's adoption of the founding legacy. Although he articulates freedom against a national mythology, his freedom is also excessive, dangerously supplemental, to that mythology. His speech threatens to be revolutionary, destabilizing customary uses of history as much as Clotel and other mulattos undermine ancestral signs of freedom. George muddles the lines of descent by avowing that black insurgents can be mistaken for and even recognized as heirs to "American revolutionists." From his biography of enslavement and miscegenation, this slave rebel articulates a politics of freedom; he appropriates a white political legacy for the theoretical use of black slave emancipation. The result is an amalgam, a hybrid narrative in which slave rebellion passes as national tradition: even as George looks and sounds like both national and plantation patriarchs, he nevertheless remains inescapably different, hostile to the men he so resembles. In the same way that the illegible face of the mulatto or the confused legacy of Jefferson and Washington jostles prevailing notions of freedom, George's amalgamated politics incites a subversive movement within the authorizing precedents of mid-nineteenth-century culture.

Proslavery thinkers devised arguments to dissipate the subversive potential of an amalgamation that was at once literal, like the mixed heritage of George, and discursive, like the mixed rebellions and contexts of George's speech. When Henry Hughes concluded in *Treatise on Sociology* (1854) that "hybridism is heinous. Impurity of race is against the law of nature. Mulattoes are monsters," he more than pronounced a vehement critique of the relaxed morals of his culture that indulged white masters. Amalgamation, he feared, would dilute the blood sovereignty of the slaveholding class, degenerating into an eventual forfeiture of white political hegemony. "Political amalgamation is ethnical amalgamation," prescribed Hughes in an uncompromising caution to beware a laxity that could ultimately imperil the clarity and supremacy of white identity. Anthropological studies similarly led J. C. Nott and George R. Gliddon in *Types of Mankind* to forecast Western civilization as a potential victim of amalgamation: "It is evident, theoretically, that the superior races ought to be kept free from all adulterations, otherwise the world will retrograde, instead of advancing, in civilization." Making sex and politics interchangeable, these supporters of slavery prophesied a national catastrophe that the mulattos of *Clotel* exemplify. With what must have been disturbing vividness, Clotel Jefferson and George Green enact an amalgamation that is at once racial and sexual. While the amalgamation of blood thus produced insulted white mistresses and confused genealogies, George's political amalgamation must have been most alarming because it does not depend upon the exchange of blood, but rather upon the seizure of beliefs. Not simply blood sovereignty, but ideological sovereignty threatened to be disseminated among the slave population. Brown, in fact, shared Hughes's opinion of mulattos as a potential incendiary element within society; however, Brown relished what he described as a smoldering "hybrid" class. Tracing the causes of the Santo Domingo slave insurrection, Brown writes: "Owing to the amalgamation between masters and slaves, there arose the mulatto population, which eventually proved to be the worst enemies of their fathers."[40] History, Brown hoped as much as Hughes feared, would repeat itself.

Biology decreed that the mulatto resemble the father; politics and history suggested he might revolt as the father. Not only did sexual amalgamation in proslavery camps constitute a threat to American liberty, but political amalgamation, that is, black repetition of a founding legacy, was feared to inspire mayhem like Nat Turner's revolt. After the suppression of that revolt, Thomas Roderick Dew published "The Abolition of Negro Slavery" (1832), which sought to discount the legitimacy of slaves following in their patriarchs' footsteps. Whereas for Dew, non-Americans such as Lafayette and Kosciuszko could wage revolution because they adopted the colonies' cause and served as generals in the Continental Army under Washington, much as George W. Custis adopted the genealogy of the father of his country, emulation of ancestral patriots by American slaves deteriorated into "hellish plots and massacres." Fearing the difference within the hybrid's sameness and threatened by the black repetition of American freedom, a proslavery political theorist went so far as to question "the doctrine of liberty" as an "*unknown idol*" around which "the blood of human victims streamed!" Rebellious slaves attained anything but the heroic status the men of 1776 achieved; as Dew argued, revolution made slaves "*parricides* instead of *patriots.*"[41] Dew's tract employs an inescapable paradox to insist on the perpetuation of race slavery: if slaves imitated their patriarchs, who in many cases were more than adopted fathers, they slayed those patriarchs. Denying slaves patriarchal knowledge did more than protect slaveowners from embarrassing reminders of sexual transgression—it ensured their survival, preventing the enactment of a history that could be claimed only by violence.

Dew's rhetoric, playing upon the kindred etymology of *parricides* and *patriots*, mingles the words only to maintain a subtle distinction. The intellect of whites, Dew suggested, understands this distinction between parricide and patriot; in contrast, the black slave, fitted by racist biology with thick hands and impoverished mental capabilities, could not wield the patriotic legacy with any degree of accuracy. As one defender of slavery commented, "Neither negroes nor mulattoes know how to use power when given to them. They always use it capriciously and tyrannically." When the scheming abolitionist in the procolonization novel *Frank Freeman's Barber Shop* (1852) tempts a slave with thoughts of rebellion by telling him "you were made for a negro Washington!" the fugitive remains loyal to Dew's logic and insists on the difference "between useless massacres and revolutions." Strict controls over the arsenal of patriotic discourse were in order: one South Carolina reverend counseled against allowing slaves to be present at Fourth of July celebrations because "their weak minds are liable to led astray—the plainest things are likely to be perverted or exaggerated."[42] Born without culturally acknowledged fathers, slaves were denied any opportunity to act as patriots without becoming parricides as well. Rather than dispel such arguments, however, fugitive slaves often implicitly agreed with part of the proslavery line by refusing to distinguish between parricide and patriotism. The blurring that occurs within this type of discursive passing allows the hybrid both to blend in as the same, playing the pious son, and simultaneously to harbor some difference, some ulterior urge to do violence to national fathers.

Parricidal impulses lurk within Douglass's presentation of Madison Washington as a patriot. This name, accorded to the hero of Douglass's lone foray into fiction, "The Heroic Slave," refers not just to two founding fathers, but to the slave who engineered the 1841 slave insurrection aboard the brig *Creole*. For the *New Orleans Daily Picayune*, the mutiny contained neither echoes of patriotic valor nor examples of courageous liberty, although the paper did print a eulogy of the captain's dog, which "fought furiously against the Negroes." No doubt Douglass felt the revolt's occluded patriotic action needed reinterpretation. Within the antebellum imagination, the slaves' violent acts were not identified as a patriotic strike for liberty, but too easily fell into Dew's parricidal sentence of slaves as lusty murderers. As William Andrews observes, during a Senate investigation, "only once in all the depositions is there even the slightest acknowledgement that the motive of the insurrectionists was liberation from their chains, not the murder of every white person on the ship."[43]

At the story's center, in the "manly form" characteristic of the ideal embodied by Douglass's *Narrative*, stands Madison Washington. Through this character Douglass reclaimed the forces of history and violence he had partially ceded to the Garrisonians in his *Narrative*. Although nominally designated a hefty share of a founding patrimony, Madison Washington enjoys none of the benefits of national ancestry. In fact, Douglass's hero receives his name from the most unauthorized source, the one who, in the legal code of the antebellum South, had cursed him with slavery—his slave mother: "Madison Washington, my mother used to call me."[44] Marked with the political nonmarkings of slave matriarchy, Madison Washington receives but a mocking, ironic incorporation into history:

> The State of Virginia is famous in American annals for multitudinous array of her statesmen and heroes. She has been dignified by some the mother of statesmen. History has not been sparing in recording their names, or in blazoning their deeds. . . . Yet not all the great ones of the Old Dominion have, by the fact of their birth-place, escaped undeserved obscurity. By some strange neglect, *one* of the truest, manliest, and bravest of her children,—one who, in after years, will, I think, command the pen of genius to set his merits forth, holds now no higher place in the records of that grand old Commonwealth than is held by a horse or an ox. Let those account for it who can, but there stands the fact, that a man who loved liberty as well

as did Patrick Henry—who deserved it as much as Thomas Jefferson,—and who fought for it with a valor as high, and arms as strong, and against odds as great, as he who led all the armies of the American colonies through the great war for freedom and independence, lives now only in the chattel records of his native State. (473–74)

In the spaces uninscribed by "American annals" and unacknowledged by national narrative, what Douglass's narrator writes is not a history of amalgamation, but a historical discourse that is itself an amalgamation. Using the name of Washington as a letter of introduction, an ex-slave composes history as amalgamated discourse: fact and fiction, prominence and obscurity, white and black mingle to create a narrative that sets forth a genealogical examination of the founding legacy to retheorize freedom, not in opposition or exclusion of slavery, but in the context of slavery.

Heroic man and heroic chattel plot a parallel course in this opening paragraph until they blur. An antebellum reader would identify "he who led all the armies of the American colonies through the great war for freedom and independence" as Washington, but that immortal name in Douglass's configuration no longer distinguishes between free citizen and slave, between American patriot and black parricide. Patriotic discourse often led the speaker to allude to George Washington without naming him, encouraging the listener to supply the name himself. Yet in Douglass's history, the filial respect that refrains from uttering the name Washington is confused with the exclusion of slave names from national history. Like the signifying disruption of the names Jefferson and Washington at the moments of Clotel's death, already in this first paragraph of "The Heroic Slave" the unspoken name Washington signifies doubly, marking both chattel and statesman. This signifying ambiguity more than implies kinship between freedom and slavery; it suggests that for both man and slave, the requirements for dignity and freedom are the same. The textual amalgamation of Washington's name causes a similar freedom to descend upon the slave and the antebellum reader. Supplying the name of the father, the citizen confirms himself as a citizen versed in the lexicon of American historical narrative. And at the same moment, the slave who affirms an unauthorized, matriarchally derived history—"Madison Washington my mother used to call me"—engages in a similar proclamation of American identity. Speaking the history of the founding father and speaking the history of the slave self yield the same yet different results; slave and citizen each realize a share of freedom by naming a patriarch—except that in Madison's case, his slave mother, though defined as an unhistorical chattel, passes as a citizen, accessing the lexicon of American historical narrative. She is not simply the site of miscegenation, but rather a subject who names her son by amalgamating a national mythos.[45]

Just as freedom was to be enacted according to the prototypes of 1776, so, too, was resistance to contain its violent implications within the example of founding patriots. In fact, the first name, Madison, grants the rebel a legalistic, constitutional authority that balances the militaristic associations of General Washington. Acting in what he called "Madisonian fashion," Lincoln also saw himself "fighting" upon *"original principles"* against the Kansas-Nebraska Act of 1854: invoking the statesman who framed key, theoretical justifications for a federal constitution, both Lincoln and Douglass sanctioned their aggressive use of the fathers' legacy to interrogate national policy.[46] Defending his actions with an appeal to the masculine virtue of the fathers, Washington subdues more than the still-struggling white crew: he also subdues an audience's fears about black parricides. He tells the white sailor attempting to retake the slaver: "We have struck for our freedom, and if a true man's heart be in you, you will honor us for the deed" (503). It is Madison Washington who declares: "We have done that which you applaud your fathers for doing, and if we are murderers, so were they" (503). Washington sees beyond the blood of violence to adopt a patriarchy to which he bears no blood connection. Within the slave's discursive passing, the fathers forfeit some of their independence that led to dominance; within amalgamated narrative, the fathers are adopted by bastard children and become dependent upon the political actions of those children.

The narrative frame surrounding Washington's manipulation of the founding fathers heightens the conditions of passing and amalgamation since the narrative of black rebellion is told by a white sailor. Although Washington calls upon the sailor to recognize his resemblance to Revolutionary ancestors, within the sailor's account, dominant cultural codes at first permit the slave no portion of a filial inheritance. The sailor admits that Washington rebels according to Revolutionary precedent only to tack on the invalidating reservation: "It was not that his principles were wrong in the abstract; for they are the principles of 1776. But I could not bring myself to recognize their application to one whom I deemed my inferior" (504). The sailor here outlines the structure of the subversive, transgressive hybrid: Madison Washington is the same yet different; he remembers national narrative—but not exactly. He is almost the same but not quite—almost the same but not white.

A political kinship exists between the fathers and the parricidal sons; however, a social hierarchy saturated with dehumanizing codes obfuscates the resemblance that the sailor intuitively recognizes. Washington confronts the wounded sailor, forcing him to admit that whether aboard a slave ship or on the battlefields of Revolutionary America, black and white rebels each realize "in the abstract" the same founding principles. "In the abstract," principles become unstuck from the lines of genealogy and patrilineal politics lose their restrictive connections to a single culturally validated color. The sailor denies any concrete connection between the Washingtons, yet he confesses that Washington has effectively adopted Washington; he grants the amalgamation of a political tradition by those most disempowered by that tradition. The sailor concludes "The Heroic Slave" by casting Madison Washington as a founding father to the people he leads into the promised land of freedom: "Uttering the wildest shouts of exultation, they marched, amidst the deafening cheers of a multitude of sympathizing spectators, under the triumphant leadership of their heroic chief and deliverer, *Madison Washington*" (505). Sealing his account and Douglass's novella with the name of Washington, the sailor's narrative resembles the fictions and juvenile biographies discussed in chapter 1 that call upon Washington to effect a closure that was at once aesthetic and political. "The Heroic Slave" implements the same strategy of closure as Cooper's *The Spy*, which ends with the finally revealed signature of "GEO. WASHINGTON." In each instance, the name Washington extends a moral authority that provides resolution and stability for a narrative where the identity or status of patriots has been in question. But within the differential context of the "The Heroic Slave," Washington's name now signifies doubly, insinuating that the univocal authority of *The Spy* is subject to alteration, bleeding into another, hybrid configuration of Revolutionary freedom.

Madison Washington exercises caution when he adopts a patriarchal legacy, for he could reinscribe himself in a situation akin to the childlike dependency from which he has just liberated himself. A look at another antebellum representation of slavery reveals how the founding fathers could foster dependency within slaves. Describing the adornments that conscript Uncle Tom to the complacent domesticity of Master Shelby's household, Harriet Beecher Stowe notices "a portrait of General Washington, drawn and colored in a manner which would certainly have astonished that hero, if ever he happened to meet with its like."[47] Though Washington stands arrayed in military garb, he whispers no stirrings of insurrection; he instills within the black slave a pattern of domesticity devoid of male resistance. Madison Washington, however, is no Uncle Tom. Instead of adopting Washington to preside over the cozy hearth, Madison summons Washington to uphold violence against white authority. Through the directionality of his adoption of political freedom (he adopts the father of his country, not the reverse) Madison preserves his independence. His adoption appears as a self-willed decision to select his own father. Looking for a patriarchal inheritance "in the abstract" and not in the restrictive peculiarities of blood, Washington insists upon the liberty to choose a patriarchal legacy. Authoring his own political genealogy, Washington enacts a rebellious narrative of the life of an American patriot in which he casts himself as the hero.

Literary critics, however, have suspiciously viewed the élan with which Washington (and Douglass) settle upon a political paternity. By fathering himself within the tradition of the founding fathers, Washington ineluctably traps himself in a historical irony; he seemingly subjects himself and his freedom to a patriotic tradition that ignores and even sanctions race slavery. The "very figures whose patriotic heritage Douglass claims for his hero won their fame by working to establish a social order in which the enslavement of blacks like Madison was a crucial component," argues Richard Yarborough.[48] William Andrews adds to this critique, questioning Douglass's historical shortsightedness, which defines Madison Washington's liberty with reference to slaveholders who doubled as patriots. The freedom Washington attains, in Andrews's understanding, remains compromised by its lingering dependency upon "the authorizing mythology of an oppressive culture." As Andrews puts it:

If Madison Washington "loved liberty" only as much as Patrick Henry or Thomas Jefferson or George Washington, all of whom

deprived hundreds of their right to enjoy liberty, then one might naturally question from the outset of his story whether Madison Washington is an exemplar at all. What can liberty mean anyway, if it is only
defined according to the norm of Jefferson or George Washington,
whose love of liberty inhibited them from allowing others to have it.[49]

Seen in the context of such questions, advocates of black rebellion
and black patriotism like Brown and Douglass trap themselves in a
rhetorical paradox that forces them once again to fetter freedom
within a history of enslavement. The important reservations that
Yarborough and Andrews raise about the political amalgamation
that occurs in "The Heroic Slave" remind us that slavery and racial
prejudice compromised the ideal of liberty so highly revered by
antebellum America. Their arguments, however, unwittingly reca-
pitulate the restrictive nature of the revolutionary inheritance about
which George Green and Madison Washington complain. These
critiques of Douglass reestablish freedom as exclusively subject to a
white primogeniture, so thoroughly decrepit that it is useless. As
Madison Washington instructs, freedom does not descend from
white-haired (or white-faced) patriarchs; nor does it constitute an
inheritance granted solely to those sons society recognizes as the
fathers' children. Instead, freedom shuns any delimitations of blood
or boundaries of discourse. Freedom, as ex-slaves repeated with
ambivalence, is transgressive.

Freedom exists as a political quality one can adopt—especially if
its guardians are unfit. George Green of *Clotel* justifies his usurpation
of the legacy of 1776 by indicting the sons who have squandered the
founding heritage:

> You boast that this is the "Land of the Free"; but a traditionary
> freedom will not save you. It will not do to praise your fathers and
> build their sepulchres. Worse for you that you have such an inher-
> itance, if you spend it foolishly and are unable to appreciate its worth.
> Sad if the genius of a true humanity, beholding you with tearful
> eyes from the mount of vision, shall fold his wings in sorrowing
> pity, and repeat the strain, "O land of Washington, how often would
> I have gathered thy children together, as a hen doth gather her brood
> under her wings, and ye would not; behold your house is left
> unto you desolate."[50]

Disputing the justice as well as the desirability of political identity
based upon restrictive genealogy, the writings of American slaves
articulate a freedom that transcends, without forgetting, the curses

and blessings of blood. They reveal themselves to be the true inheritors of American freedom: proving that the freedom promulgated by the founders eludes the facts and confines of patriarchal descent, ex-slaves best recalled the founding promise. Precisely because ex-slaves once were enslaved, writers like Douglass and Brown vitally understand how any conception or practice of American freedom remains bound to American slavery. They assert a freedom alien to the legal genealogy and life of a slave; theirs is an affirmation that enables freedom to move beyond a politics limited to descent.

A white genealogy, betrayed by its own dissolution, reappears throughout slave narratives, accusing the avowed sons as poor stewards of freedom. Placing freedom in the hands of the post-Revolutionary generation was placing freedom in the hands of the prodigal son. The plantation patriarch, Solomon Northup recalls, transmitted to his son a perverse freedom that forced others to remember the painful conditions of their bondage: "Mounted on his pony, he [the master's eldest son] often rides into the field with his whip, playing the overseer, greatly to his father's delight. Without discrimination, at such times, he applies the rawhide, urging the slaves forward with shouts, and occasional expressions of profanity, while the old man laughs, and commends him a thorough-going boy." Brandy, gambling, improvident management of the father's fortune, and an unhealthy commitment to leisure all recur in the slave narratives as signs of the sons' inability to wield responsibly their inheritance. An abolitionist traveling incognito in "The Heroic Slave" stops at a tavern and notes that, "like everything else peculiar to Virginia," the once noble edifice, adorned with pillars and portico, echoes of classic republican civilization, has slipped into disrepair and decay (489). If not junior tyrants, consumptive and licentious offspring meekly step forward in the slave narratives as the heirs of the fathers' freedom. Plantation patriarchs rarely escape portrayals that cast them as short-sighted and impotent; again and again within slave narratives and fictions, manumission papers remain unsigned at the master's unexpected death. The sons rarely inherit the principles of wise governance; as Jefferson noted, slavery disfigured the development of the legitimate son, causing him to be "nursed, educated, and daily exercised in tyranny."[51]

Whereas Yarborough and Andrews demarcate freedom as a restrictive domain enclosed and forever tainted by prodigal fathers, slave narrators formulate an understanding of freedom that resists the ties of patrimonial testaments. Certainly, the founding fathers exercised freedom, but no matter how much they intended and no matter how zealously white sons tried, freedom could not be inherited as though it were a commodity. Yarborough and Andrews seem daunted by the political sepulcher of the fathers and express a hesitancy lest slave rebels be seen as repeating history and perpetuating the same conditions of domination. Douglass and Brown obviate the need for these worries; within their mimicking of national narrative, the aligned practices of signifyin(g), discursive passing, and political amalgamation repeat history without producing the same content. In their mirrorings of and confrontations with history, slave narrators evade the oppressive weight of history and escape the nihilistic "dry bones of the past" to structure an affirmation. Ralph Ellison's *Invisible Man*, a novel signifying upon the slave narrative, offers a vision of this affirmation of freedom transcending, rather than descending from the founding fathers. Meditating upon his grandfather's deathbed counsel, the narrator of *Invisible Man* decides: "He *must* have meant the principle, that we were to affirm the principle on which the country was built and not the men, or at least the men who did the violence."[52] The words of the white sailor narrating Madison Washington's revolt now take on a fuller resonance. When he states "It was not that his principles were wrong in the abstract," he does more than attempt to separate the real actions of Madison Washington from the remembered heroism of George Washington. Instead, he reveals how through its reiterations, freedom is necessarily altered, abstracted from its own corrupt origins.

NOT THE SAME (EMERSONIAN) STORY

It is important to understand, however, that the abstraction of freedom does not involve a transcendence of the Emersonian sort, in which the self rises above the tainted world, forgetting the institutions, practices, precedents, and slave codes that impact the everyday. The dominant strain of New England abolitionism was subject to this ether of moral transcendence; as one critic observes, for many Northern reformers, "slavery became not really a social problem but a moral abstraction."[53] For them, freedom had to be abstracted from its corrupt origins if it was ever going to be practiced in a way that was not dehumanizing to American blacks, and yet slave narrators asserted that those corrupt origins are not to be forgotten. *Clotel*, "The Heroic Slave," and slave narratives stand as acts of memory, fused with personal recollections and marginalized black history, that counter the narrative of American freedom. Even though the sin of race slavery has always disrupted confident articulation of a founding legacy, Douglass and Brown show that a republican enactment of freedom depends upon remembering the discontinuites and aberrations within freedom's origins. Though they may be unfounded and culturally unfathered, slave narrators thus act as genealogists. In narratives inscribing subjectivity, ex-slaves stress how their existence and their illegitimate histories introduce contradictions and interruptions within a national narrative that has tended toward uncritical readings of Jamestown, the Declaration of Independence, George Washington, Thomas Jefferson, all as chapters proclaiming the contours of freedom. The slave's genealogy, on a literal level is shadowed in rumor and illegitimacy, but on a political and textual level, this nonauthoritative residue of knowledge formulates a critical practice that recovers "a dangerous legacy . . . [that] disturbs what was previously considered immobile; it fragments what was thought unified; it shows the heterogeneity of what was imagined consistent with itself."[54]

Like their fathers before them, the antebellum white sons who listened to Lincoln urge them to perpetuate the republican tradition in his address before the Young Men's Lyceum transmitted a freedom that was inconsistent and incomplete—and called it perfect. In contrast, unrecognized black sons wrote themselves as truer inheritors of the republican fathers who never saw them as kin or citizens. It took those without complete genealogies to remember a more complete genealogy of freedom. Narrating an unrecognized history of incompleteness disruptive to American freedom, the writing of ex-slaves continues to do violence to an ossified national narrative. Violence, in this sense, is a critical assault upon a ritualized and unquestioned past. Republicanism entails remembrance of the past, but it does not intend to solemnize the past with the myth of inviolate origins. Rather, republicanism as a genealogical practice acknowledges the blood and the violence: like Machiavelli, it acknowledges that Rome was founded upon fratricide; like Nietzsche, it marks the beginnings of civilization in sacrifice, mutilation, and torture; like

Foucault, it embraces a historiography that assumes that the authority of origins deserves to be dissipated and toppled. And as a theoretical site of freedom, slave narratives pass along forgotten limitations, ruptures, and contradictions fundamental to the slave's negotiated subscription to freedom and central to republican genealogy. Just as the genealogical criticism of slave narrative defies linear inscriptions of freedom from plantation father to legal heir, ex-slave writings upset the lines of American narrative that would inscribe freedom as a concept and an experience without incongruous angles, unsettling gaps, or uncomfortable questions.

Remembering the contradictions of freedom within national narrative, African American writing before the Civil War sought to imagine political experiences within a narrative frame that would not be coincident with the nation. Neither resolution nor coherence were the goal; instead, the African American genealogical project, an endeavor that finds similarities in the thinking of Melville and, at times, Lincoln, dismembered the nation so that freedom could be retold within different forms. The ambivalence of memory remains the cornerstone of this project: only by recalling the ironies of freedom within national history could the variations and discrepancies between freedom and nation appear. National disarticulation suggests uncompleted possibilities for meaningful and revolutionary political articulation.

Notes

INTRODUCTION

1. Abraham Lincoln, "Address before the Young Men's Lyceum," in *The Collected Works of Abraham Lincoln*, 9 vols., ed. Roy P. Basler, (New Brunswick, N.J.: Rutgers University Press, 1953), 1:112, 1:109, 1:110.

2. Ibid., 1:110.

3. Ibid., 1:112, 1:109–10.

4. Ibid., 112.

5. Ibid., 1:115. Other critics have noted the importance of Lincoln's innovative irreverence toward the founding fathers in this speech. See Eric J. Sundquist, "Slavery, Revolution, and the American Renaissance," in *The American Renaissance Reconsidered: Selected Papers from the English Institute, 1982–83*, ed. Walter Benn Michaels and Donald Pease (Baltimore: Johns Hopkins University Press, 1985), 4; Robert J. Ferguson, *Law and Letters in American Culture* (Cambridge, Mass.: Harvard University Press, 1984), 309.

6. Jefferson Davis, "Farewell Address," *The Papers of Jefferson Davis*, 7 vols., ed. Lynda Lasswell Crist and Mary Seaton (Baton Rouge: Louisiana State University Press, 1992), 7:22. In this farewell address to the United States Senate, Davis, like Lincoln more than twenty years earlier, emphasizes the genealogical character of the nation, interpreting rebellion as the means to "transmit [rights] unshorn to our children, " 7:22.

7. Lewis Clarke and Milton Clarke, *Narratives of the Sufferings of Lewis and Milton Clarke, Sons of a Soldier of the Revolution, During a Captivity of More Than Twenty Years among the Slaveholders of Kentucky, One of the So Called Christian States of North America* (Boston: Bela Marsh, 1846), 43.

8. Lincoln, "Address before the Young Men's Lyceum," *Collected Works*, 1:114, 1:108.

9. By "national narrative," I mean to imply a consistent narrative line reflected in all the artifacts deployed by a culture (and the list is diverse, encompassing more than literary texts and including painting, architecture, mapping, oratory, legal decisions, constitutional debates, and anthropological description) that provide a meaningful political grammar that is fluid enough, while still internally structured, to accommodate scattered people to homogeneous imaginings of themselves as a nation. I further elaborate the strategies of national narrative below in chapter 1. It is important to mention at this point, however, that what I am calling national narrative may be dominant but by no means is hegemonic. Not all narratives partake of the

terms or techniques of patriarchal genealogy. Catherine Maria Sedgwick's *Hope Leslie* (1827; reprint, New Brunswick, N.J.: Rutgers University Press, 1987) and Harriet Jacobs's *Incidents in the Life of a Slave Girl, Written by Herself,* ed. Jean Fagan Yellin (1861; Cambridge, Mass.: Harvard University Press, 1987) suggest instances of political community derived through matriarchal remembering as opposed to patriarchal descent. Yet in terms of the discussion and debates surrounding the past, ownership, authority, and political being, the narrative of founding fathers was preeminent in antebellum culture.

10. Homi K. Bhabha, "DissemiNation: Time, Narrative, and the Margins of the Modern Nation," in *Nation and Narration* ed. Homi K. Bhabha (New York: Routledge, 1990), 319. Discussing American culture in terms of Bhabha's ideas about national narrative, hybridity, and cultural difference might seem unexpected, since the formation of a nation in the United States was markedly different from postcolonial situations. Yet without obscuring the significant distinctions between American history and colonial, neocolonial, and postcolonial encounters, we can read the counter-memories within imperialism, federalism, and slavery in the United States as creating ambivalences and disruptions that are comparable to the discursive struggles Bhabha and others observe in non-Western sites. On reading eighteenth-century and nineteenth-century American authors as postcolonial writers, see also Thomas Gustafson, *Representative Words: Politics, Literature, and the American Language, 1776-1865* (Cambridge: Cambridge University Press, 1992), 21.

11. By "America," I want to suggest a narrativized entity that both undergirds and exceeds the geopolitical United States. "America" suggests a mythic and ritualized set of associations and practices through which citizens mark their shared allegiances as well as their profound differences. I draw this understanding of America in part from Lauren Berlant, who defines America as "an assumed relation, an explication of ongoing collective practices, and also an occasion for exploring what it means that national subjects already share not just a history, or a political allegiance, but a set of forms and the affect that makes these forms meaningful." *The Anatomy of National Fantasy: Hawthorne, Utopia, and Everyday Life* (Chicago: University of Chicago Press, 1991), 4.

12. Lincoln, "Address before the Young Men's Lyceum," *Collected Works,* 1:114

13. Ibid., 1:115; George B. Forgie, *Patricide in the House Divided: A Psychological Interpretation of Lincoln and His Age* (New York: Norton, 1979), 8.

14. Jacobs, *Incidents,* 78; Michel Foucault, "Nietzsche, Genealogy, History," in *Language, Counter-Memory, Practice: Selected Essays and Interviews,* trans. Donald F. Bouchard and Sherry Simon (Ithaca: Cornell University Press, 1972), 146.

15. Daniel Webster, *The Orations on Bunker Hill Monument, The Character of Washington, and The Landing at Plymouth* (New York: American Book

Company, 1894), 21; Frederick Douglass, "The Meaning of the Fourth of July for the Negro," in *The Life and Writings of Frederick Douglass*, 5 vols., ed. Philip S. Foner (New York: International Publishers, 1950), 2:186, 2:201; William Wells Brown, *St. Domingo: Its Revolutions and its Patriots, A Lecture Delivered Before the Metropolitan Athanaeum, London, May 16, and at St. Thomas' Church, Philadelphia, December 20, 1854* (1855; reprint, Philadelphia: Rhistoric, 1969), 37. Eric J. Sundquist suggests that antebellum ambivalence toward the fathers, and parricide in the extreme, unsettles narrative. Working from Freud's *Totem and Taboo*, he looks at nineteenth-century texts to demonstrate how "the authority a writer's own performance implements will be sanctioned by violence at the same time it is hedged by his unconscious invocation and veneration of the ancestors whose placed he has usurped." *Home as Found: Authority and Genealogy in Nineteenth-Century American Literature* (Baltimore: Johns Hopkins University Press, 1979), xiii.

16. Friedrich Nietzsche, *The Genealogy of Morals*, in *The Birth Tragedy and The Genealogy of Morals*, trans. Francis Golffing (New York: Doubleday, 1956), 197; Foucault, "Nietzsche, Genealogy, History," 143.

17. *Dred Scott v. Sandford*, 60 U.S. 702 (1856).

18. Ibid., 702–3, 703.

19. Ibid., 703.

20. Edward W. Said, *Beginnings: Intention and Method* (New York: Columbia University Press, 1985), xiii. Michel Foucault also assesses the authority of origins in "What is an Author?" in *Language, Counter-Memory, and Practice*, 113–38, and "Nietzsche, Genealogy, History," 139–64.

21. *Dred Scott v. Sandford*, 702. Yancey is quoted in George M. Fredrickson, *The Black Image in the White Mind: The Debate on Afro-American Character and Destiny, 1817–1914* (New York: Harper & Row, 1971), 61.

22. For more information concerning the filial character of antebellum political culture, one might turn to Melville's *Pierre*, which treats at some length the crisis occurring in filial consciousness when a patriot father ceases to speak unambiguously. Also see Forgie, *Patricide in the House Divided*, and Michael Paul Rogin, *Subversive Genealogy: The Politics and Art of Herman Melville* (New York: Knopf, 1983), who examines how family history combines with national concerns in Melville's texts.

23. For implications of the etymology of *authority*, see Said, *Beginnings*, 83, and Sundquist, *Home as Found*, xiii.

24. *Dred Scott v. Sandford*, 700, 701, 703.

25. Ibid., 706.

26. Of course, Clotel Jefferson is not her legal name, and Brown's narrator never goes so far as to grant her share of a patrimony that is legally denied. I give her the name of her purported grandfather to underscore her disjunctive history.

27. Michel Foucault, *Power/Knowledge: Selected Interviews and Other Writings, 1972–1977*, ed. Colin Gordon, trans. Colin Gordon, Leo Marshall, John Mepham, and Kate Soper (New York: Pantheon, 1980), 82, 84.

28. Elsewhere, such as in *The Archaeology of Knowledge,* Foucault sees that humanist discourse in general shares these same tendencies of organization, hierarchy, categorization, and codification with "scientific discourse."

29. Lincoln, "Address before the Young Men's Lyceum," *Collected Works,* 1:108.

30. Foucault, *Power/Knowledge,* 85.

31. Sacvan Bercovitch, "The Rites of Assent: Rhetoric, Ritual, and the Ideology of American Consensus," in *The American Self: Myth, Ideology, and Popular Culture,* ed. Sam Girgus (Albuquerque: University of New Mexico Press, 1981), 29; *The Rites of Assent: Transformations in the Symbolic Construction of America* (New York: Routledge, 1993), 356. For rewritings of the Declaration, see Philip S. Foner, *We, the Other People: Alternative Declarations of Independence by Labor Groups, Farmers, Women's Rights Advocates, Socialists, and Blacks, 1829–1975* (Urbana: University of Illinois Press, 1976). Thoreau, who took up residence in the woods on July 4, suggests *Walden* functions as a declaration of independence.

32. Bercovitch, *Rites of Assent,* 364.

33. Jonathan Arac, "Nationalism, Hypercanonization, and *Huckleberry Finn,*" *boundary 2* 19 (spring 1992): 19.

34. Bercovitch, *The American Jeremiad* (Madison: University of Wisconsin Press, 1978), 191; *The Office of The Scarlet Letter* (Baltimore: Johns Hopkins University Press, 1991), 17, 31, 112; Foucault, *Power/Knowledge,* 142; Jonathan Arac and Harriet Ritvo, introduction, to *Macropolitics of Nineteenth-Century Literature: Nationalism, Exoticism, Imperialism,* ed. Jonathan Arac and Harriet Ritvo (Philadelphia: University of Pennsylvania Press, 1991), 1.

35. Bhabha, "DissemiNation," 313; "Of Mimicry and Man: The Ambivalence of Colonial Discourse," *October* 28 (spring 1984): 130; and "Signs Taken for Wonders: Questions of Ambivalence and Authority under a Tree Outside Delhi, May 1817," *Critical Inquiry* 12 (autumn 1985): 157, 150. Bhabha's "DissemiNation" addresses these issues through the concept of "supplements" that augment and revise national narratives. See especially 312–15. These essays have since been collected in *The Location of Culture* (New York: Routledge, 1994). Other chapters of this volume further explore notions of the hybrid; see especially "Interrogating Identity: Frantz Fanon and the Postcolonial Prerogative" and "By Bread Alone: Signs of Violence in the Mid-Nineteenth Century."

36. Bhabha, "Signs Taken for Wonders," 155. Bhabha's emphasis on "discontinuous history" of course shares much with Foucault's idea of genealogy. See Bhabha's invocation of the "genealogical gaze" in "Of Mimicry and Man," 129.

37. Herman Melville, *Moby-Dick; or, The Whale* (Boston: Houghton Mifflin, 1956), 427, 418–19. Janet Reno, for instance, understands *Moby-Dick* as Ishmael's way to move beyond the catastrophic experiences of the *Pequod* and enter another community, a community of readers. Janet Reno, *Ishmael Alone Survived* (Lewisburg, Pa.: Bucknell University Press, 1990); see especially 48, 106–7, 136.

38. Frederick Douglass, "The Heroic Slave," in *Life and Writings*, 5:474. Despite this comparison, which comes at the level of the narrative frame, within "The Heroic Slave," women are figured as a debilitating force in the struggle for freedom. The slave women aboard the *Creole* play no part in rebellion, and Madison's own independence is jeopardized by his return to rescue his wife. Several important studies do examine women's role in the nation. Foremost, in my mind, is Lauren Berlant's *The Anatomy of National Fantasy*, but also see Cathy N. Davidson, *Revolution and the Word: The Rise of the Novel in America* (New York: Oxford University Press, 1986); Mary V. Dearborn, *Pocohantas's Daughters: Gender and Ethnicity in American Culture* (New York: Oxford University Press, 1986); Jean Fagan Yellin, *Women and Sisters: The Antislavery Feminists in American Culture* (New Haven: Yale University Press, 1989); *The Culture of Sentiment: Race, Gender, and Sentimentality in Nineteenth-Century America*, ed. Shirley Samuels (New York: Oxford University Press, 1992); Karen Sánchez-Eppler, *Touching Liberty: Abolition, Feminism, and the Politics of the Body* (Berkeley: University of California Press, 1993); and the chapters on Stowe in Jane Tompkins, *Sensational Designs: The Cultural Work of American Fiction, 1790–1860* (New York: Oxford University Press, 1985).

39. Melville, *Moby-Dick*, 58.

40. Herman Melville, *Pierre; or, The Ambiguities*, in *Pierre, or the Ambiguities; Israel Potter, His Fifty Years of Exile; The Piazza Tales; The Confidence-Man, His Masquerade; Uncollected Prose; Billy Budd, Sailor (An Inside Narrative)* (New York: Library of America, 1984), 27. Future citations of works included in this volume will refer to it as the Library of America edition.

41. Frederick Douglass, *My Bondage and My Freedom* (New York: Arno Press, 1968), 34–35. See Eugene D. Genovese, *Roll, Jordan, Roll: The World the Slaves Made* (New York: Vintage, 1976).

42. Ralph Waldo Emerson, "Lecture on Slavery," in *Emerson's Antislavery Writings*, ed. Len Gougeon and Joel Myerson (New Haven: Yale University Press, 1995), 106.

CHAPTER 1

1. Of course, the coherence of American national foundations is only storied. The fact that the United States can point to two founding documents—the Constitution and the Declaration of Independence—is indicative of this fictive though strained consistency. It is therefore more appropriate to speak of national foundations and origins in the plural, as contestatory and divided. On the lack of univocality and determinate meanings in the language and documents of the founding fathers, see Gustafson, *Representative Words*, 55–57.

2. Edmund Jackson, "The Effects of Slavery," in *The Liberty Bell* (Boston: Massachusetts Anti-Slavery Fair, 1842), 41; E. M. Hudson, *The Second War of Independence in America* (London: Longman, Green, Longman, Roberts, and Green, 1863), 146; Isaac Jefferson, *Memoirs of a Monticello Slave, As Dictated*

to Charles Campbell in the 1840's by Isaac, One of Thomas Jefferson's Slaves (Charlottesville: University of Virginia Press, 1951), 31, 22. Isaac Jefferson's recollections were recorded in 1847, but not published until 1951.

3. Jay Fliegelman, *Prodigals and Pilgrims: The American Revolution against Patriarchal Authority* (Cambridge: Cambridge University Press, 1982), 199.

4. Washington is quoted in Paul Leceister Ford, *The True George Washington* (Philadelphia: J. B. Lippincott, 1896), 154. On Washington's Farewell Address and the question of slavery see Walter H. Mazyack, *George Washington and the Negro* (New York: Associated, 1932), 132.

5. C. M. Kirkland, *Memoirs of Washington* (New York: Appleton, 1857), vi, 204–5.

6. Benson J. Lossing, *The Home of Washington and Its Associations, Historical, Biographical, and Pictorial* (1859; reprint, New York: W. A. Townsend, 1866), 285; Kirkland, *Memoirs*, 422.

7. Kirkland, *Memoirs*, 472; Washington Irving, *The Life of George Washington*, 5 vols. (New York: G. P. Putnam, 1859), 5:298.

8. Sundquist, "Slavery, Revolution, and the American Renaissance," 7.

9. Clay is quoted in William A. Bryan, "George Washington: Symbolic Guardian of the Republic, 1850–1861" *William and Mary Quarterly* 7 (January 1950): 54; Thomas Jefferson is quoted in Barry Schwartz, *George Washington: The Making of an American Symbol* (New York: Free Press, 1987), 88.

10. Berlant, *The Anatomy of National Fantasy*, 20; Timothy Brennan, "The National Longing for Form," in *Nation and Narration*, ed. Homi K. Bhabha (New York: Routledge, 1990), 49; Bhabha, "DissemiNation," 297; Benedict Anderson, *Imagined Communities: Reflections of the Origins and Spread of Nationalism*, rev. ed. (New York: Verso, 1991). In addition to these critics, see Edward W. Said, *Culture and Imperialism* (New York: Knopf, 1993), xii-xxvi; Donald Pease, "National Identities, Postmodern Artifacts, and Postnational Narratives" *boundary 2* 19 (spring 1992): 3–4; and Arac, "Nationalism, Hypercanonization, and *Huckleberry Finn*," 15–16. This grouping should not be read as an indication that all these critics share a common definition of national narrative. Much of the usefulness of national narrative as a concept, I have found, comes from the various inflections given to it. Subtle differences exist among these writers' use of the term. For instance, Arac seems to understand national narrative as a genre of discourse distinct from literary narrative in which texts purvey a monocultural impression. This view is aligned with that of Anderson, whose study powerfully demonstrates how novels in particular have a formative role in the conception of the modern nation. Bhabha takes a slightly different tack, applying the term "national narrative" not to single texts so much as to the received codes, myths, histories, novels, laws, and "truths" that combine to produce a coherent image of the nation. My purpose here is not to detail the distinctions between these critics; assuredly, I have drawn from all their accounts. My own placement among this grouping is elaborated below.

11. Etienne Balibar, "The Nation Form: History and Ideology," in Etienne Balibar and Immanuel Wallerstein, *Race, Nation, Class: Ambiguous Identities*, trans. of Balibar by Chris Turner (New York: Verso, 1991), 97; Anderson, *Imagined Communities*, 174.

12. John Winthrop, *A Model of Christian Charity*, in *The Norton Anthology of American Literature*, 2 vols., 3rd ed., ed. Nina Baym et al. (New York: Norton, 1989), 40, 36, 37; John Beverley, *Against Literature* (Minneapolis: University of Minnesota Press, 1993), viii.

13. Thomas Hobbes, *Leviathan* (New York: Pelican, 1968), 217; Michael Paul Rogin, *Ronald Reagan, The Movie: and Other Episodes in Political Demonology* (Berkeley: University of California Press, 1987), see especially 81–86, 298–300; Mason Locke Weems, *The Life of Washington*, ed. Marcus Cunliffe (1809; Cambridge: Cambridge University Press, 1962), 182.

14. On the political demonology of presidential bodies, see Rogin, *Ronald Reagan, The Movie*, especially "The King's Two Bodies." Michael Kammen notes that in addition to Washington, other Revolutionary figures such as Patrick Henry experienced rhetorical divisions in the antebellum period. *A Season of Youth: The American Revolution and the Historical Imagination* (New York: Knopf, 1978), 18.

15. Edmund S. Morgan, *American Slavery, American Freedom: The Ordeal of Colonial Virginia* (New York: Norton, 1975), 376; Harriet Beecher Stowe, "The Two Altars; or, Two Pictures in One," in *Dred: A Tale of the Great Dismal Swamp together with Anti-Slavery Tales and Papers*, 2 vols. (New York: AMS Press, 1967), 2:253. For a different account of how New England revolutionaries recognized the inconsistencies of slavery and freedom, see Leon F. Litwack, *North of Slavery: The Negro in the Free States, 1790–1860* (Chicago: University of Chicago Press, 1961), 4–13. Also see Orlando Patterson, *Slavery and Social Death: A Comparative Study* (Cambridge, Mass.: Harvard University Press, 1982), which discusses the strange kinship between freedom and slavery.

16. Daniel Webster, "The Character of Washington," in *The Works of Daniel Webster*, 6 vols. (Boston: Little and Brown, 1851) 1:230; John C. Calhoun, "Speech on the Slavery Question, Delivered in the Senate, March 4th, 1850," in *The Works of John C. Calhoun*, 6 vols., ed. Richard K. Crallé (New York: D. Appleton, 1854–1860) 4:562; E. Cecil [pseud.?], *The Life of Washington, Written for Children* (Boston: Crosby, Nichols, 1859), 99; The Confederate verse is quoted in William Alfred Bryan, *George Washington in American Literature, 1775–1865* (New York: Columbia University Press, 1952), 165; Herman Melville, "Lee in the Capitol," in *Poems, Containing Battle-Pieces, John Marr and Other Sailors, Timoleon, and Miscellaneous Poems*, vol. 16 of *The Standard Edition of the Works of Herman Melville* (New York: Russell and Russell, 1963), 164. Alan Heimert, "*Moby-Dick* and American Political Symbolism," *American Quarterly* 15 (winter 1963): 498–534, places such contradictory invocations in the context of widespread rhetorical production in the antebellum era. For a rendering of the need for coherence at the level of

political parties, see Eric Foner, who discusses attempts to form a national political party with a "universal" ideology capable of defeating sectionalism. *Politics, Ideology, and the Origins of the American Civil War* (New York: Oxford University Press, 1980), 34–53.

17. Fliegelman, *Prodigals and Pilgrims,* 199. In light of Fliegelman's critical evaluation of psychohistory, it should be remembered that the story of Oedipus is not solely a psychological fable. It is foremost a drama of political dimensions, a story of a tyrant enacted within Athenian democracy.

18. Frederick Douglass, "The Meaning of the Fourth of July for the Negro," in *Life and Writings,* 2:187–88.

19. Toni Morrison, *Playing in the Dark: Whiteness and the Literary Imagination* (Cambridge, Mass.: Harvard University Press, 1992), 63.

20. John N. Norton, *Life of General Washington* (New York: General Protestant Episcopal Sunday School Union and Church Book Society, 1860), 375, 379.

21. Phillips is quoted in Forgie, *Patricide in the House Divided,* 130.

22. Frank Kermode, *The Sense of an Ending* (New York: Oxford University Press, 1966), 7, 62.

23. Hayden White, *The Content of the Form: Narrative Discourse and Historical Representation* (Baltimore: Johns Hopkins University Press, 1987), 11.

24. Herman Melville, *The Confidence-Man: His Masquerade* (New York: Norton, 1971), 58.

25. Herman Melville, *Billy Budd,* in the Library of America edition, 1431.

26. Melville, *The Confidence-Man,* 217; *Billy Budd,* 1432, 1433.

27. Carolyn Porter, "Call Me Ishmael, or How to Make Double-Talk Speak," in *New Essays on Moby-Dick,* ed. Richard Brodhead (New York: Cambridge University Press, 1986), 93. In distinction to "News from the Mediterranean," the narrator's understanding of authority (both the authority of Captain Vere and his own as narrator) remains in suspension, denied any sense of closure.

28. White, *The Content of the Form,* 25.

29. Bhabha, "DissemiNation," 309; Morrison, *Playing in the Dark,* 8. On the idea of closure, see Hayden White, who suggests that the telos in narrative discourse is always connected to "integrative structures such as the 'folk,' the 'nation,' or the 'culture.'" *Metahistory: The Historical Imagination in Nineteenth-Century Europe* (Baltimore, Johns Hopkins University Press, 1973), 16.

30. George Washington Parke Custis, *Recollections and Private Memoirs of Washington, by His Adopted Son, G. W. Parke Custis* (Washington, D.C.: W. H. Moore, 1859), 12.

31. Fredric Jameson, *The Political Unconscious: Narrative as a Socially Symbolic Act* (Ithaca: Cornell University Press, 1981), 139.

32. Uncle Juvinell [Morrison Heady], *The Farmer Boy, and How He Became Commander-in-Chief* (Boston: Walker, Wise, 1864), 3.

33. Ibid., 36–37, 43, 45.

34. Ibid., 45; Winthrop, *Model of Christian Charity,* 31. It should be re-

membered that Winthrop's famous sermon is not a doctrine of equality, but a justification for an inegalitarian class structure. One can witness this proslavery distortion of Winthrop's notion of hierarchy in a 1701 pamphlet by John Saffin, who argued that the idea that "all men have equal right to Liberty" contradicts "the order that God hath set in the World, who hath ordained different degrees and orders of men, some to be High and Honourable, some to be Low and Despicable . . . yea some to be born Slaves, and so to remain during their lives." Quoted in William Sumner Jenkins, *Pro-Slavery Thought in the Old South* (Chapel Hill, University of North Carolina Press, 1935), 5. Young George's willingness to sacrifice his body reaffirms what Frederick Douglass notes as an ideological imperative of the patriarchal institution: "It is better that a dozen slaves should suffer under the lash, than that the overseer should be convicted, in the presence of the slaves, of having been at fault." *Narrative of the Life of Frederick Douglass, An American Slave, Written by Himself* (1845; reprint, New York: Signet, 1968), 38.

35. Lydia Maria Child, *Hobomok and Other Writings on Indians*, ed. Carolyn L. Karcher (New Brunswick, N.J.: Rutgers University Press, 1986), 3; Doris Summer, "Irresistible Romance: The Foundational Fictions of Latin America" in *Nation and Narration*, ed. Homi K. Bhabha (New York: Routledge, 1990), 76. Charles Powell Clinch, drawing heavily upon Cooper's language, produced a dramatic version of the novel that first appeared in March 1822. See Clinch, *The Spy: A Tale of Neutral Ground (From the Novel of That Name): A Dramatic Romance in Three Acts*, in *Metamora and Other Plays*, ed. Eugene R. Page (Princeton: Princeton University Press, 1941). By the time of the drama's opening, *The Spy* was in its third edition. For information concerning the reception of *The Spy* and its central importance as a prototype for the genre of American historical fiction, see Kammen, *A Season of Youth*, 148, 154.

36. James Fenimore Cooper, *The Spy: A Tale of Neutral Ground* (New York: Hafner, 1960), 12. Subsequent references are to this edition and will be included in the text. Of course, Washington also appears disguised as Harper in the novel. Yet he does so without evoking the threats to hierarchy that accompany class, gender, or racial cross-dressing. He remains a gentleman, dignified, religious, respectful, even when disguised.

37. Clinch, *The Spy . . . in Three Acts*, 89. Cooper himself later expressed reservations about uttering the name of Washington in fiction. To some readers, it seemed inappropriate to place Washington in secret interviews with the peddler-spy. Indeed, when *The Spy* reached the New York stage, Washington's character was omitted from the drama.

38. Ibid., 92.

39. Calhoun "Speech on the Slavery Question," 4:561.

40. Cooper, *The American Democrat; or, Hints on the Social and Civic Relations of the United States of America* (New York: Vintage, 1956), 172. Although Harvey Birch says at one point "In heaven there is no distinction of colour," the novel hardly suggests that the same sentiment should hold true for this historical world (391). Cooper does include a spokesman for emancipation

without exciting any tensions that could strain the hierarchal harmony of his novel. One evening after battle, Dr. Sitgreaves waxes idealistic and predicts "the manumission of our slaves" (193). Yet Sitgreaves's status as a doctor and not a soldier, as an idle philosopher and not a man of action, tends to undercut his liberal views. After the good doctor expresses his reservations about the institution first imported by the British, Cooper invalidates his position by stating: "It will be remembered that Doctor Sitgreaves spoke forty years ago" (193). History proves Sitgreaves to be a visionary, a social dreamer lost atop ethereal mastheads.

41. Cooper, *The American Democrat*, 147, 174, 137, 45, 171. Critics have characterized *The Spy* as an ideological rupture with democratic faith devoted to staving off any further revolutionary action that might threaten class distinctions. On this point, see Robert Clark, "Rewriting Revolution: Cooper's War of Independence," in *James Fenimore Cooper: New Critical Essays*, ed. Robert Clark (London: Vision, 1985), 191. Kammen similarly notes the manner in which historical romances about the Revolution have tended to de-revolutionize its political character; see *A Season of Youth*, 64, 211–13, 219.

42. Eric Lott marks a similar irony in his understanding of how use of a cultural form—blackface minstrelsy—to suture national divisions in antebellum America could work to expose and intensify that crisis. *Love and Theft: Blackface Minstrelsy and the American Working Class* (New York: Oxford University Press, 1993), especially 201–10.

43. Samuel Ringgold Ward, *Autobiography of a Fugitive Negro: His Anti-Slavery Labours in the United States, Canada, & England* (1855; reprint, New York: Arno Press, 1968), 114.

44. Uncle Juvinell, *The Farmer Boy*, 4. For more on the preface, see Jacques Derrida, *Dissemination*, trans. Barbara Johnson (Chicago: University of Chicago Press, 1981), 44–45. Helpful in understanding Derrida's conception of the preface-text relation is Gayatri Chakravorty Spivak's translator's preface to *Of Grammatology* (Baltimore: Johns Hopkins University Press, 1976): "The preface is a necessary gesture of homage and parricide, for the book (the father) makes a claim of authority or origin which is both true and false" (xi). In calling the preface "the *critical* instance of the text," Derrida implies the subversive nature inherent to the preface. *Dissemination*, 27 n.

45. Derrida, *Dissemination*, 44, 45.

46. Abraham Lincoln, "Fragment on the Constitution and the Union," in *Collected Works*, 4:169.

CHAPTER 2

1. Melville, *Moby-Dick*, 246. All subsequent citations in this chapter are to the Houghton Mifflin edition cited in the introduction and will appear parenthetically in the text.

2. John Seelye has also compared the kinetic, linear quality of Ahab's story to the static, discursive circularity of Ishmael's musings. *Melville: The Ironic Diagram* (Evanston, Ill.: Northwestern University Press, 1970), 6, 63–66.

3. Melville, "Hawthorne and His Mosses," in the Library of America edition, 1154. Nina Baym underscores Melville's discomfort with narrative

in "Melville's Quarrel with Fiction," *PMLA* 94 (October 1979): 909–24. She suggests that "Melville abandoned narrative principles and did not use normative fictional genres. . . . [He experienced] a rapid disenchantment with fiction both as a mode of truth telling and as a mode of truth seeking" (913).

4. Various critics have noted *Moby-Dick's* allusive treatment of Manifest Destiny and the political crisis it produced. See, for instance, John McWilliams, Jr., *Hawthorne, Melville, and the American Character: A Looking-Glass Business* (Cambridge: Cambridge University Press, 1984); Rogin, *Subversive Genealogy*; and Heimert, "*Moby-Dick* and the American Political Symbolism," 510.

5. Ezra B. Chase, *Teachings of Patriots and Statesmen; or the "Fathers of the Republic" on Slavery* (Philadelphia: J. W. Bridley, 1860), 6, 12. On Clay's reverential faith in Washington's Farewell Address, see Bryan, "George Washington," 54. Few figures questioned the prevailing political retrospection as Melville did. For a rare exception, see Albert Brisbane, who in 1840 criticized the leading statesmen of the day for putting their faith in "the policy of a Washington or a Jefferson, and not in new principles or organic changes. . . . It is clear that our politicians are all looking backwards." *Social Destiny of Man: or, Association and Reorganization of Industry* (New York: Burt Franklin, 1968) viii.

6. My use of "truth" as a category of knowledge is not meant to imply a transcendent or universal intelligence. Rather I follow both Melville and Foucault in subjecting "truth" to the critical perspective of genealogy. As I will argue below, for Melville, "truth" did not denote universals, but instead a historically specific and racially contextual belief in democracy.

7. Melville, "Hawthorne and His Mosses," 1160, 1162; Michel Foucault, "The Discourse on Language," in *The Archaeology of Knowledge*, trans. A. M. Sheridan Smith (New York: Harper & Row, 1972), 224; *Power/Knowledge*, 131.

8. Melville, "Hawthorne and His Mosses," 1160.

9. In trying to evade slipping *dans le vrai*, Ishmael thus resists the "author-function" also described by Foucault in "What Is an Author?" in *The Foucault Reader*, ed. Paul Rabinow (New York: Pantheon, 1984), 101–20.

10. Three recent studies of *Moby-Dick* raise similar questions. Wai-chee Dimock's *Empire for Liberty: Melville and the Poetics of Individualism* (Princeton: Princeton University Press, 1989), Rogin's *Subversive Genealogy*, and Carolyn L. Karcher's *Shadow over the Promised Land: Slavery, Race, and Violence in Melville's America* (Baton Rouge: Louisiana State University Press, 1980) all understand Herman Melville as a profound critic of a national mission that sanctioned the domination of Native Americans, the enslavement of African Americans, and the imperialist aggression of the Mexican-American War.

11. Nathaniel Hawthorne, *The Scarlet Letter* (New York: Signet, 1980) 16, 42, 21, 44; Derrida, *Dissemination*, 41; Edgar Allan Poe, *The Narrative of Arthur Gordon Pym of Nantucket*, (New York: Penguin, 1986) 44; Jacobs, *Incidents*, 3.

12. *The Letters of Herman Melville*, ed. Merrell R. Davis and William H. Gilman (New Haven: Yale University Press, 1960), 96.

13. Karcher, *Shadow over the Promised Land*, 11, and see her discussion of further accounts of Melville's variance from potential colleagues, 9–26.

14. Melville, *Letters*, 127, 78.

15. Donald Pease, *Visionary Compacts: American Renaissance Writings in Cultural Context* (Madison: University of Wisconsin Press, 1987), 46; Charles H. Foster, "Something in Emblems: A Reinterpretation of *Moby-Dick*," in *New England Quarterly* 34 (March 1961): 11; Melville, *Letters*, 127, 128.

16. Melville, "Hawthorne and His Mosses," 1160; Ralph Ellison, *Shadow and Act* (New York: Random House, 1964), 40–41. Edgar Dryden has also paid attention to the thematic content of Melville's form, noting especially its metaphysical dimensions. Dryden argues that in Melville's hands, the novel acts as a metaphysical attempt to formulate an "experience which is both particular and unified" (7). My focus on the political content of narrative form, however, suggests that *Moby-Dick* often struggles against the implicit coherence and unity of and of narrative. See *Melville's Thematics of Form: The Great Art of Telling the Truth* (Baltimore: Johns Hopkins University Press, 1968).

17. Frederick Douglass, "To The Lynn Anti-Slavery Sewing Circle, August 18, 1846," in *Life and Writings*, 1:187. The range of *Moby-Dick's* narratives, according to Baym, confused readers, and early reviews were "unable to determine its genre." "Melville's Quarrel with Fiction," (917–18).

18. Richard Brodhead, *Hawthorne, Melville, and the Novel* (Chicago: University of Chicago Press, 1976), 20, 4.

19. Carolyn Porter, "Call Me Ishmael," 102, 101, 100; Brodhead, *Hawthorne, Melville, and the Novel*, 151. John Samson underscores Porter's discussion of how Ishmael subverts authorized discourses of antebellum America. Working from insights supplied by Bakhtin and Foucault, Samson stresses how Melville developed an anti-authoritarian stance toward a national culture that was becoming increasingly monolithic. *White Lies: Melville's Narratives of Facts* (Ithaca: Cornell University Press, 1989), 11–16. Anacharsis Clootz was a radical democrat and German-born leader of the French Revolution who headed a delegation he proclaimed as an "embassy of the human race." He was sent to the guillotine in March 1794.

20. Melville, *Letters*, 127.

21. Eleanor E. Simpson, "Melville and the Negro: From *Typee* to *Benito Cereno*," *American Literature* 41 (March 1969): 28.

22. This displacement of Queequeg from the "dark continent" to the imaginary Kokovoko serves as an misdirection that corresponds to Melville's theory of truth telling. As Ishmael says of Kokovoko, "It is not down in any map; true places never are" (62).

23. The *Richmond Enquirer* is quoted in Rogin, *Ronald Reagan, the Movie*, 53; Hudson, *The Second War of Independence in America*, 150.

24. Henry Hughes, *Treatise on Sociology, Theoretical and Practical* (1854, reprint; New York: Negro Universities Press, 1968), 227, 214; J. C. Nott and George R. Gliddon, *Types of Mankind* (Philadelphia: Lippencott, Grambo, 1855), 403, 404. Karcher's *Shadow over the Promised Land* provides excellent

readings and background of antebellum ethnology and its representation in Melville's texts. For instance, in her chapter "A Jonah's Warning to America in *Moby-Dick*," she discusses at length how Queequeg rescues Ishmael from color prejudices instilled by contemporary scientific discourses (62–69). Also helpful is George Fredrickson's *The Black Image in the White Mind*.

25. Therefore Ishmael allows Melville to criticize the discriminating actions of judges like his father-in-law Lemuel Shaw, whose decision to uphold racially segregated schooling in the case of *Sarah C. Roberts v. City of Boston* (1849) later acted as the foundation of the doctrine of "separate but equal." See Karcher, *Shadow over the Promised Land*, 10.

26. William A. Smith, *Lectures on the Philosophy and Practice of Slavery, As Exhibited in the Institution of Domestic Slavery in the United States: With the Duties of Masters to Slaves* (1856, reprint.; Miami Fla.: Mnemosyne, 1969), 223, 223–24. Ishmael here undercuts the declaration he later extrapolates from his observations of Pip: "For blacks, the year's calendar should show naught but three hundred and sixty-five Fourth of Julys and New Year's Days" (319). In fact, Ishmael's own association with Queequeg, as well as his descriptions of Daggoo, should logically contradict his "findings" here. Also noteworthy is the severe irony of Ishmael's statement when considered alongside of Frederick Douglass's comments on the meaning of the Fourth of July to the Negro, or Harriet Jacobs's description of New Year's Day as a time of uncertainty and separation for the slave mother who sits "watching the children who may all be torn from her the next morning." *Incidents*, 16.

27. Richard Chase, *Herman Melville: A Critical Study* (New York: Macmillan, 1949), 42. Chase's classic study traces the Prometheus motif throughout Melville's work. See, especially, 45–48.

28. Michael Walzer suggests that "symbolic action" is key to political manipulations. "The union of men," writes Walzer "can only be symbolized; it has no palpable shape or substance." "On the Role of Symbolism in Political Thought," *Political Science Quarterly* 82 (June 1967): 194. For accounts of the struggle for narrative authority between Ishmael/Melville and Ahab, see See F. O. Matthiessen, *American Renaissance: Art and Expression in the Age of Whitman and Emerson*, (New York: Oxford University Press, 1941), 445–47; Nicholas Canaday, *Melville and Authority*, (Gainesville: University of Florida Press, 1968), 52; Robert L. Caserio, *Plot, Story, and the Novel: From Dickens to Poe in the Modern Period* (New Jersey: Princeton University Press, 1979), 137; and, Seelye, *Melville*, 63–71.

29. Charles Olson, *Call Me Ishmael*, (New York: Grove Press, 1947), 53.

30. Rogin similarly notes that Ahab makes ceremonial use of the pagan harpooners to invest his rule with a mystical, religious power. *Subversive Genealogy*, 129–31.

31. Melville, *Letters*, 133, 142.

32. Melville, "Hawthorne and His Mosses," 1159, 1158. On the Puritan understanding of the relation of symbolism to allegory, see Charles Feidleson, *Symbolism and American Literature* (Chicago: University of Chicago Press, 1953). In *Typee* (1846), the ship's captain attempts a similar manipulation of

dark bodies as part of an effort to curb his crew's desires for "liberty" or shore leave: "if you'll take my advice, every mother's son of you will stay aboard, and keep out of the way of the bloody cannibals altogether. . . . for if those tattooed scoundrels get you a little ways back into their valleys, they'll nab you—that you may certain of. Plenty of white men have gone ashore here and never been seen any more." Herman Melville, *Typee* (Evanston, Ill.: Northwestern University Press, 1968), 34.

33. Melville, "Hawthorne and His Mosses," 1159.

34. Pease, *Visionary Compacts*, 245. On Ahab's ability to distort the covenant into a form of possession, notice his appraisal of Starbuck after the ritual of "The Quarter-Deck": "Starbuck is now mine; cannot oppose me now, without rebellion" (140).

35. James Baldwin, "Everybody's Protest Novel," in *Notes of a Native Son*, (Boston: Beacon, 1955), 16. Michel Foucault, *Discipline and Punish: The Birth of the Prison*, trans. Alan Sheridan (New York: Vintage, 1979), 25. Foucault continues to say that the political involvement of the body establishes "the 'body politic' as a set of material elements and techniques that serve as weapons, relays, communications routes and supports for the power and knowledge relations that invest human bodies and subjugate them by turning them into objects of knowledge" (28). On female abolitionists'/suffragists' use of the black body, see Karen Sánchez-Eppler's fine article, "Bodily Bonds: The Intersecting Rhetorics of Abolition and Feminism," *Representations* 24 (Fall 1988): 28–59.

36. For further commentary on the theatrical dynamics between Ahab and Pip, see Canaday, *Melville and Authority*, 45, and Karcher, *Shadow over the Promised Land*, 84–88.

37. John Schaar, "The Uses of Literature for the Study of Politics: The Case of Melville's 'Benito Cereno,'" in *Legitimacy in the Modern State* (New Brunswick, N.J.: Transaction, 1981), 77. These redemptive moments, of course, have strong components of male eroticism and homosexuality, which Melville understood as fulfilling desires that are at once political and sexual. On this point, see Robert K. Martin, *Hero, Captain, Stranger: Male Friendship, Social Critique, and Literary Form in the Sea Novels of Herman Melville* (Chapel Hill: University of North Carolina Press, 1986).

38. Homi Bhabha equates this reduction of narratives with nationalism: "For the political unity of the nation consists in a continual displacement of its irredeemably plural modern space, bounded by different, even hostile nations, into a signifying space that is archaic and mythical, paradoxically representing the nation's modern territoriality, in the patriotic, atavistic temporality of Traditionalism. Quite simply, the difference of space returns as the Sameness of time, turning Territory into Tradition, turning the People into One." "DissemiNation," 300.

39. *The Congressional Globe: New Series, Containing Sketches of the Debates and Proceedings of the First Session of the Thirty-First Congress* (City of Washington: John C. Rives, 1850), 246.

40. There are, however, studies that read *Moby-Dick's* characters as having real-world referents in the antebellum political scene. Foster thus reads Ahab as Daniel Webster in "Something in Emblems," while Alan Heimert positions John C. Calhoun as Ahab in *"Moby-Dick* and American Political Symbolism." I resist this strict type of allegorical reading. I agree more readily with Rogin's strategy for reading Melville in *Subversive Genealogy*: "The intention here is neither to make Melville's romances real by reducing them to some preexistent reality, nor to recover American history in Melville in order to unmask the truth behind his fiction, but rather to understand Melville's constructions in the light of the material from which they were made" (23). Rogin thus writes: "Melville was a realist in his attention to a political rhetoric which, in the literary definition of that term, was not realist. Unlike that public language, however, Melville's version of American history was no celebratory romance" (41). Likewise, David S. Reynolds argues that "historical source study can be delimiting" and focuses his critical energies on the rhetoric, not the message, of reform movements of Melville's era. See *Beneath the American Renaissance: The Subversive Imagination in the Age of Emerson and Melville* (New York: Knopf, 1988), 156.

CHAPTER 3

1. "Editor's Table," *Harper's New Monthly Magazine* 5 (November 1852), 839. William Wells Brown, *Clotel; or the President's Daughter. A Narrative of Slave Life in the United States.* (1853; reprint, New York: Carol, 1969), 72.

2. On the structural imperatives within citizenship that erase local identities with abstract affiliations, see Lauren Berlant, "National Brands/National Body: *Imitation of Life,"* in *Comparative American Identities: Race, Sex, and Nationality in the Modern Text,* ed. Hortense Spillers (New York: Routledge, 1991), 113–14.

3. "Editor's Table," 839; Melville, *Moby-Dick,* 153. Important studies of economic and territorial expansion in relation to American literature and culture include Leo Marx, *The Machine in the Garden: Technology and the Pastoral Ideal in America* (New York: Oxford University Press, 1964); Alan Trachtenberg, *The Incorporation of America: Culture and Display in the Gilded Age* (New York: Hill and Wang, 1982); and Carolyn Porter, *Seeing and Being: The Plight of the Participant Observer in Emerson, James, Adams, and Faulkner* (Middletown: Wesleyan University Press, 1982).

4. Berlant, *The Anatomy of National Fantasy,* 5.

5. Ralph Waldo Emerson, *Nature,* in *Essays and Lectures,* ed. Joel Porte (New York: Library of America, 1983), 17. All further references to Emerson in this chapter that use this edition will be cited in the text. I follow Hayden White, who discusses the difference between narrating and narrativizing by defining narration as a discourse that "openly adopts a perspective and reports it" and narrative as a discourse that "feigns to make the world speak itself and speak itself *as a story."* "The Value of Narrativity in the Repre-

sentation of Reality," in *On Narrative* ed. W. J. T. Mitchell (Chicago, University of Chicago Press, 1981), 2–3.

6. Friedrich Nietzsche, "On the Uses and Disadvantages of History for Life," in *Untimely Meditations*, trans. R. B. Hollingdale (New York: Cambridge University Press, 1983), 68–70, 62, 64.

7. Edward Everett, "The Bunker Hill Monument," in *Orations and Speeches on Various Occasions*, 4 vols. (Boston: Little, Brown, 1850), 1:362; George Washington Warren, *The History of the Bunker Hill Monument Association during the First Century of the United States of America* (Boston: J. R. Osgood, 1877), 375; Daniel Webster, "The Completion of the Bunker Hill Monument," in *Works*, 1:86; Daniel Kemmis, *Community and the Politics of Place* (Norman: University of Oklahoma Press, 1990), 86; Nietzsche, "On the Uses and Disadvantages of History," 71.

8. Thomas Jefferson, *Notes on the State of Virginia*, in *The Life and Selected Writings of Thomas Jefferson*, ed. Adrienne Koch and William Peden (New York: Modern Library, 1972), 205, 196. Frank Kermode's study of the *translatio* discusses biological aspects informing American exceptionalism. See *The Classic* (London: Faber and Faber, 1975), 100.

9. Thomas Cole, *The Collected Essays and Prose Sketches*, ed. Marshall Tymn (St. Paul, Minn.: John Colet Press, 1980), 16, 10. Cole's nativist tone reverberates with themes of Manifest Destiny. The waters of the Hudson, the American prairie, the "margin of the distant Oregon," are "his [the American's] own land; its beauty, its magnificence, its sublimity—all are his" (3). David C. Hunington, *The Landscapes of Frederic Edwin Church: Vision of an American Era* (New York: George Braziller, 1966), 10.

10. John Sears, *Sacred Places: American Tourist Attractions in the Nineteenth Century* (New York: Oxford University Press, 1989), 12. The Boston preacher is quoted in Elizabeth McKinsey, *Niagara Falls: Icon of the American Sublime* (Cambridge: Cambridge University Press, 1985), 107. Sears, *Sacred Places*, 3–30, and McKinsey, *Niagara Falls*, 100–16, are indispensable in explaining the national and popular resonance of Niagara Falls in nineteenth-century America. Also important in understanding the national appeal of landscape painting in this period is Angela Miller, "Everywhere and Nowhere: The Making of the National Landscape," *American Literary History* 2 (summer 1992): 207–29. "In the absence of a shared race history," she argues, visual representations from the Hudson River School "proffered a sense of national identity" (213). My understanding of collective imagining draws upon Anderson's discussion of the logo in "Census, Map, Museum," *Imagined Communities*, 163–85.

11. Lincoln, "Fragment on Niagara Falls," in *Collected Works*, 2:10–11.

12. Hunington, *The Landscapes of Frederic Edwin Church*, 70; for a discussion of the radical dimensions of Church's *Niagara*, see 69; McKinsey, *Niagara Falls*, 206. Hunington states that "Frederic Church and the United States of America were one" (61) in his argument that Church was the artist of Manifest Destiny. Such a view, I think, is essentially correct, though in the absence of further commentary, this interpretation risks reproducing the

ideological message of Church's painting insofar as it understands *Niagara* as an uncomplicated, grand patriotic expression without remarking upon the less glorious aspects that reside in American expansionism and its artistic imaginings. In addition, I want to insist that my grouping of Church and his mentor Cole is not an attempt to collapse the differences between the two. Cole's landscape paintings—often punctuated with tree stumps that suggest an ambivalence about American inroads into the wilderness—cast a more sombre tone than Church's works. Cole's apprehensions culminate in his *Course of Empire* series, whose ruined classical monuments bespeak reservations about American exceptionalism. For detailed descriptions of the differences between specific works by Cole and Church, see Franklin Kelly, *Frederic Edwin Church and the National Landscape* (Washington, D.C.: Smithsonian Institution Press: 1988). Adam Badeau's description of Church's *Niagara* underscores how the antebellum art patron was disposed to imagine herself or himself at the scene, or better yet, how via the image, he or she outdistanced spatial restrictions to stand at the site of a homogeneous polity: "The idea of motion he [Church] has imparted to his canvass, the actual feeling you have of the tremble of the fall." *The Vagabond* (New York: Rudd and Carleton, 1859), 123.

13. Cole is quoted in Barbara Novak, *American Painting of the Nineteenth-Century: Realism, Idealism, and the American Experience* (New York: Praeger, 1969), 63; Badeau, *The Vagabond*, 123–24. For a reading of Cole's *Niagara Falls* as an evocation of cosmic unity, see McKinsey, *Niagara Falls*, 213–14. It is important to remember that the sublime works to elevate humans even as it diminishes them. In many nineteenth-century landscapes, faint views of civilization suggest praise for human endeavors that are able to secure a foothold for settlement within the awesome splendor of the wilderness. Thus, Sears argues that the elevated perspective of American landscapes brings to mind "a faintly sacred point of vision that recalls Moses's view of the Promised Land from Mount Pisgah." *Sacred Places*, 54. Angela Miller extends the implications of this insight, stating that the allusion to Moses's view of the Promised Land was "repeated by Americans like an incantation throughout the period of settlement as they sought to subdue the wilderness and make it blossom as the rose." "Everywhere and Nowhere," 214.

14. Thomas Jefferson, *Notes on the State of Virginia*, in *Life and Selected Writings*, 197.

15. Cole is quoted in Novak, *American Painting of the Nineteenth Century*, 64. Donald A. Ringe, in *The Pictorial Mode: Space and Time in the Art of Bryant, Irving, and Cooper* (Lexington: University Press of Kentucky, 1971), examines how the expanse of American nature influenced the consciousness and productions of nineteenth-century painters and writers. And also see Hunington, *The Landscapes of Frederic Edwin Church*, xi, and McKinsey, *Niagara Falls*, 247, for instance, who argue that Emersonian principles underlay aspects of Church's and Cole's work.

16. Melville, *Pierre*, in the Library of America edition, 3. Angela Miller elaborates the political dimensions of nineteenth-century landscape paint-

ing. She argues that the tension between part and whole in aesthetic composition replicates the tension between the remoteness of local jurisdiction and the abstractness of federal centralism. See "Everywhere and Nowhere," especially 208–9, 219.

17. John L. O'Sullivan, "The Great Nation of Futurity," in *Manifest Destiny*, ed. Norman A. Graebner (New York: Bobbs-Merrill, 1968), 19–20; Melville, *Moby-Dick*, 103, 105, 106. Anderson, *Imagined Communities*, 22–36. See also Heimert, who discusses how the distinct geographic origins of the *Pequod*'s mates exemplify positions in the national debates of the mid-century United States. "*Moby-Dick* and American Political Symbolism," 502.

18. Simms is quoted in Kammen, *A Season of Youth*, 162; the review of Melville is quoted in Brian Higgins and Hershel Parker, *Critical Essays on Melville's 'Pierre; or, The Ambiguities'* (Boston: G. K. Hall, 1983), 38; Perry Miller, *The Raven and the Whale: The War of Wits and Words in the Era of Poe and Melville* (New York: Harcourt Brace, 1956), 31; Melville, "Hawthorne and His Mosses," 1165.

19. Badeau, *The Vagabond*, 154.

20. Daniel Webster, "The Character of Washington," *Works*, 1:230; J. Lansing Burrows, "Address Before the Mount Vernon Association, July 4th, 1855," *Southern Literary Messenger* 21 (1855), 515.

21. Kirkland, *Memoirs of Washington*, 57.

22. McKinsey, *Niagara Falls*, 104. The diminutive figures at the base of the falls, enveloped and partially obscured by the spray from the falls, further makes incidental—and forgettable—Native Americans, suggesting their incompatibility within the monumental nation. Wai-chee Dimock demonstrates how the extermination of Native Americans was made to conform to larger narratives of American destiny: "The Indian, as he is described by antebellum ethnographers and politicians, is therefore always the subject of a predestined narrative in which he is responsible for, guilty of, and committed to a fated course of action, in which he appears as . . . a legible sign of his own inexorable end." "Ahab's Manifest Destiny," in *Macropolitics of Nineteenth-Century Literature*, ed. Jonathan Arac and Harriet Ritvo (Philadelphia: University of Pennsylvania Press, 1991), 190.

23. Ibid. McKinsey discusses the engraving *America* in terms of "harmony." But is unity the only message that this engraving can narrativize? In chapter 4, I suggest that Williams Wells Brown presents a different strategy of reading sublime national narrative that listens to the story the muted slave of *America* might tell.

24. Thomas Jefferson, *Notes on the State of Virginia*, in *Life and Selected Writings*, 197. Given Webster's message, it is not surprising to hear his speech described as illustrative of federalism, as unifying, as "sublime": "The conception of the whole discourse was magnificent; and, being grandly sustained in all its parts, its effect upon the immense auditory, carried away by his lofty sentiments, mingled into one mass, and wrought up as one man to the highest pitch of enthusiasm, was really sublime." Warren, *History of the*

Bunker Hill Monument Association, 150; Webster, "Completion of The Bunker Hill Monument," *Works*, 1:59

25. Berlant, *The Anatomy of National Fantasy*, 186.

26. "Editor's Table," 702; Weems, *Life of Washington*, 5.

27. Berlant makes a similar point: nationalism produces a "powerful politically sanctioned ideology of amnesia" that leads to the erasure of local memory. *The Anatomy of National Fantasy*, 194. While I agree with Berlant, at the same time, I want to suggest that national history leads to a forgetting of not just local memory, but of national history itself.

28. Weems, *Life of Washington*, 22; Jared Sparks, *The Life of George Washington* (New York: Miller, Orton, Mulligan, 1855), iv.

29. Nietzsche, "On the Uses and Disadvantages of History," 62, 71.

30. For the sake of clarity and simplification, I will hereafter refer to the Washington Monument in Baltimore as the Baltimore Monument, and the obelisk in Washington, D.C. as the Washington Monument. My suggestion of an equivalence between Emerson's writing and the national narratives of American monuments deserves further comment. The volume of Emerson's corpus, and its contradiction and diversity, must be somewhat overlooked in order to argue for a sympathy between Emerson and monumental architecture, and yet, as Donald Pease suggests, Emerson's thought, particularly his popular notions of self-reliance and transcendence, proved susceptible to this sort of seamless rendering by the antebellum public. "Emerson himself was not careful to distinguish what he meant by self-reliance from what the term was popularly understood to mean," writes Pease. "His essays and orations exploited the confusion between what he meant and what the public understood." *Visionary Compacts*, 205. In short, then, my invocations of Emerson are designed as explications of those discrete elements of his thinking that can be taken up to ratify the projects and philosophy of monumental culture. Following Foucault's "What is an Author?" I read Emerson not so much as an autonomous writer, but as a discursive subject whose writing is infused with various cultural forces including the transcendent imagining of the nation. Champion of Young America and critic of national policy, devotee of American exceptionalism and antagonist of United States social institutions, Emerson represents a complexity and a contradiction, not all of whose ideas filtered equally throughout the republic. Like imperial America, my interest lies in Emerson's notions especially conducive to the monumental project.

31. Everett is quoted in Warren, *History of the Bunker Hill Monument Association*, 115; Melville, *Moby-Dick*, 132. In addition, to fabled New World political advancements, the Bunker Hill Monument gave testimony to a progressing and more efficient American ingenuity. One of the first railroads built on the American continent ran between Quincy and Bunker Hill, transporting the granite blocks used in construction. While expenditures for the Baltimore structure totalled two hundred and twenty thousand dollars, the Bunker Hill monument, containing twice the amount of cubic feet and

sixty feet higher, was estimated at one hundred and twenty thousand dollars. See Richard Frothingham, *History of the Siege of Boston, and the Battles of Lexington, Concord, and Bunker Hill*, (Boston: C. C. Little and J. Brown, 1849), 353–54.

32. Pease, *Visionary Compacts*, 217. John Bodnar reads monuments such as the Vietnam Veterans Memorial as instances in which "official culture" tries to override "ordinary" culture by using nationalism to predominate the "profane" experiences of "ordinary people and ordinary emotions." He suggests that Webster's speeches at Bunker Hill, by championing the middle classes, worked to foreground this ordinary citizen, but I find it hard not to see Webster's praise as a ratification of a common, undifferentiated culture committed to prosperity and progress. In Webster's era, so much of what was considered to be "common" or "ordinary" was understood as coincident with America itself. See John Bodnar, *Remaking America: Public Memory, Commemoration, and Patriotism in the Twentieth Century* (Princeton: Princeton University Press, 1992), 7, 25.

33. Weems, *Life of Washington*, 9; Everett is quoted in Warren, *History of the Bunker Hill Monument Association*, 116; William W. Wheildon, *Memoir of Solomon Willard, Architect and Superintendent of the Bunker Hill Monument* (Boston: Monument Association, 1865), 223. Just as contributions and certificates permitted the citizen to imagine himself or herself as part of national history, at Niagara Falls the souvenirs, guide books, and certificates from trips to Termination Rock were all directed at "tourists who stepped out of their ordinary routines, their familiar and obscure surroundings, and stepped onto the stage of history." Sears, *Sacred Places*, 23–24.

34. Wheildon, *Memoir of Solomon Willard*, 191; Frederick Loviad Harvey, *History of the Washington National Monument and the Washington National Monument Society* (Washington, D.C.: Elliot Printing, 1902), 72. Traces of division still disfigure the Washington Monument even though it was completed in 1886. The visible discrepancy in the shading of the marble blocks between the lower and upper portions of the monument preserves memory of the cessation of national construction in the Civil War era.

35. Melville, *Moby-Dick*, 141; see Anderson, *Imagined Communities*, 24–25.

36. Webster, "Completion of the Bunker Hill Monument," *Works*, 1:86–87, 105. Hannah Arendt outlines this republican notion of the past and *religare* in "What is Authority?" in *Between Past and Future: Eight Exercises in Political Thought* (New York: Viking, 1968). Arendt describes how the Roman republic saw itself moving into a future that extended to the foundations of the past.

37. Foucault, *Discipline and Punish*, 202–3. The entire chapter on Panopticism (195–228) is key to understanding Foucault's ideas about the intersection of visibility and disciplinary individualism. In light of Foucault's investigations, one is struck by the fact that the granite for the Bunker Hill Monument, an icon of democratic freedom, was prepared by forced labor at the state prison.

38. Pease, *Visionary Compacts*, 45. By saying that American monumentalism does not make individuals visible, I do not intend to discount that within the United States, individuals are also highly visible registers of,simultaneously, power, knowledge, and resistance. The existence of extensive police forces, public-opinion polls, and the popularity of psychological therapy may be taken as signs of panopticism.

39. Webster, "Completion of the Bunker Hill Monument," *Works*, 1:83.

40. Foucault, *Discipline and Punish*, 201, 207.

41. Melville, *Letters*, 210.

42. Herman Melville, *Israel Potter: His Fifty Years of Exile* in the Library of America edition, 425. All further references made to this edition will be included in the text.

43. Melville, *Letters*, 170; "Editor's Table," 701. Daniel Reagan, in "Melville's *Israel Potter* and the Nature of Biography," *American Transcendental Quarterly* 3 (September 1989): 257–76, though he may misrepresent an elitist tendency of Emerson's notions of biography by concentrating upon *Representative Men*, is helpful in generating a historical context for nineteenth-century American biography. For the monarchical tension within Melville's authorship, see chapter 2 of Dimock, *Empire for Liberty*.

44. Chase's classic work, *Herman Melville*, locates many of Melville's figures within the American folk tradition; for further treatment of the folk influences in *Israel Potter*, see 176–83.

45. Brodhead, *Hawthorne, Melville, and the Novel*, 191.

46. Melville, *Letters*, 78. For an exploration of the parallels between Melville and Bartleby, see Leo Marx, "Melville's Parable of the Walls," in *Herman Melville's 'Billy Budd,' "Benito Cereno," "Bartleby the Scrivener," and Other Tales*, ed. Harold Bloom (New York: Chelsea House, 1987), 11–29. John Seelye further elaborates on metaphysical grounds the differences between Melville and Emerson. *Melville*, 7–8.

47. "Editor's Table," 701. In his account of monumental history, Nietzsche describes a situation relevant to Israel's effacement, emphasizing the pitfalls of neglect, of smoothing out "what is individual": "If, therefore, the monumental mode of regarding the past *rules* . . . the past itself suffers *harm*: whole segments of it are forgotten, despised, and flow away in an uninterrupted colourless flood." "On the Uses and Disadvantages of History," 69, 70–71.

48. Perhaps inadvertently, Warren records the ways in which the monumental forgets and pushes the individual toward oblivion. Warren notes that "it was promised in the beginning that the names of all those who should give a single dollar would be preserved in perpetual remembrance," only to apologize that such a project remained to be realized. *History of the Bunker Hill Monument Association*, vii. Peter J. Bellis's discussion supports the idea that *Israel Potter* identifies amnesia and alienation as key elements of the monumental. Melville's "reinscription" of Potter's autobiography as biography works to "*discredit* the notion of historical narrative as simple 'rec-

ollection'; history is, he insists, a fictionalizaton, a reinscription that obscures the reality of alienation and loss." *"Israel Potter*: Autobiography as History as Fiction," *American Literary History* 2 (winter 1990): 610.

49. Hannah Arendt, *The Human Condition* (Chicago: University of Chicago Press, 1958), 179; Frothingham, *History of the Siege of Boston*, 344; Webster, "Completion of the Bunker Hill Monument," *Works*, 1:86. Wu Hung's essay on Tiananmen Square provides a helpful account of how monuments can act to implement a fixed, temporal order. The Goddess of Democracy that sprang up under much different auspices than the official state buildings in the square, he suggests, offers an almost antimonumental posture insofar as "it was prepared to be destroyed." It is this ephemeral nature that connotes the political for Arendt. "Tiananmen Square: A Political History of Monuments," *Representations* 35 (summer 1991): 113.

50. Webster, "Completion of the Bunker Hill Monument," *Works*, 1:107; Lincoln, "Address before the Young Men's Lyceum," *Collected Works*, 1:112, 1:115. This understanding of Lincoln's politics emerges from my reading of Arendt, who describes politics as a human realm of interconnection that is necessarily transitory and fragile. See *The Human Condition*, especially 199–200.

51. Nietzsche, "On the Uses and Disadvantages of History," 72.

52. Carolyn Porter, "Reification and American Literature," in *Ideology and Classic American Literature*, ed. Sacvan Bercovitch and Myra Jehlen (Cambridge: Cambridge University Press, 1986), 203. See also Pease, who comments on the "incomprehensible," nonactual aspect of this passage. *Visionary Compacts*, 227.

53. See Bellis, *"Israel Potter,"* for a thorough accounting of the differences between Melville's biography and Potter's autobiography. Bellis sums up the significance of these differences by suggesting that *Israel Potter* is a "critique of narrative representation that is at once a theoretical or self-reflexive gesture and an attack on the mythmaking that supports an ideology of national progress" (622).

54. In his discussion of *Pierre*, Sundquist suggests a relation between parody and parricide. *Home as Found*, 177–82. For an illuminating account of contemporary resistance to the official history of the monumental, see Marita Sturken, "The Wall, the Screen, and the Image: The Vietnam Veterans Memorial" *Representations* 35 (summer 1991): 118–42.

55. Israel R. Potter, *Life and Remarkable Adventures of Israel R. Potter* (1824, reprint; New York: Corinth Books, 1962), 50. As Melville remarks in his preface, despite the original's autobiographical form, it was written by another, most probably its publisher, Trumbull.

56. Arendt, *The Human Condition*, 186; Bellis, *"Israel Potter,"* 607.

57. Foucault, *Power/Knowledge*, 82, 81; Berlant, *The Anatomy of National Fantasy*, 149, 105.

58. Nietzsche, "On the Uses and Disadvantages of History," 76. See also Bhabha, "DissemiNation," for a discussion of how alterity and difference

such as is found in *Israel Potter* represents the nation as an "ambivalent, ragbag narrative" (318).

59. Nietzsche, "On the Uses and Disadvantages of History," 69, 71. Laughter performs another vital function by guarding against the excessive use of critical history, which can destroy life. Critical history can lead to an outlook that declares "For all that exists is *worthy* of perishing. So it would be better if nothing existed" (76). For further elaboration of the need to temper critical history with metaphor and tragedy, see White, *Metahistory*, 332–72.

CHAPTER 4

1. Melville, "Hawthorne and His Mosses," 1161; Berlant, *The Anatomy of National Fantasy*, 29.

2. O'Sullivan, "The Great Nation of Futurity," 20. McWilliams provides interesting background about O'Sullivan; see *Hawthorne, Melville, and the American Character*, 13–15. Not only was O'Sullivan Una Hawthorne's godfather, but he figured as the godfather of the Young America movement. Perry Miller's *The Raven and the Whale* still stands as one of the most comprehensive treatments of literary nationalism during the American Renaissance. Other commentators include Kammen, *A Season of Youth*, 161–69; McWilliams, 1–21, and Joel Porte, *In Respect to Egotism: Studies in American Romantic Writing* (Cambridge: Cambridge University Press, 1991), 16–19.

3. Melville, "Hawthorne and His Mosses," 1165.

4. Theodore Parker, *The American Scholar*, ed. George Willis Cooke (Boston: American Unitarian Association, 1907), 33–34, 44; Melville, "Hawthorne and His Mosses," 1164.

5. Parker, *The American Scholar*, 37. Despite Parker's determination that slave narratives were "original," these works often adapted and cunningly manipulated more established literary forms, among them the picaresque, the sentimental novel, and the travel narrative. That slavery and race provided an "original," if not embarrassing, cultural nationalism is evident in the context of minstrelsy in addition to that of the slave narrative. See Eric Lott on the intersections of the popular culture of blackface and national culture. *Love and Theft*, 89–107.

6. Toni Morrison, "Unspeakable Things Unspoken: The Afro-American Presence in American Literature" *Michigan Quarterly Review* 28 (winter 1989): 6, 12–13, 11, 13. The intersection of monumentalism and race could also examine the United States government's attitude toward Native Americans. Beginning with the Hudson River School, art and literature portrayed Native Americans relinquishing the grandeur of Nature to the white settler. In Ann S. Stephens's *Malaeska: The Indian Wife of the White Hunter* (1860; reprint, New York: John Day, 1929), for instance, the disappearance of Native Americans is carefully staged against a monumental landscape. This real dispossession from the land saw the symbolic inclusion of Native Americans within an iconic and monumental history. Treaties with tribes were often ratified with

peace medals engraved with the president's image. On this point, see the iconic medallion emblazoned with an image of Washington that Chingach-gook wears in *The Pioneers*. In addition, representatives from tribes formed part of the formal ceremonies consecrating the Washington Monument, and some of its stones, whose inscriptions face inside, were donated from tribes.

7. Ibid., 14; Bercovitch, "The Rites of Assent," and see also the final chapter of *The American Jeremiad*. Douglass, *Narrative of the Life*, vii.

8. Bercovitch, *The American Jeremiad*, 176.

9. Burrows, "Address Before the Mount Vernon Association," 515; Marion Harland [Mary Virginia Terhune], *Moss-Side* (New York: Derby, Jackson, 1857), 55; E.D.H., "The Fugitive Slave's Apostrophe to Niagara," in Joseph T. Buckingham, *Personal Memoirs and Recollections of Editorial Life* (Boston: Ticknor, Reed, Fields, 1852), 194. This poem's author is identified by only the three initials, and evidence suggests that it is not the production of a fugitive slave, despite the work's title. Impersonal, distancing expressions such as "the bondman's breast" (192) and "the Negro's God" (194) indicate the poem as the creation of a white abolitionist.

10. Austin Steward, *Twenty-Two Years a Slave, and, Forty Years a Freeman: Embracing a Correspondence of Several Years, while President of Wilberforce Colony, London, Canada West* (1856; reprint, New York: Negro Universities Press, 1968), 303–4; Samuel Ringgold Ward, *Autobiography of a Fugitive Negro*, 158.

11. William Wells Brown, *The Anti-Slavery Harp: A Collection of Songs for Anti-Slavery Meetings, Compiled by William W. Brown, a Fugitive Slave* (1848; reprint, Philadelphia: Rhistoric, 1969), 23; Ralph Waldo Emerson, "The American Scholar," in *Essays and Lectures*, 69.

12. William Wells Brown, *The Narrative of William W. Brown, A Fugitive Slave, Written by Himself* (1847), in *Four Fugitive Slave Narratives*, ed. Robin W. Winks, et al. (Reading, Mass.: Addison-Wesley, 1969), 43, 1; *St. Domingo*, 25, 32.

13. Brown, *Narrative*, 1.

14. For the different editions and changing details of Brown's autobiography, see Larry Gara's introduction to the *Narrative*, xi.

15. William Wells Brown, *The Black Man: His Antecedents, His Genius, and His Achievements* (1863; reprint, New York: Johnson Reprint, 1969), 109–10. Not all critics have agreed on the significance of William Wells Brown. Arthur P. Davis, introducing J. Noel Herrmance's *William Wells Brown and 'Clotelle': A Portrait of the Artist in the First Negro Novel* (Hamden, Conn.: Shoe String Press, 1969), belies Brown's significance as cultural critic. He considers Brown a "limited and pedestrian" writer and continues to state: "Brown was not a five-talent man like Frederick Douglass; he was a one-talent, at best a two-talent man. . . . When we think of these circumstances, we tend to forget some of the artistic shortcomings of Mr. Brown. The surprising thing is that he wrote at all" (vii, viii).

16. William Wells Brown, "A Visit of a Fugitive Slave to the Grave of Wilberforce," in *Autographs for Freedom*, ed. Julia Griffiths, (1853; Rochester, N.Y.: Wagner, Beardley, 1854), 71.

17. Frederick Douglass used "colonize" in this sense of racial segregation when he denounced the prejudice "that colored people should be separated and sent up stairs—colonized." See Doulgass, *Life and Writings*, 2:123. William A. Craigie cites two examples particularly relevant to connotations of deportation. In 1863, Thomas Prentice Kettel recorded in *History of the Great Rebellion*: "The President alluded to the efforts he had made in relation to emancipation, and also in relation to colonizing the emancipated blacks." In 1854, Maria Cummins wrote in the sensationally popular *The Lamplighter*: "The house is pretty considerable full just now, to be sure, but maybe you can get colonized out. . . . 'One room, in the next street!' cried the doctor. 'Ah, that's being colonized out, is it?'" *A Dictionary of American English on Historical Principles*, 4 vols., ed. William A. Craigie, et al. (Chicago: University of Chicago Press, 1960), 1:558–59).

18. Brown, "A Visit of a Fugitive Slave," 71; *The Black Man*, 34.

19. Brown, *Narrative*, 46.

20. George Lippard, *The Legends of the American Revolution, 1776; or, Washington and His Generals*, (1847; reprint, Philadelphia: Leary, Stewart, 1876), 360, 368.

21. Ibid., 361–62. This passage nicely illustrates Lippard's understanding of the ideological contradictions posed by the figure of the black slave, but even more contradictory for him was the figure of white slave of industrial labor. David S. Reynolds writes: "Though painfully conscious of the southern Negro's plight, Lippard was more concerned with the white slavery in northern factories than with black slavery on southern plantations." *George Lippard* (Boston: Twayne, 1982), 59.

22. Lippard, *Legends of the American Revolution*, 361; William Lloyd Garrison, "No Compromise with Slavery," in *The Liberty Bell* (Boston: Massachusetts Anti-Slavery Fair, 1844), 216; Abraham Lincoln, "Address to the New Jersey Senate at Trenton, New Jersey," in *Collected Works*, 4:236. The fuller context of Lincoln's speech makes clear that his concerns about national duration are rooted at the level of narrative. He remembers "that away back in my childhood, the earliest days of my being able to read, I got hold of a small book . . . 'Weems' Life of Washington'"(4:235). In the face of secessionist fever in early 1861, his own presidency could hardly be so securely emplotted.

23. From the Greek, meaning "to put in beside," parenthesis implies a hiatus having no grammatical connection to the passage into which it is inserted. Often the lack of connection is contextual as well, in the sense of a digression that steps outside the supposed process of the discourse. Within a sentence, parenthesis destroys unity, producing a dislocation that interrupts the progress, promised to all sentences, from beginning to end. Hugh Blair writes: "I proceed to a third rule for preserving the Unity of Sentences; which is, to keep clear of all Parentheses in the middle of them . . . for the most part, their effect is extremely bad; being a sort of wheels within wheels; sentences in the midst of sentences, which a writer wants art to introduce in its proper place." *Lectures on Rhetoric and Belles Lettres*, 2 vols., ed. Harold F.

Harding (1783; reprint, Carbondale: Southern Illinois University Press, 1965), 1:222.

24. Anthony Kemp, *The Estrangement of the Past: A Study in the Origins of Modern Historical Consciousness* (New York: Oxford University Press, 1991), 137–39, 142. See especially 82–87 for his discussion of parenthesis. I do not mean to say that with the decline of the Puritan community, historical consciousness became wholly secular and that Rome replaced Canaan as the destination of memory. American politics carried, and still do carry, strong religious overtones. Washington's resistance of the dictatorial impulse can fit a religious allegory as well. Lippard, for instance, speaks of Washington as "the redeemer" (77) and imagines a temptation in the American wilderness when British general William Howe tries to seduce Washington from the cause of independence with offers of a dukedom.

25. Forgie, *Patricide in the House Divided*, 49. In addition to this anecdote about Monroe, Forgie's book is stocked with examples of attempts either to preserve or to throw off the founding past.

26. Brown, *Clotel*, 64. Bercovitch makes this argument about dissent/consent in several places, but see *The American Jeremiad*, especially the final chapter.

27. Bercovitch, *The Office of the Scarlet Letter*, 70.

28. Herman Melville, "The Bell-Tower," in the Library of America edition, 819. All subsequent references are to this edition.

29. Lincoln, "Address before the Young Men's Lyceum," *Collected Works*, 1:108. Lincoln's Lyceum speech was motivated by outbreaks of mob violence that seemed to indicate the present's distorted understanding of democracy. It is not insignificant that he took as one of his examples the lynching of a black man in St. Louis.

30. Various critics have noted the dimensions of both wage slavery and race slavery in "The Bell-Tower." See especially Karcher, *Shadow over a Promised Land*; Marvin Fisher, *Going Under: Melville's Short Fiction and the American 1850's* (Baton Rouge: Louisiana State University Press, 1977), as well as "Melville's 'Bell-Tower:' a Double Thrust," in *American Quarterly* 18 (summer 1966): 200–207.

31. Earlier in his career, Bannadonna participates in founding. He reminds one of the magistrates: "Some years ago, you may remember, I graved a small seal for your republic, bearing, for its chief device, the head of your ancestor, its illustrious founder" (825).

32. Other commentators have noted the correspondence between Bannadonna's bell and the Liberty Bell. See, for instance, Karcher, *Shadow over a Promised Land*, 156, and Fisher, "Melville's 'Bell-Tower,'" 206.

33. Historical legends present other dates than Washington's birthday 1846 for the cracking of the Liberty Bell. Among them are the arrival of Lafayette in 1824, the Catholic Emancipation Act of 1828, the death of John Marshall in 1835, and Washington's birthday in 1835. See Justin Kramer, *Cast in America* (Los Angeles: Justin Kramer, 1975), 77; Rev. John Baer Stoudt, *The Liberty Bells of Pennsylvania* (Philadelphia: William J. Campbell, 1920), 120–21.

On February 26, 1846, the *Public Ledger* assessed the status of the bell after Washington's birthday:

> The old Independence Bell rang its last clear note on Monday last in honor of the birthday of Washington and now hangs in the great city steeple irreparably cracked and dumb. It had been cracked before but was set in order for that day by having the edges of the fractures filed so as not to vibrate against each other, as there was a prospect that the church bells would chime on that occasion. It gave out clear notes and loud . . . [but] it [is] completely out of tune and left . . . mere wreck of what it was. We were lucky enough to get a small fragment of it and shall keep it sacred in memory of the good and glory achieved by the old herald of Independence in times long past and ever to be remembered.
>
> Quoted from Victor Rosewater,
The Liberty Bell: Its History and Significance
(New York: Appleton, 1926), 102.

34. David S. Reynolds discusses the popular veracity of Lippard's creations in *George Lippard*, 49. Sensing the inextricable blurring of historical fact and popular fabrication, one historian wrote in 1926: "The Legends of the Bell have secured unquestioning acceptance and enjoyed a popularity not only among the unlearned but also among people priding themselves upon being especially critical; in faith, they have accomplished as much as its true history in widening a pall of sacredness about it and making it venerated far and wide as a precious relic." Rosewater, *The Liberty Bell*, 110—11).

35. Lippard, *Legends of the American Revolution*, 392; Lincoln, "Address before the Young Men's Lyceum," *Collected Works*, 1:108.

36. Lippard, *Legends of the American Revolution*, 392. Lincoln, "Address before the Young Men's Lyceum," *Collected Works*, 1:115.

37. Lippard, *Legends of the American Revolution*, 393.

38. John Locke, *Second Treatise of Government* (New York: Liberal Arts Press, 1952), 57; Lincoln, "Address before the Young Men's Lyceum," *Collected Works*, 1:115.

39. Locke, *Second Treatise of Government*, 58.

40. Abraham Lincoln, "Address at Cooper Institute, New York City," in *Collected Works*, 3:523, 534–35. Although Lincoln here entertained critiques of the national patriarchy, later in the same speech he displaced the threat of parricide by pointing to Southern sectionalists: "It was not we, but you, who discarded the old policy of fathers" (3:538).

41. David Donald, *Lincoln Reconsidered: Essays of the Civil War Era*, 2nd ed. (New York: Knopf, 1972), 16; Frederick Douglass, *Life and Times of Frederick Douglass, Written By Himself* (1892; reprint, New York: Collier, 1962), 485, 484. Also important is Douglass's reminder that Lincoln spoke from a much different place than did most social critics and reformers of the antebellum era. Evaluating Lincoln's statements during his debates with Stephen A. Douglas, Douglass recognized the position of the politician: "These were not the words of an abolitionist—branded a fanatic, and carried away by an enthusiastic devotion to the Negro—but the calm, cool, deliberate utterance of a statesman." *Life and Times*, 295.

42. Abraham Lincoln, "Emancipation Proclamation," in *Collected Works*, 6:29; Benjamin Quarles, *Lincoln and the Negro* (New York: Oxford University Press, 1962), 146. Lincoln's view of the Emancipation Proclamation is quoted on 151. For the problematics of Lincoln's views and policies toward blacks, see Don E. Fehrenbacher, "Only His Stepchildren: Lincoln and the Negro," *Civil War History* 20 (December 1974): 293–310, and George M. Fredrickson, "A Man but Not a Brother: Abraham Lincoln and Racial Equality" *Journal of Southern History* 41 (February 1975): 39–58.

43. Abraham Lincoln, "Address at Sanitary Fair, Baltimore, Maryland," in *Collected Works*, 7:301–2.

44. Abraham Lincoln, "Address Delivered at the Dedication of the Cemetery at Gettysburg," in *Collected Works*, 7:23; Douglass, "Comments on Gerrit Smith's Address," in *Life and Writings*, 1:375.

CHAPTER 5

1. Douglass, *Narrative*, 114; "The Heroic Slave," in *Life and Writings*, 5:503. All further references to "The Heroic Slave" in this chapter will be cited parenthetically in the text.

2. Daniel Webster, "Completion of The Bunker Hill Monument," *Works*, 1:59; Emerson, *Nature*, in *Essays and Lectures*, 7. Recent studies examining America's national patriarchy include Forgie, *Patricide in the House Divided*; Rogin, *Subversive Genealogy* and *Fathers and Children: Andrew Jackson and the Subjugation of the American Indian* (New York: Vintage, 1976), and Sundquist, "Slavery, Revolution, and the American Renaissance" and *To Wake the Nations: Race in the Making of American Literature* (Cambridge: Harvard University Press, 1993). Also relevant are Michael Kammen, *A Season of Youth*, and Jay Fleigelman, *Prodigals and Pilgrims*.

3. Natalie Zemon Davis and Randolph Stern, introduction to a special issue on memory and counter-memory, *Representations* 26 (spring 1989): 2; for a further description of *topoi* as related to memory, see 2–3.

4. Mary Henderson Eastman, *Aunt Phillis's Cabin; or, Southern Life As It Is* (1852; reprint, New York: Negro Universities Press, 1968), 205; Burrows, "Address Before the Mount Vernon Association," 517; Edmund Jackson, "The Effects of Slavery," 41.

5. Brown, *Narrative*, xxv, 91.

6. Bhabha, "Of Mimicry and Man," 126, 130. Also see Bhabha's account of the hybrid, "Signs Taken for Wonders," 153–57, and his account of "cultural difference"in "DissemiNation," 312–15.

7. Henry Louis Gates, Jr., *The Signifying Monkey: A Theory of Afro-American Literary Criticism* (New York: Oxford University Press, 1988), xxii–xxiii, 75, 42–54.

8. Douglass, *My Bondage and My Freedom*, 191; *Dred Scott v. Sandford*, 703.

9. Douglass, *Narrative*, 21. Certainly, Douglass's 1845 autobiography is an integral document of American history and not simply a personal narrative. I am commenting, however, on the editor's efforts to limit the dis-

cursive scope of the *Narrative*. Sundquist provides a discussion on the important changes Doulgass made in his history and representation of America in moving from the *Narrative* to *My Bondage and My Freedom*. *To Wake the Nations*, 83–93.

10. Douglass, *Narrative*, 93; *My Bondage and My Freedom*, 361.

11. See James Olney, "The Founding Fathers—Frederick Douglass and Booker T. Washington," in *Slavery and the Literary Imagination: Selected Papers from the English Institute, 1987*, ed. Deborah E. McDowell and Arnold Rampersad (Baltimore: Johns Hopkins University Press, 1989). Olney reads Douglass's *Narrative* as a "revolutionary document" that signifies upon the Declaration of Independence (6). Also see Sundquist's chapters on Douglass and Nat Turner in *To Wake the Nations* and Maggie Sale, "Critiques from Within: Antebellum Projects of Resistance," *American Literature* 64 (December 1992): 695–718.

12. I refer to "amalgamation" instead of "miscegenation" because the latter term was not invented until 1863, and was coined then to express a specific anxiety concerning how black emancipation would affect sexual relations between the races. See Forrest Wood, *Black Scare: The Racist Response to Emancipation* (Berkeley: University of California Press, 1970), 53–55.

13. Brown, *Clotel*, 226. Sundquist makes use of the duality of the Mayflower—vessel to freedom and slave trade ship—to discuss the "elementary doubleness of America's political origins." "Slavery, Revolution, and the American Renaissance," 7. He also examines the patriotic implications of Nat Turner's rebellion, see "Slavery, Revolution, and the American Renaissance," 14, and *To Wake the Nations*, 65.

14. William Andrews, *To Tell a Free Story: The First Century of Afro-American Autobiography, 1760–1865* (Urbana: University of Illinois Press, 1986); Hazel Carby, *Reconstructing Womanhood: The Emergence of the Afro-American Woman Novelist* (New York: Oxford University Press, 1987); Henry Louis Gates, Jr., *Figures in Black: Words, Signs, and the "Racial" Self* (New York, Oxford University Press, 1987) and *The Signifying Monkey*; Valerie Smith, *Self-Discovery and Authority in Afro-American Literature* (Cambridge, Mass.: Harvard University Press, 1987); Robert Stepto, *Behind the Veil: A Study of Afro-American Narrative* (Urbana: University of Illinois Press, 1979).

15. Foucault, "Nietzsche, Genealogy, and History," in *The Foucault Reader*, 87, 88; Bhabha, "DissemiNation," 312.

16. Octavia V. Rogers Albert, *The House of Bondage; or, Charlotte Brooks and Other Slaves* (1890; reprint, New York: Oxford University Press, 1988), 158–59.

17. Patterson, *Slavery and Social Death*, 337. James Olney and Henry Louis Gates, Jr. have discussed the problematics of memory for the slave narrator. See Olney, "'I Was Born': Slave Narratives, Their Status as Autobiography and as Literature," in *The Slave's Narrative*, ed. Charles T. Davis and Henry Louis Gates, Jr. (New York: Oxford University Press, 1985), 149–152; and Gates, *Figures in Black*, 100–104; Melville, *Pierre*, 27. Hortense Spillers' article, "Mamma's Baby, Papa's Maybe: An American Grammar Book" *Diacritics* 17

(summer 1987): 65–81, which examines the historical and rhetorical construction and effacement of black womanhood, is instrumental in understanding the disruptions in gender and family identity caused by slavery. It is important to point out, however that my remarks concern the slave narrative and do not necessarily concern the slave community. In addition, it should be noted that my study seeks to understand conceptions of freedom largely within men's slave narratives. Women's slave narratives proffer much different notions of freedom, ones that are less individual and more family-oriented. See Sale, "Critiques from Within," especially 701–13.

18. See John Thompson, *The Life of John Thompson, A Fugitive Slave, Containing His History of Twenty-Five Years in Bondage, and His Providential Escape: Written by Himself* (1856; reprint, New York: Negro Universities Press, 1968). Solomon Northup, *Twelve Years a Slave; Narrative of Solomon Northup, a Citizen of New York, Kidnapped in Washington City in 1841, and Rescued in 1853, from a Cotton Plantation, near the Red River, in Louisiana*, in *Puttin' On Ole Master: The Slave Narratives of Henry Bibb, William Wells Brown, and Solomon Northup*, ed. Gilbert Osofsky (1853; New York: Harper & Row, 1969), 406, 229.

19. Ward, *Autobiography of a Fugitive Negro*, 280; Albert Taylor Bledsoe, *An Essay on Liberty and Slavery* (Philadelphia: J. B. Lippincott, 1856), 131; James Roberts, *The Narrative of James Roberts, Soldier in the Revolutionary War and at the Battle of New Orleans* (1858; reprint, Hattiesburg, Miss.: The Book Farm, 1945), 31. In suggesting that black patriarchy was slighted in national consciousness, I do not mean to indicate that blacks did not exercise fatherhood or that they were merely incidental to American founding history. Indeed, Brown's own studies, such as *The Black Man* and *The Negro in the American Rebellion* (1867; reprint, New York: Citadel Press, 1971), oppose the antebellum predisposition to ignore or declare invalid black fathers, within both actual social structures and constructed national history.

20. James W. C. Pennington, *The Fugitive Blacksmith; or, Events in the History of James W. C. Pennington, Pastor of a Presbyterian Church, New York, Formerly a Slave in the State of Maryland*, in *Great Slave Narratives*, ed. Arna Bontemps (Boston: Beacon, 1969), 201.

21. Gates, *Figures in Black*, 100; Patterson, in *Slavery and Social Death*, provides a range of cross-cultural examples of "social death."

22. C. W. Larison, *Silvia Dubois (Now 116 Years Old), A Biografy of the Slav Who Wipt Her Mistres and Gand Her Fredom* (1883; reprint, New York: Oxford University Press, 1988), 76.

23. S. A. Cartwright, *Slavery in the Light of Ethnology*, in *'Cotton is King,' and Pro-slavery Arguments: Comprising the Writings of Hammond, Harper, Christy, Stringfellow, Hodge, Bledsoe, and Cartwright on this Important Subject*, ed. E. N. Elliot (1860; New York: Johnson Reprint, 1968), 722.

24. John Brown, *Slave Life in Georgia: A Narrative of the Life, Sufferings, and Escape of John Brown, A Fugitive Slave, Now in England* (1855; reprint, Savannah, Ga.: Beehive Press, 1972), 98. Brown dictated his narrative to Louis Alex Chamerovzow. On the slave narrator's strategies to gain authority and authenticity, see Stepto, *Behind the Veil*, and Olney, "'I Was Born.'"

25. Byrd is quoted in Genovese, *Roll, Jordan, Roll,* 75.

26. Roberts, *Narrative,* 10.

27. On the indispensability of history for human subjectivity, see Nietzsche, "On the Uses and Disadvantages of History," 60–61.

28. Douglass, *Narrative,* 21–22.

29. William Craft, *Running a Thousand Miles for Freedom; or, the Escape of William And Ellen Craft from Slavery* (1860; reprint, Salem, Mass.: Ayer, 1991), 2, 57. Samuel Ringgold Ward also uses a textual metaphor to describe the mulatto: "Ah! the slaveholders are publishing, as in so many legibly written volumes, in the faces of their mulatto offspring, the sad, sickening evidences of their abominable immoralities." *Autobiography of a Fugitive Negro,* 205.

30. Craft, *Running a Thousand Miles for Freedom,* v; the proslavery pamphlet is quoted in Thomas Wentworth Higginson, *Black Rebellion: A Selection from Travellers and Outlaws* (1889; reprint, New York: Arno Press, 1969), 272; *Dred Scott v. Sandford* 702–3.

31. Craft, *Running a Thousand Miles for Freedom,* 2, 60. These and other scenes from the Crafts' history are adapted by Brown in *Clotel,* 170–76, 204. On the sexual and psychological dangers of the miscegenated body, see Dearborn, *Pocohontas's Daughters,* 131–58.

32. Moses Roper, *A Narrative of the Adventures and Escape of Moses Roper, from American Slavery* (1838; reprint, Philadelphia: Rhistoric, 1969), 1–2; Brown, *Narrative,* 59; and *Clotel,* 158, 159. The mistress's actions in *Clotel* are a perfect example of what Barbara Jeanne Fields calls "society in the act of inventing race." "Slavery, Race, and Ideology in the United States of America" *New Left Review* (May-June 1990): 95–118.

33. William Andrews examines fictive slave narratives, including *Clotel* and "The Heroic Slave," and points to the ways in which African American texts confuse fictional and factual discourse to acquire narrative authority. "The Novelization of Voice in Early African American Narrative" *PMLA* 105 (January 1990): 23–34.

34. The newspaper reviews of Brown are quoted in William Edward Farrison, *William Wells Brown, Author and Reformer* (Chicago: University of Chicago Press, 1969), 259, 288. In *Behind the Veil,* Stepto treats the complex relationship of the slave narrative to the editor's preface.

35. Douglass, *My Bondage and My Freedom,* xxxi; Frederick Douglass, Letter to Charles Sumner, September 2, 1852, in *Life and Writings,* 2:210; Sundquist, *To Wake the Nations,* 104.

36. Eric J. Sundquist, introduction to *Frederick Douglass: New Literary and Historical Essays,* ed. Eric J. Sundquist (Cambridge: Cambridge University Press, 1990), 12; Brown, *Clotel,* 245.

37. Patterson, *Slavery and Social Death,* 340.

38. Brown, *Clotel,* 217. Douglass recounts a similar episode of a slave woman's suicide/escape in his "An Appeal to the British People, May 12, 1846," in *Life and Writings,* 1:159.

39. Brown, *Clotel,* 224, 226. Yet the conclusion of *Clotel* suggests reservations about how effective this militant political strategy is in the United

States. It is not insignificant that the close of the novel finds George living happily in Europe, passing as a white man, and Clotel dead. The "tragic mulatto," as Werner Sollors has argued, had no place in American society, finding only suicide as the pathetic outcome of a resolve to remain in the United States. Those fictional characters who removed to Europe, in contrast, fared more successfully. See Werner Sollors, "'Never was Born': The Mulatto, An American Tragedy," *Massachusetts Review* 27 (summer 1986): 300. In later versions of *Clotel*, entitled *Miralda; or, the Beautiful Quadroon* (1860) and *Clotelle; or, the Colored Heroine* (1864), the mulatto, George Green, becomes the black rebel Jerome. For the significance of these changes, see Jean Fagan Yellin, *The Intricate Knot: Black Figures in American Literature, 1776–1863* (New York: New York University Press, 1972), 174–77. Both the chronological setting of *Clotel* (1831) and George's genealogy—"He too could boast that his father was an American statesman. His name was George"—make it plausible that he is the son of a founding father. The ambiguity of whose name is George ("his" logically refers to "father") creates suggestive speculations about which Virginia statesman named George gave birth to this rebel.

40. Hughes, *Treatise on Sociology,* 239–40, 240; Nott and Gliddon, *Types of Mankind,* 405; Brown, *The Black Man,* 92.

41. Bledsoe, *Essay on Liberty and Slavery,* 10; Thomas Roderick Dew, "The Abolition of Negro Slavery," in *The Ideology of Slavery: Proslavery Thought in the Antebellum South, 1830–1860,* ed. Drew Gilpin Faust (Baton Rouge: Louisiana State University Press, 1981), 59.

42. Cartwright, *Slavery in the Light of Ethnology,* 725; Baynard Hall, *Frank Freeman's Barber Shop; A Tale* (New York: Charles Scribner, 1852), 210; the South Carolina reverend is quoted in Eugene D. Genovese, *From Rebellion to Revolution: Afro-American Slave Revolts in the Making of the Modern World* (Baton Rouge, Louisiana State University Press, 1979), 127. Sundquist also discusses Dew's use of the words *parricides* and *patriots* in the context of Nat Turner and Douglass. *To Wake the Nations,* 35, 115.

43. *New Orleans Daily Picayune,* December 3, 1841; Andrews, "The Novelization of Voice," 28.

44. Frederick Douglass, "The Heroic Slave," in *Life and Writings,* 5:479. All further references to this text are to volume 5 this edition. For the historical circumstances of the *Creole* affair, see Howard Jones, "The Peculiar Institution and National Honor: The Case of the *Creole* Slave Revolt," *Civil War History* 21 (March 1975): 28–50. Andrews offers a similar view of the subversive quality of fictive discourse within Douglass's story. He argues that "The Heroic Slave" sabotages "natural" discourse by authorizing the representation of history within fictive discourse. "The Novelization of Voice," 29–31.

45. Robert B. Stepto has suggested the significance of naming in this first paragraph of "The Heroic Slave." Stepto writes: "Douglass advances his comparison of heroic statesman and heroic chattel, and does so quite ingeniously by both naming and *not* naming them in such a way that we are led

to discover that statesmen and slaves may share the same name and be heroes and Virginians alike." "Storytelling in Early Afro-American Fiction: Frederick Douglass' 'The Heroic Slave,'" *Georgia Review* 36 (1982): 362.

46. Abraham Lincoln, "First Debate with Stephen A. Douglas at Ottawa, Illinois," in *Collected Works*, 3:19.

47. Harriet Beecher Stowe, *Uncle Tom's Cabin; or, Life among the Lowly* (New York: Penguin Books, 1984), 68. Stepto's essay "Storytelling in Early Afro-American Fiction" also marks Madison Washington's example of violent resistance as a significant opposition to the Christ-like passivity and sufferings of Uncle Tom. Andrews makes a similar point in *To Tell a Free Story*, 186. Still, it should not be forgotten that Uncle Tom's Washington is dressed up in blackface as well—a fact that, especially after the appearance of Eric Lott's *Love and Theft*, makes this portrait the site of complex negotiations between ethnic, national, and gender identities. While not radical for Uncle Tom, this blackface Washington offers subversive readings for Northern audiences, acting as a "racialized mediator of northern conflicts in southern guise" (199).

48. Richard Yarborough, "Race, Violence, and Manhood: The Masculine Ideal in Frederick Douglass's 'The Heroic Slave,'" in *New Essays on Frederick Douglass*, 180.

49. Andrews, *To Tell a Free Story*, 187. Maggie Sale argues against the positions of Yarborough and Andrews as well: "this criticism of Douglass's strategies rests on the notion that one can exist, indeed one can think, in a place outside of culture, outside the language systems" that constitute the material and imaginative worlds of nineteenth-century America (711). And see Sundquist in *To Wake the Nations*: "the notion that the language of the Revolution was but a new form of totalizing imprisonment, a thorough mockery of freedom, is a view that would have been anathema to Douglass" (121). Indeed, Douglass seems to anticipate the arguments of Yarborough and Andrews and attempts to sort out the complex legacy of Washington and the other founders in his speech on the Dred Scott decision. See *Life and Writings*, 2:407–24, especially 422–23.

50. Brown, *Clotel*, 226–27.

51. Northup, *Twelve Years a Slave*, 370; Thomas Jefferson, *Notes on the State of Virginia*, in *Life and Selected Writings*, 278.

52. Ralph Ellison, *Invisible Man* (New York: Random House, 1952), 433.

53. Stanley Elkins, *Slavery: A Problem in American Institutional and Intellectual Life* (Chicago: University of Chicago Press, 1968), 170.

54. Foucault, "Nietzsche, Genealogy, and History," 82.

Works Cited

Albert, Octavia V. Rogers. *The House of Bondage; or, Charlotte Brooks and Other Slaves*. 1890. Reprint, New York: Oxford University Press: 1988.

Anderson, Benedict. *Imagined Communities: Reflections on the Origin and Spread of Nationalism*. Rev. ed. New York: Verso, 1991.

Andrews, William L. "The Novelization of Voice in Early African American Narrative." *PMLA* 105 (January 1990): 23–34 .

―――. *To Tell a Free Story: The First Century of Afro-American Autobiography, 1760–1865*. Urbana: University of Illinois Press, 1986.

Arac, Jonathan. "Nationalism, Hypercanonization, and *Huckleberry Finn*." *boundary 2* 19 (spring 1992): 14–33.

Arac, Jonathan, and Harriet Ritvo. Introduction to *Macropolitics of Nineteenth-Century Literature: Nationalism, Exoticism, Imperialism*. Edited by Jonathan Arac and Harriet Ritvo. Philadelphia: University of Pennsylvania Press, 1991.

Arendt, Hannah. *Between Past and Future: Eight Exercises in Political Thought*. New York: Viking, 1968.

―――. *The Human Condition*. Chicago: University of Chicago Press, 1958.

Badeau, Adam. *The Vagabond*. New York: Rudd and Carleton, 1859.

Baldwin, James. *Notes of a Native Son*. Boston: Beacon, 1955.

Balibar, Etienne. "The Nation Form: History and Ideology." In Etienne Balibar and Immanuel Wallerstein, *Race, Nation, Class: Ambiguous Identities*. Translation of Balibar by Chris Turner. New York: Verso, 1991.

Baym, Nina. "Melville's Quarrel with Fiction." *PMLA* 94 (October 1979): 909–23.

Bellis, Peter J. "*Israel Potter*: Autobiography as History as Fiction." *American Literary History* 2 (winter 1990): 607–26.

Bercovitch, Sacvan. *The American Jeremiad*. Madison: University of Wisconsin Press, 1978.

―――. *The Office of The Scarlet Letter*. Baltimore: Johns Hopkins University Press, 1991.

―――. "The Rites of Assent: Rhetoric, Ritual, and the Ideology of American Consensus." In *The American Self: Myth, Ideology, and Popular Culture*. Edited by Sam Girgus. Albuquerque: University of New Mexico Press, 1981.

―――. *The Rites of Assent: Transformations in the Symbolic Construction of America*. New York: Routledge, 1993.

Berlant, Lauren. *The Anatomy of National Fantasy: Hawthorne, Utopia, and Everyday Life*. Chicago: University of Chicago Press, 1991.

———. "National Brands / National Body: *Imitation of Life*." In *Comparative American Identities: Race, Sex, and Nationality in the Modern Text*. Edited by Hortense Spillers. New York: Routledge, 1991.

Beverley, John. *Against Literature*. Minneapolis: University of Minnesota Press, 1993.

Bhabha, Homi K. "DissemiNation: Time, Narrative, and the Margins of the Modern Nation." In *Nation and Narration*. Edited by Homi K. Bhabha. New York: Routledge, 1990.

———. *The Location of Culture*. New York: Routledge, 1994.

———. "Of Mimicry and Man: The Ambivalence of Colonial Discourse." *October* 28 (spring 1984): 125–33.

———. "Signs Taken for Wonders: Questions of Ambivalence and Authority under a Tree Outside Delhi, May 1817." *Critical Inquiry* 12 (autumn 1985): 145—65.

Blair, Hugh. *Lectures on Rhetoric and Belles Lettres*. 2 vols. Edited by Harold F. Harding. 1783. Reprint, Carbondale: Southern Illinois University Press, 1965.

Bledsoe, Albert Taylor. *An Essay on Liberty and Slavery*. Philadelphia: J. B. Lippincott, 1856.

Bodnar, John. *Remaking America: Public Memory, Commemoration, and Patriotism in the Twentieth Century*. Princeton: Princeton University Press, 1992.

Brennan, Timothy. "The National Longing for Form." In *Nation and Narration*. Edited by Homi K. Bhabha. New York: Routledge, 1990.

Brisbane, Albert. *Social Destiny of Man: Or, Association and Reorganization of Industry*. 1840. Reprint, New York: Burt Franklin, 1968.

Brodhead, Richard. *Hawthorne, Melville, and the Novel*. Chicago: University of Chicago Press, 1976.

Brown, John. *Slave Life in Georgia: A Narrative of the Life, Sufferings, and Escape of John Brown, A Fugitive Slave, Now In England*. 1855. Reprint, Savannah, Ga.: Beehive Press, 1972.

Brown, William Wells. *The Anti-Slavery Harp: A Collection of Songs for Anti-Slavery Meetings, Compiled by William W. Brown, a Fugitive Slave*. 1848. Reprint, Philadelphia: Rhistoric, 1969.

———. *The Black Man: His Antecedents, His Genius, and His Achievements*. 1863. Reprint, New York: Johnson Reprint, 1969.

———. *Clotel; or, the President's Daughter. A Narrative of Slave Life in the United States*. 1853. Reprint, New York: Carol, 1969.

———. "A Lecture Delivered Before the Female Anti-Slavery Society of Salem at Lyceum Hall, Nov. 14, 1847." In *Four Fugitive Slave Narratives*. Introductions by Robin W. Winks et al. Reading, Mass.: Addison-Wesley, 1969.

————. *The Narrative of William W. Brown, A Fugitive Slave, Written by Himself.* In *Four Fugitive Slave Narratives.* Introductions by Robin W. Winks et al. Reading, Mass.: Addison-Wesley, 1969.

————. *The Negro in the American Rebellion.* 1867. Reprint, New York: Citadel Press, 1971.

————. *St. Domingo: Its Revolutions and its Patriots; A Lecture Delivered Before the Metropolitan Athenaeum, London, May 16, and at St. Thomas' Church, Philadelphia, December 20, 1854.* 1855. Reprint, Philadelphia: Rhistoric, 1969.

————. "A Visit of a Fugitive Slave to the Grave of Wilberforce." In *Autographs for Freedom.* Edited by Julia Griffiths. Rochester, N.Y.: Wagner, Beardley, 1854.

Bryan, William Alfred. *George Washington in American Literature, 1775–1865.* New York: Columbia University Press, 1952.

————. "George Washington: Symbolic Guardian of the Republic, 1850–1861." *William and Mary Quarterly* 7 (January 1950): 55–63.

Buckingham, Joseph T. *Personal Memoirs and Recollections of Editorial Life.* Boston: Ticknor, Reed, Field, 1852.

Burrows, J. Lansing. "Address Before the Mount Vernon Association, July 4th, 1855." *Southern Literary Messenger* 21 (1855).

Calhoun, John C. *The Works of John C. Calhoun.* 7 vols. Edited by Richard K. Crallé. New York: D. Appleton, 1854–1860.

Canaday, Nicholas. *Melville and Authority.* Gainesville: University of Florida Press, 1968.

Carby, Hazel. *Reconstructing Womanhood: The Emergence of the Afro-American Woman Novelist.* New York: Oxford University Press, 1987.

Cartwright, S. A. *Slavery in the Light of Ethnology.* In *'Cotton is King,' and Pro-slavery Arguments: Comprising the Writings of Hammond, Harper, Christy, Stringfellow, Hodge, Bledsoe, and Cartwright on this Important Subject.* Edited by E. N. Elliot. 1860. Reprint, New York: Johnson Reprint, 1968.

Caserio, Robert L. *Plot, Story, and the Novel: From Dickens to Poe in the Modern Period.* Princeton: Princeton University Press, 1979.

Cecil, E. [pseud.?]. *The Life of Washington, Written for Children.* Boston: Crosby, Nichols, 1859.

Chase, Ezra B. *Teachings of Patriots and Statesmen; or, the "Fathers of the Republic" on Slavery.* Philadelphia: J. W. Bridley, 1860.

Chase, Richard. *Herman Melville: A Critical Study.* New York: Macmillan, 1949.

Child, Lydia Maria. *Hobomok and Other Writings on Indians.* Edited by Carolyn L. Karcher. New Brunswick, N.J.: Rutgers University Press, 1986.

Clark, Robert. "Rewriting Revolution: Cooper's War of Independence." In *James Fenimore Cooper: New Critical Essays.* Edited by Robert Clark. London: Vision, 1985.

Clarke, Lewis, and Milton Clarke. *Narratives of the Sufferings of Lewis and Milton Clarke, Sons of a Soldier of the Revolution, During a Captivity of More Than Twenty Years among the Slaveholders of Kentucky, One of the So Called Christian States of North America.* Boston: Bela Marsh, 1846.

Clinch, Charles Powell. *The Spy: A Tale of Neutral Ground (From the Novel of That Name): A Dramatic Romance in Three Acts.* In *Metamora and Other Plays.* Edited by Eugene R. Page. Princeton: Princeton University Press, 1941.

Cole, Thomas. *The Collected Essays and Prose Sketches.* Edited by Marshall Tymn. St Paul, Minn.: John Colet Press, 1980.

The Congressional Globe: New Series, Containing Sketches of the Debates and Proceedings of the First Session of the Thirty-First Congress. City of Washington: John C. Rives, 1850.

Cooper, James Fenimore. *The American Democrat; or, Hints on the Social and Civic Relations of the United States of America.* New York: Vintage, 1956.

———. *The Pioneers.* New York: Dodd, Mead, 1958.

———. *The Spy: A Tale of Neutral Ground.* New York: Hafner, 1960.

Craft, William. *Running a Thousand Miles for Freedom; or, the Escape of William And Ellen Craft from Slavery.* 1860. Reprint, Salem, Mass.: Ayer, 1991.

Custis, George Washington Parke. *Recollections and Private Memoirs of Washington, by His Adopted Son, G. W. Parke Custis.* Washington, D.C.: W. H. Moore, 1859.

Davidson, Cathy N. *Revolution and the Word: The Rise of the Novel in America.* New York: Oxford University Press, 1986.

Davis, Jefferson. *The Papers of Jefferson Davis.* 7 vols. Edited by Lynda Lasswell Crist and Mary Seaton. Baton Rouge: Louisiana State University Press, 1992.

Davis, Natalie Zemon, and Randolph Stern. Introduction to a special issue on memory and counter-memory. *Representations* 26 (spring 1989): 1–7.

Dearborn, Mary V. *Pocohantas's Daughters: Gender and Ethnicity in American Culture.* New York: Oxford University Press, 1986.

Derrida, Jacques. *Dissemination.* Translated by Barbara Johnson. Chicago: University of Chicago Press, 1981.

———. *Of Grammatology.* Translated by Gayatri Chakravorty Spivak. Baltimore: Johns Hopkins University Press, 1976.

Dew, Thomas Roderick. "The Abolition of Negro Slavery." In *The Ideology of Slavery: Proslavery Thought in the Antebellum South, 1830–1860.* Edited by Drew Gilpin Faust. Baton Rouge: Louisiana State University Press, 1981.

Dimock, Wai-chee. "Ahab's Manifest Destiny." In *Macropolitics of Nineteenth-Century Literature: Nationalism, Exoticism, Imperialism.* Edited by Jonathan Arac and Harriet Ritvo. Philadelphia: University of Pennsylvania Press, 1991.

———. *Empire for Liberty: Melville and the Poetics of Individualism*. Princeton: Princeton University Press, 1989.

Donald, David. *Lincoln Reconsidered: Essays of the Civil War Era*. 2nd ed. New York: Knopf, 1972.

Douglass, Frederick. *Life and Times of Frederick Douglass, Written By Himself*. 1892. Reprint, New York: Collier, 1962.

———. *My Bondage and My Freedom*. 1855. New York: Arno Press, 1968.

———. *Narrative of the Life of Frederick Douglass, An American Slave, Written by Himself*. 1845. Reprint, New York: Signet, 1968.

———. *The Life and Writings of Frederick Douglass*. 5 vols. Edited by Philip S. Foner. New York: International Publishers, 1950.

Dryden, Edgar. *Melville's Thematics of Form: The Great Art of Telling the Truth*. Baltimore: Johns Hopkins University Press, 1968.

Dumond, Dwight L. *Southern Editorials on Secession*. New York: Century, 1931.

E.D.H. [pseud.]. "The Fugitive Slave's Apostrophe to Niagara." In Joseph T. Buckingham, *Personal Memoirs and Recollections of Editorial Life*. Boston: Ticknor, Reed, Fields, 1852.

Eastman, Mary Henderson. *Aunt Phillis's Cabin; or, Southern Life As It Is*. 1852. Reprint, New York: Negro Universities Press, 1968.

Elkins, Stanley. *Slavery: A Problem in American Institutional and Intellectual Life*. Chicago: University of Chicago Press, 1968.

Ellison, Ralph. *Invisible Man*. New York: Random House, 1952.

———. *Shadow and Act*. New York: Random House, 1964.

Emerson, Ralph Waldo. *Emerson's Antislavery Writings*. Edited by Len Gougeon and Joel Myerson. New Haven: Yale University Press, 1995.

———. *Essays and Lectures*. Edited by Joel Porte. New York: Library of America, 1983.

Everett, Edward. *Orations and Speeches on Various Occasions*. 4 vols. Boston: Little, Brown, 1850.

Farrison, William Edward. *William Wells Brown, Author and Reformer*. Chicago: University of Chicago Press, 1969.

Feidleson, Charles. *Symbolism and American Literature*. Chicago: University of Chicago Press, 1953.

Fehrenbacher, Don E. "Only His Stepchildren: Lincoln and the Negro." *Civil War History* 20 (December 1974): 293–310.

Ferguson, Robert J. *Law and Letters in American Culture*. Cambridge, Mass.: Harvard University Press, 1984.

Fields, Barbara Jeanne. "Slavery, Race, and Ideology in the United States of America." *New Left Review*. (May–June 1990): 95–118.

Fisher, Marvin. *Going Under: Melville's Short Fiction and the American 1850's*. Baton Rouge: Louisiana State University Press, 1977.

———. "Melville's 'Bell-Tower': a Double Thrust." *American Quarterly* 18 (summer 1966): 200–207.

Fliegelman, Jay. *Prodigals and Pilgrims: The American Revolution against Patriarchal Authority*. Cambridge: Cambridge University Press, 1982.

Foner, Eric. *Politics, Ideology, and the Origins of the American Civil War.* New York: Oxford University Press, 1980.

Foner, Philip S. *We, the Other People: Alternative Declarations of Independence by Labor Groups, Farmers, Women's Rights Advocates, Socialists, and Blacks, 1829–1975.* Urbana: University of Illinois Press, 1976.

Ford, Paul Leceister. *The True George Washington.* Philadelphia: J. B. Lippincott, 1896.

Forgie, George, B. *Patricide in the House Divided: A Psychological Interpretation of Lincoln and His Age.* New York: Norton, 1979.

Foster, Charles H. "Something in Emblems: A Reinterpretation of *Moby-Dick.*" *New England Quarterly* 34 (March 1961): 3–35.

Foucault, Michel. *The Archaeology of Knowledge.* Translated by A. M. Sheridan Smith. New York: Harper & Row, 1972.

———. *Discipline and Punish: The Birth of the Prison.* Translated by Alan Sheridan. New York: Vintage, 1979.

———. *The Foucault Reader.* Edited by Paul Rabinow. New York: Pantheon, 1984.

———. *Language, Counter-Memory, Practice: Selected Essays and Interviews.* Translated by Donald F. Bouchard and Sherry Simon. Ithaca: Cornell University Press, 1972

———. *Power/Knowledge: Selected Interviews and Other Writings, 1972–1977.* Edited by Colin Gordon. Translated by Colin Gordon, Leo Marshall, John Mepham, and Kate Soper. New York: Pantheon, 1980.

Fredrickson, George M. *The Black Image in the White Mind: The Debate on Afro-American Character and Destiny, 1817–1914.* New York: Harper & Row, 1971.

———. "A Man but Not a Brother: Abraham Lincoln and Racial Equality." *Journal of Southern History* 41 (February 1975): 39–58.

Frothingham, Richard. *History of the Siege of Boston, and the Battles of Lexington, Concord, and Bunker Hill.* Boston: C. C. Little and J. Brown, 1849.

Garrison, William Lloyd. "No Compromise with Slavery." In *The Liberty Bell.* Boston: Massachusetts Anti-Slavery Fair, 1844.

Gates, Henry Louis, Jr. *Figures in Black: Words, Signs, and the "Racial" Self.* New York: Oxford University Press, 1987.

———. *The Signifying Monkey: A Theory of Afro-American Literary Criticism.* New York: Oxford University Press, 1988.

Genovese, Eugene D. *From Rebellion to Revolution: Afro-American Slave Revolts in the Making of the Modern World.* Baton Rouge, Louisiana State University Press, 1979.

———. *Roll, Jordan, Roll: The World the Slaves Made.* New York: Vintage, 1976.

Gustafson, Thomas. *Representative Words: Politics, Literature, and the American Language, 1776-1865.* Cambridge: Cambridge University Press, 1992.

Hall, Baynard. *Frank Freeman's Barber Shop; A Tale*. New York: Charles Scribner, 1852.

Marion Harland [Mary Virginia Terhune]. *Moss-Side*. New York: Derby, Jackson, 1857.

Harvey, Frederick Loviad. *History of the Washington National Monument and the Washington National Monument Society*. Washington, D.C.: Elliot Printing, 1902.

Hawthorne, Nathaniel. *The Scarlet Letter*. New York: Signet, 1980.

Heimert, Alan. "*Moby-Dick* and American Political Symbolism." *American Quarterly* 15 (winter 1963): 498–534.

Herrmance, J. Noel. *William Wells Brown and 'Clotelle': A Portrait of the Artist in the First Negro Novel*. Hamden, Conn.: Shoe String Press, 1969.

Higgins, Brian, and Hershel Parker. *Critical Essays on Melville's 'Pierre; or, The Ambiguities.'* Boston: G. K. Hall, 1983.

Higginson, Thomas Wentworth. *Black Rebellion: A Selection from Travellers and Outlaws*. 1889. Reprint, New York: Arno Press, 1969.

Hobbes, Thomas. *Leviathan*. New York: Pelican, 1968.

Hudson, E. M. *The Second War of Independence in America*. London: Longman, Green, Longman, Roberts, and Green, 1863.

Hughes, Henry. *Treatise on Sociology, Theoretical and Practical*. 1854. Reprint, New York: Negro Universities Press, 1968.

Hunington, David C. *The Landscapes of Frederic Edwin Church: Vision of an American Era*. New York: George Braziller, 1966.

Irving, Washington. *The Life of George Washington*. 5 vols. New York: G. P. Putnam, 1859.

Jackson, Edmund. "The Effects of Slavery." In *The Liberty Bell*. Boston: Massachusetts Anti-Slavery Fair, 1852.

Jacobs, Harriet Ann. *Incidents in the Life of a Slave Girl, Written by Herself*. Edited by Jean Fagan Yellin. 1861. Cambridge, Mass.: Harvard University Press, 1987.

Jameson, Fredric. *The Political Unconscious: Narrative as a Socially Symbolic Act*. Ithaca: Cornell University Press, 1981.

Jefferson, Isaac. *Memoirs of a Monticello Slave, As Dictated to Charles Campbell in the 1840's by Isaac, One of Thomas Jefferson's Slaves*. Charlottesville: University of Virginia Press, 1951.

Jefferson, Thomas. *The Life and Selected Writings of Thomas Jefferson*. Edited by Adrienne Koch and William Peden. New York: Modern Library, 1972.

Jenkins, William Sumner. *Pro-Slavery Thought in the Old South*. Chapel Hill: University of North Carolina Press, 1935.

Jones, Howard. "The Peculiar Institution and National Honor: The Case of the *Creole* Slave Revolt." *Civil War History* 21 (March 1975): 28–50.

Kammen, Michael. *A Season of Youth: The American Revolution and the Historical Imagination*. New York: Knopf, 1978.

Karcher, Carolyn L. *Shadow over the Promised Land: Slavery, Race, and Violence in Melville's America*. Baton Rouge: Louisiana State University Press, 1980.

Kelly, Franklin. *Frederic Edwin Church and the National Landscape*. Washington, D.C.: Smithsonian Institution Press: 1988.

Kemmis, Daniel. *Community and the Politics of Place*. Norman: University of Oklahoma Press, 1990.

Kemp, Anthony. *The Estrangement of the Past: A Study in the Origins of Modern Historical Consciousness*. New York: Oxford University Press, 1991.

Kermode, Frank. *The Classic*. London: Faber and Faber, 1975.

———. *The Sense of an Ending*. New York: Oxford University Press, 1966.

Kirkland, C. M. *Memoirs of Washington*. New York: Appleton, 1857.

Kramer, Justin. *Cast in America*. Los Angeles: Justin Kramer, 1975.

Larison, C. W. *Silvia Dubois (Now 116 Years Old), A Biografy of the Slav Who Wipt Her Mistres and Gand Her Fredom*. 1883. Reprint, New York: Oxford University Press, 1988.

Lincoln, Abraham. *The Collected Works of Abraham Lincoln*. 9 vols. Edited by Roy P. Basler. New Brunswick, N.J.: Rutgers University Press, 1953.

Lippard, George. *The Legends of the American Revolution, 1776; or, Washington and His Generals*. 1847. Reprint, Philadelphia: Leary, Stewart, 1876.

Litwack, Leon F. *North of Slavery: The Negro in the Free States, 1790–1860*. Chicago: University of Chicago Press, 1961.

Locke, John. *Second Treatise of Government*. New York: Liberal Arts Press, 1952.

Lossing, Benson J. *The Home of Washington and Its Associations, Historical, Biographical, and Pictorial*. 1859. Reprint, New York: W. A. Townsend, 1866.

Lott, Eric. *Love and Theft: Blackface Minstrelsy and the American Working Class*. New York: Oxford University Press, 1993.

McKinsey, Elizabeth. *Niagara Falls: Icon of the American Sublime*. Cambridge: Cambridge University Press, 1985.

McWilliams, John, Jr. *Hawthorne, Melville, and the American Character: A Looking-Glass Business*. Cambridge: Cambridge University Press, 1984.

Martin, Robert K. *Hero, Captain, Stranger: Male Friendship, Social Critique, and Literary Form in the Sea Novels of Herman Melville*. Chapel Hill: University of North Carolina Press, 1986.

Marx, Leo. *The Machine in the Garden: Technology and the Pastoral Ideal in America*. New York: Oxford University Press, 1964.

———. "Melville's Parable of the Walls." In *Herman Melville's 'Billy Budd,' "Benito Cereno," "Bartleby the Scrivener," and Other Tales*. Edited by Harold Bloom. New York: Chelsea House, 1987.

Matthiessen, F. O. *American Renaissance: Art and Expression in the Age of Whitman and Emerson*. New York: Oxford University Press, 1941.

Mazyack, Walter H. *George Washington and the Negro.* New York: Associated, 1932.

Melville, Herman. *The Confidence-Man: His Masquerade.* New York: Norton, 1971.

———. *The Letters of Herman Melville.* Edited by Merrell R. Davis and William H. Gilman. New Haven: Yale University Press, 1960.

———. *Moby-Dick; or, The Whale.* Boston: Houghton Mifflin, 1956.

———. *Pierre, or the Ambiguities; Israel Potter, His Fifty Years of Exile; The Piazza Tales; The Confidence Man, His Masquerade; Uncollected Prose; Billy Budd, Sailor (An Inside Narrative).* New York: Library of America, 1984.

———. *Poems, Containing Battle-Pieces, John Marr and Other Sailors, Timoleon, and Miscellaneous Poems.* Vol. 16 of *The Standard Edition of the Works of Herman Melville.* New York: Russell and Russell, 1963.

———. *Typee.* Evanston: Northwestern University Press, 1968.

Miller, Angela. "Everywhere and Nowhere: The Making of the National Landscape." *American Literary History* 2 (summer 1992): 207–29.

Miller, Perry. *The Raven and the Whale: The War of Wits and Words in the Era of Poe and Melville.* New York: Harcourt Brace, 1956.

Morgan, Edmund S. *American Slavery, American Freedom: The Ordeal of Colonial Virginia.* New York: Norton, 1975.

Morrison, Toni. *Playing in the Dark: Whiteness and the Literary Imagination.* Cambridge, Mass.: Harvard University Press, 1992.

———. "Unspeakable Things Unspoken: The Afro-American Presence in American Literature." *Michigan Quarterly Review* 28 (winter 1989): 1–34.

Nietzsche, Friedrich. *The Birth Tragedy and The Genealogy of Morals.* Translated by Francis Golffing. New York: Doubleday, 1956.

———. "On the Uses and Disadvantages of History for Life." In *Untimely Meditations.* Translated by R. B. Hollingdale. New York: Cambridge University Press, 1983.

Northup, Solomon. *Twelve Years a Slave; Narrative of Solomon Northup, a Citizen of New York, Kidnapped in Washington City in 1841, and Rescued in 1853, from a Cotton Plantation, near the Red River, in Louisiana.* In *Puttin' On Ole Master: The Slave Narratives of Henry Bibb, William Wells Brown, and Solomon Northup.* Edited by Gilbert Osofsky. New York: Harper & Row, 1969.

Norton, John N. *Life of General Washington.* New York: General Protestant Episcopal Sunday School Union and Church Book Society, 1860.

Nott, J. C., and George R. Gliddon. *Types of Mankind.* Philadelphia: Lippincott, Grambo, 1855.

Novak, Barbara. *American Painting of the Nineteenth-Century: Realism, Idealism, and the American Experience.* New York: Praeger, 1969.

Olney, James. "The Founding Fathers—Frederick Douglass and Booker T. Washington." In *Slavery and the Literary Imagination: Selected Papers from the English Institute, 1987.* Edited by Deborah E. McDowell and Arnold Rampersad. Baltimore: Johns Hopkins University Press, 1989.

————. "'I was Born': Slaves Narratives, Their Status as Autobiography and Literature." In *The Slave's Narrative*. Edited by Charles T. Davis and Henry Louis Gates, Jr. New York: Oxford University Press, 1985.

Olson, Charles. *Call Me Ishmael*. New York: Grove Press, 1947.

O'Sullivan, John L. "The Great Nation of Futurity." In *Manifest Destiny*. Edited by Norman A. Graebner. New York: Bobbs-Merrill, 1968.

Parker, Theodore. *The American Scholar*. Edited by George Willis Cooke. Boston: American Unitarian Association, 1907.

Patterson, Orlando. *Slavery and Social Death: A Comparative Study*. Cambridge, Mass.: Harvard University Press, 1982.

Pease, Donald. "National Identities, Postmodern Artifacts, and Postnational Narratives." *boundary 2* 19 (spring 1992): 1–13.

————. *Visionary Compacts: American Renaissance Writings in Cultural Context*. Madison: University of Wisconsin Press, 1987.

Pennington, James W. C. *The Fugitive Blacksmith; or, Events in the History of James W. C. Pennington, Pastor of a Presbyterian Church, New York, Formerly a Slave in the State of Maryland*. In *Great Slave Narratives*. Edited by Arna Bontemps. Boston: Beacon, 1969.

Poe, Edgar Allan. *The Narrative of Arthur Gordon Pym of Nantucket*. New York: Penguin, 1986.

Porte, Joel. *In Respect to Egotism: Studies in American Romantic Writings*. Cambridge: Cambridge University Press, 1991.

Porter, Carolyn. "Call Me Ishmael, or How to Make Double-Talk Speak." In *New Essays on Moby-Dick*. Edited by Richard Brodhead. Cambridge: Cambridge University Press, 1986.

————. "Reification and American Literature." In *Ideology and Classic American Literature*. Edited by Sacvan Bercovitch and Myra Jehlen. Cambridge: Cambridge University Press, 1986.

————. *Seeing and Being: The Plight of the Participant Observer in Emerson, James, Adams, and Faulkner*. Middletown, Conn.: Wesleyan University Press, 1982.

Potter, Israel R. *Life and Remarkable Adventures of Israel R. Potter*. 1824. Reprint, New York: Corinth Books, 1962.

Quarles, Benjamin. *Lincoln and the Negro*. New York: Oxford University Press, 1962.

Reagan, Daniel. "Melville's *Israel Potter* and the Nature of Biography." *American Transcendental Quarterly* 3 (September 1989): 257–76.

Reno, Janet. *Ishmael Alone Survived*. Lewisburg, Pa.: Bucknell University Press, 1990.

Reynolds, David S. *Beneath the American Renaissance: The Subversive Imagination in the Age of Emerson and Melville*. New York: Knopf, 1988.

————. *George Lippard*. Boston: Twayne, 1982.

Ringe, Donald A. *The Pictorial Mode: Space and Time in the Art of Bryant, Irving, and Cooper*. Lexington: University Press of Kentucky, 1971.

Roberts, James. *The Narrative of James Roberts, Soldier in the Revolutionary War and at the Battle of New Orleans*. 1858. Reprint, Hattiesburg, Miss.: The Book Farm, 1945.

Rogin, Michael Paul. *Fathers and Children: Andrew Jackson and the Subjugation of the American Indian*. New York: Vintage, 1976.

———. *Ronald Reagan, The Movie: and Other Episodes in Political Demonology*. Berkeley: University of California Press, 1987.

———. *Subversive Genealogy: The Politics and Art of Herman Melville*. New York: Knopf, 1983.

Roper, Moses. *A Narrative of the Adventures and Escape of Moses Roper, from American Slavery*. 1838. Reprint, Philadelphia: Rhistoric, 1969.

Rosewater, Victor. *The Liberty Bell: Its History and Significance*. New York: Appleton, 1926.

Said, Edward W. *Beginnings: Intention and Method*. New York: Columbia University Press, 1985.

———. *Culture and Imperialism*. New York: Knopf, 1993.

Sale, Maggie. "Critiques from Within: Antebellum Projects of Resistance." *American Literature* 64 (December 1992): 695–718.

Samson, John. *White Lies: Melville's Narratives of Facts*. Ithaca: Cornell University Press, 1989.

Samuels, Shirley, ed. *The Culture of Sentiment: Race, Gender, and Sentimentality in Nineteenth-Century America*. New York: Oxford University Press, 1992.

Sánchez-Eppler, Karen. "Bodily Bonds: The Intersecting Rhetorics of Abolition and Feminism." *Representations* 24 (fall 1988): 28–59.

———. *Touching Liberty: Abolition, Feminism, and the Politics of the Body*. Berkeley: University of California Press, 1993.

Schaar, John. *Legitimacy in the Modern State*. New Brunswick, N.J.: Transaction, 1981.

Schwartz, Barry. *George Washington: The Making of an American Symbol*. New York: Free Press, 1987.

Sears, John. *Sacred Places: American Tourist Attractions in the Nineteenth Century*. New York: Oxford University Press, 1989.

Sedgwick, Catherine Maria. *Hope Leslie*. 1827. Reprint, New Brunswick, N.J.: Rutgers University Press, 1987.

Seelye, John. *Melville: The Ironic Diagram*. Evanston, Ill.: Northwestern University Press, 1970.

Simpson, Eleanor E. "Melville and the Negro: From *Typee* to *Benito Cereno*." *American Literature* 41 (March 1969): 19–39.

Smith, William A. *Lectures on the Philosophy and Practice of Slavery, As Exhibited in the Institution of Domestic Slavery in the United States: With the Duties of Masters to Slaves*. 1856. Reprint, Miami, Fla.: Mnemosyne, 1969.

Smith, Valerie. *Self-Discovery and Authority in Afro-American Literature*. Cambridge, Mass.: Harvard University Press, 1987.

Sollors, Werner. "'Never was Born': The Mulatto, An American Tragedy." *Massachusetts Review* 27 (summer 1986): 293–316.

Sparks, Jared. *The Life of George Washington.* New York: Miller, Orton,
Mulligan, 1855.

Spillers, Hortense. "'Mamma's Baby, Papa's Maybe: An American Grammar Book." *Diacritics* 17 (summer 1987): 65–81.

Stephens, Ann S. *Malaeska: The Indian Wife of the White Hunter.* 1860. Reprint, New York: John Day, 1929.

Stepto, Robert B. *Behind the Veil: A Study of Afro-American Narrative.* Urbana: University of Illinois Press, 1979.

———. "Storytelling in Early Afro-American Fiction: Frederick Douglass'
'The Heroic Slave.'" *Georgia Review* 36 (1982): 355–68.

Steward, Austin. *Twenty-Two Years a Slave, and, Forty Years a Freeman:
Embracing a Correspondence of Several Years, while President of Wilberforce
Colony, London, Canada West.* 1856. Reprint, New York: Negro Univer-
sities Press, 1968.

Stoudt, Rev. John Baer. *The Liberty Bells of Pennsylvania.* Philadelphia:
William J. Campbell, 1920.

Stowe, Harriet Beecher. "The Two Altars; or, Two Pictures in One." In
*Dred: A Tale of the Great Dismal Swamp together with Anti-Slavery Tales
and Papers.* 2 vols. New York: AMS Press, 1967.

———. *Uncle Tom's Cabin; or, Life among the Lowly.* New York: Penguin
Books, 1984.

Sturken, Marita. "The Wall, the Screen, and the Image: The Vietnam Veterans Memorial." *Representations* 35 (summer 1991): 118–42.

Summer, Doris. "Irresistible Romance: The Foundational Fictions of Latin
America." in *Nation and Narration.* Edited by Homi K. Bhabha. New
York: Routledge, 1990.

Sundquist, Eric J. *Home as Found: Authority and Genealogy in Nineteenth-
Century American Literature.* Baltimore: Johns Hopkins University
Press, 1979.

———. "Slavery, Revolution, and the American Renaissance." In *The
American Renaissance Reconsidered: Selected Papers from the English Insti-
tute, 1982–83.* Edited by Walter Benn Michaels and Donald E. Pease.
Baltimore: Johns Hopkins University Press, 1985.

———. *To Wake the Nations: Race in the Making of American Literature.*
Cambridge, Mass.: Harvard University Press, 1993.

———, Introduction to *Frederick Douglass: New Literary and Historical Essays.* Edited by Eric J. Sundquist. Cambridge: Cambridge University
Press, 1990.

Thompson, John. *The Life of John Thompson, A Fugitive Slave, Containing
His History of Twenty-Five Years in Bondage, and His Providential Escape:
Written by Himself.* 1856. Reprint, New York: Negro Universities Press,
1968.

Tompkins, Jane. *Sensational Designs: The Cultural Work of American Fiction,
1790–1860.* New York: Oxford University Press, 1985.

Trachtenberg, Alan. *The Incorporation of America: Culture and Display in the Gilded Age*. New York: Hill and Wang, 1982.

Uncle Juvinell [Morrison Heady]. *The Farmer Boy, and How He Became Commander-in-Chief*. Boston: Walker, Wise, 1864.

Walzer, Michael. "On the Role of Symbolism in Political Thought." *Political Science Quarterly* 82 (June 1967): 191–204.

Ward, Samuel Ringgold. *Autobiography of a Fugitive Negro: His Anti-Slavery Labours in the United States, Canada, & England*. 1855. Reprint, New York: Arno Press, 1968.

Warren, George Washington. *The History of the Bunker Hill Monument Association during the First Century of the United States of America*. Boston: J. R. Osgood, 1877.

Webster, Daniel. *The Orations on Bunker Hill Monument, The Character of Washington, and The Landing at Plymouth*. New York: American Book Company, 1894.

———. *The Works of Daniel Webster*. 6 vols. Boston: Little and Brown, 1851.

Weems, Mason Locke. *The Life of Washington*. Edited by Marcus Cunliffe. 1809. Cambridge: Cambridge University Press, 1962.

Wheildon, William W. *Memoir of Solomon Willard, Architect and Superintendent of the Bunker Hill Monument*. Boston: Monument Association, 1865.

White, Hayden. *The Content of the Form: Narrative Discourse and Historical Representation*. Baltimore: Johns Hopkins University Press, 1987.

———. *Metahistory: The Historical Imagination in Nineteenth-Century Europe*. Baltimore, Johns Hopkins University Press, 1973.

———. "The Value of Narrativity in the Representation of Reality." In *On Narrative*. Edited by W. J. T. Mitchell. Chicago: University of Chicago Press, 1981.

Winthrop, John. "A Model of Christian Charity." In *The Norton Anthology of American Literature*. 2 vols. 3rd ed. Edited by Nina Baym et al. New York: Norton, 1989.

Wood, Forrest. *Black Scare: The Racist Response to Emancipation*. Berkeley: University of California Press, 1970.

Wu Hung. "Tiananmen Square: A Political History of Monuments." *Representations* 35 (summer 1991): 84–117.

Yarborough, Richard. "Race, Violence, and Manhood: The Masculine Ideal in Frederick Douglass's 'The Heroic Slave.'" In *New Essays on Frederick Douglass*. Edited by Eric J. Sundquist. Cambridge: Cambridge University Press: 1990.

Yellin, Jean Fagan. *The Intricate Knot: Black Figures in American Literature, 1776–1863*. New York: New York University Press, 1972.

———. *Women and Sisters: The Antislavery Feminists in American Culture*. New Haven: Yale University Press, 1989.

Index

Adams, Henry, 203
Adams, John, 7
Albert, Octavia V. Rodgers (*The House of Bondage*), 200
amalgamation. *See* miscegenation
America (engraving), 126–28, 165
Anderson, Benedict, 37, 116, 121, 135–37, 234n10, 244n10
Andrews, William, 199, 219, 223–24, 225–26, 259n33, 260n44, 261n49
Arac, Jonathan, 21, 22, 234n10
Arendt, Hannah, 148, 153, 248n36, 250n50
Attucks, Crispus, 168
Aunt Phillis's Cabin (Eastman) 191
authority: breakdown of, 42–44, 54–55, 57–59, 61–66, 81–87, 100, 102, 143; colonial, 22–23, 87, 194; cultural, 46, 51, 72–75, 77, 80; of ethnology, 87–90; etymology of, 14; foundational, 11, 13, 104, 161–62, 176, 184, 187–88; monumental, 109–10, 113, 126; narrative, 43–46, 48–51, 68, 70–78, 80–81, 91; of national narrative, 12, 27, 60–62, 65, 85–87; patriarchal, 6–7, 12–16, 33–34, 49–52, 60, 68, 137–38, 207; in slave narratives, 77–78, 167, 197–98, 200–201, 203–6, 210–12, 221; subversion of, 87–90, 93, 105, 153–54, 190, 194, 207, 216, 223, 228; Washington as, 33–34, 48–56, 70, 138, 222
authorized discourse, 80, 86, 97, 194; parodied 75, 82

Badeau, Adam (*The Vagabond*), 118, 244–45n12
Bakhtin, Mikhail, 82
Baldwin, James, 98
Balibar, Etienne, 37
Baym, Nina, 238–39n3
Bellis, Peter, 153, 249–50n48, 250n53
Bercovitch, Sacvan, 19–22, 160, 174, 176–77
Berlant, Lauren, 108–9, 129, 154, 157, 230n11, 247n27

Beverly, John, 38
Bhabha, Homi K.: on colonial discourse, 87, 194; on hybridity, 22–23; idea of "discontinuous history," 232n36: on national narrative, 6, 46, 190, 200, 230n10, 232n35, 234n10, 242n38, 250–51n58
Blair, Montgomery, 170
Bodnar, John, 248n32
Brodhead, Richard, 82, 144
Brown, John (abolitionist), 62
Brown, John (ex-slave, *Slave Life in Georgia*), 205
Brown, William Wells: autobiographies of, 27, 161, 165–67, 170–71, 193; critique of national patriarchy, 12, 17, 20, 25, 28–29, 65–66, 157, 161, 173, 176–77, 185, 214, 246n23; and monumentalism, 164–71, 177, 183, 202; as orator, 211, 213, 252n15; republican thinking of, 162, 227; and Santo Domingo, 9, 166. Works: *The Black Man*, 167–68, 258n19; *Clotel*, 17–18, 28, 32, 49, 106–7, 166, 167, 176, 185, 190, 193, 199, 210, 212–17, 220, 224–27, 231n26, 259nn31,32,33, 259–60n39; "Jefferson's Daughter," 164–65
Bryan, William Alfred, 239n5
Bryant, William Cullen, 119
Bunker Hill Monument: Brown's critique of, 170–71; Melville's ironic representation of, 142, 146–51, 155–56; as national icon, 4, 8, 24, 28, 108, 110, 111–14, 120, 128, 129, 132, 134–35, 137–38, 154, 167, 191, 247–48n31; as panoptic structure, 140, 248n37
Byrd, William, 205

Calhoun, John C., 32, 40–41, 51, 65, 87, 90, 243n40
Carby, Hazel, 199
Cecil, E. (*Life of Washington*), 41
Chase, Ezra B. (*Teachings of Patriots and Statesmen*), 69–71
Chase, Richard, 91–92

Compositor: Braun-Brumfield, Inc.
Text: Palatino
Display: Palatino
Printer and Binder: Braun-Brumfield, Inc.